THE RIGHT WAR?

To declare oneself a conservative in American foreign policy is to enter immediately into a fractious, long-standing debate. Should America retreat from the world, deal with the world as it is, or try to transform it in its own image? Which school of thought – traditionalist, realist, or neoconservative – is truest to the country's ideals and interests?

With the dramatic shift in American foreign policy since 9/11, these differences have been brought into stark relief, especially by the Bush administration's decision to go to war in Iraq. This book brings together the most articulate and influential voices in the debate among conservatives over the tactics and strategy of America's engagement in Iraq. Its contents run the gamut from protests to second thoughts to full-throated endorsements, and represent a vivid sampling of the ideological currents likely to influence the Bush administration as it tries to make good on its ambitious goals for Iraq and the wider Middle East.

Gary Rosen is the managing editor of *Commentary*. A member of the Council on Foreign Relations, he holds a Ph.D. in political science from Harvard and is the author of *American Compact: James Madison and the Problem of Founding*. His articles and reviews have appeared in *Commentary*, the *New York Times*, the *Wall Street Journal*, and the *Washington Post*.

The Right War?

THE CONSERVATIVE DEBATE ON IRAQ

Edited by

GARY ROSEN

CAMBRIDGE
UNIVERSITY PRESS

CAMBRIDGE UNIVERSITY PRESS
Cambridge, New York, Melbourne, Madrid, Cape Town, Singapore, São Paulo

Cambridge University Press
40 West 20th Street, New York, NY 10011-4211, USA

www.cambridge.org
Information on this title: www.cambridge.org/9780521856812

First published 2005

Printed in the United States of America

A catalog record for this publication is available from the British Library.

Library of Congress Cataloging in Publication Data

The right war? : the conservative debate on Iraq / edited by Gary Rosen.
p. cm.
Includes index.
ISBN 0-521-85681-7 – ISBN 0-521-67318-6 (alk. paper)
1. Iraq War, 2003. 2. United States – Politics and government – 2001–
3. Iraq – Politics and government – 2003– I. Rosen, Gary, 1966–
DS79.76.R54 2005
956.7044′3 – dc22 2005011486

ISBN-13 978-0-521-85681-2 hardback
ISBN-10 0-521-85681-7 hardback

ISBN-13 978-0-521-67318-1 paperback
ISBN-10 0-521-67318-6 paperback

Contents

List of Contributors

Fouad Ajami is Majid Khadduri Professor of Middle Eastern Studies at the School of Advanced International Studies of Johns Hopkins University and the author of *The Dream Palace of the Arabs: A Generation's Odyssey* (1998).

Andrew J. Bacevich is professor of international relations at Boston University. His latest books are *American Empire: The Realities and Consequences of U.S. Diplomacy* (2004) and *The New American Militarism: How Americans Are Seduced by War* (2005).

Max Boot is a columnist for the *Los Angeles Times*, a senior fellow at the Council on Foreign Relations, and the author of *The Savage Wars of Peace: Small Wars and the Rise of American Power* (2003).

David Brooks is a columnist for the *New York Times.*

Patrick J. Buchanan was twice a candidate for the Republican presidential nomination and was the Reform Party's candidate in 2000. A syndicated columnist and television political analyst, he is a founder and editor of the *American Conservative.*

Eliot A. Cohen is Robert E. Osgood Professor at the School of Advanced International Studies of Johns Hopkins University and the author of *Supreme Command: Soldiers, Statesmen, and Leadership in Wartime* (2002).

Robert F. Ellsworth is vice chairman of the board of directors of the Nixon Center. He served in the U.S. House of Representatives from 1961 to 1967 and as American ambassador to NATO from 1969 to 1971.

Francis Fukuyama is Bernard L. Schwartz Professor of International Political Economy at the School of Advanced International Studies of

Johns Hopkins University and the author of, most recently, *State-Building: Governance and World Order in the 21st Century* (2004).

Reuel Marc Gerecht is a resident fellow at the American Enterprise Institute and a contributing editor of the *Weekly Standard*. From 1985 to 1994, he was a Middle East specialist at the Central Intelligence Agency.

Victor Davis Hanson teaches classics at California State University in Fresno. A senior fellow of the Hoover Institution at Stanford and a columnist for *National Review Online*, he is the author of, most recently, *A War Like No Other: How the Athenians and Spartans Fought the Peloponnesian War* (2005).

Owen Harries is a senior fellow at the Center for Independent Studies in Sydney, Australia, and was the editor of the American foreign-policy journal the *National Interest* from 1985 to 2001. His article is taken from his 2003 Boyer lectures prepared for the Australian Broadcasting Corporation.

Robert Kagan is a contributing editor of the *Weekly Standard*, a senior associate at the Carnegie Endowment for International Peace, and the author of *Of Paradise and Power: America and Europe in the New World Order* (2003).

Charles R. Kesler is the associate director of the Henry Salvatori Center at Claremont McKenna College and the editor of the *Claremont Review of Books*. He is a senior fellow of the Claremont Institute.

Henry A. Kissinger was U.S. Secretary of State from 1973 to 1977.

Charles Krauthammer is a syndicated columnist for the *Washington Post* and an essayist for *Time*.

William Kristol is the editor of the *Weekly Standard* and the co-author (with Lawrence F. Kaplan) of *The War Over Iraq: Saddam's Tyranny and America's Mission* (2003).

James Kurth is the Claude Smith Professor of Political Science at Swarthmore College and the editor of *Orbis*.

Norman Podhoretz, editor-at-large of *Commentary*, is the author of ten books, including *The Norman Podhoretz Reader* (2004). He was recently awarded the Presidential Medal of Freedom, the nation's highest civilian honor.

Dimitri K. Simes is the founding president of the Nixon Center and co-publisher of the *National Interest*.

Andrew Sullivan is a senior editor at the *New Republic* and a columnist for *Time*. He writes a weblog at *andrewsullivan.com*.

George F. Will is a columnist for the *Washington Post*.

Fareed Zakaria is the editor of *Newsweek International* and the author of *The Future of Freedom: Illiberal Democracy at Home and Abroad* (2003).

GARY ROSEN

Introduction

THIS VOLUME IS NOT A HISTORY OF THE WAR IN IRAQ, NOR IS IT A systematic exploration of the issues raised by the war. It contains no government documents or presidential pronouncements, and there is not a single public official among its contributors. Though a diverse collection of opinion pieces and journal articles, it does not pretend to cover the full range of views on the American effort to overthrow and replace the regime of Saddam Hussein. It is a sampling taken exclusively from writers who belong, by self-identification or by the character of their arguments, to the political right. It is partial, partisan, incomplete – and yet it represents what is perhaps the most interesting and consequential foreign-policy discussion now going on in the United States.

This is true, in the first instance, because the levers of American foreign policy are in the hands of a Republican administration whose outlook has been shaped decisively by certain currents of conservative thought. George W. Bush's decision to go to war in Iraq did not spring directly from the pages of the *Weekly Standard*, *Commentary*, or the *Wall Street Journal*, but the influence of these and like-minded publications on the actions and rhetoric of the administration is unmistakable. The Bush Doctrine, with its combination of military assertiveness and democratic idealism, may have been declared in the wake of 9/11, but the intellectual groundwork for it was laid years before by the editors, pundits, academics, and think-tank denizens who call themselves – and are now widely recognized as – neoconservatives.

Because this group of thinkers has had so obvious an impact on the Bush administration, neoconservatism has been the object of a great deal of critical scrutiny by liberal and radical opponents of the war in Iraq. Some of this criticism has been constructive; much of it has been irresponsible, even hysterical, particularly in suggesting that the White House has fallen prey to a secretive foreign-policy cabal. The irony of these dark mutterings is that, whatever their other faults, neoconservatives have never been shy about announcing and promoting their agenda. They are famously eager intellectual combatants, always ready to butt heads with opponents on the left or, for that matter, critics on their own side of the political aisle.

Indeed, what has often been overlooked in the attention paid to liberal unhappiness with the Bush Doctrine is the extent to which it has divided the right as well, especially on the issue of Iraq. Though the Republican rank-and-file has been overwhelmingly supportive of the war, conservative intellectuals of various stripes have been among the administration's most persistent critics. They have pointed to a range of failures in the planning and execution of the American occupation, raised serious doubts about the feasibility of bringing democracy to the Middle East, and questioned the justice and necessity of the war itself. Lacking the partisan hostility of other critics of the U.S. engagement in Iraq, these conservative dissenters have probed the claims of the Bush administration more fairly and intelligently, I would suggest, than the great bulk of their counterparts on the left.

In selecting items for *The Right War?*, I have tried to bring together the leading voices in this intramural debate. Conservative print journalism takes many different forms these days, and the articles included here reflect that diversity. They range from short, punchy newspaper pieces by columnists like David Brooks, George F. Will, and Max Boot to ambitious, long-form journal articles by writers like Norman Podhoretz, Francis Fukuyama, and Charles Krauthammer. They are drawn from the nation's leading newspapers as well as from the universe of opinion magazines in which conservative thought is welcome, from the *New Republic* on the hawkish left to the *American Conservative* on the cranky, alienated right. The merits of individual arguments aside, the contributions to this volume give some idea of the breadth and sophistication of a conservative movement too often caricatured for its supposed conformity and simple-mindedness.

* * *

As students of the American right know, today's internecine battles are nothing new. Even in the final decades of the Cold War, when the various factions of the Republican coalition were relatively united in their concern about the Soviet threat, declaring oneself a conservative on foreign policy was to enter immediately into a fractious debate. The administrations of Richard Nixon, Gerald Ford, Ronald Reagan, and George H.W. Bush were marked by bitter disagreements over the international priorities of the United States.

For neoconservatives – most of them refugees from an increasingly dovish Democratic Party – the task of the U.S. in its confrontation with the Soviet Union was to raise high the banner of the "free world," answering Communist aggression with no less determined American resistance. Unswayed by the purported reasonableness of this or that Soviet leader, they pointed to the irredeemable character of the Soviet system itself; the regime and its destructive ideology were what mattered. Compromise with totalitarian evil was out of the question.

Conservative practitioners of realpolitik, by contrast, put forward a very different agenda. Concerned more about stability and peace than about promoting American principles, these "realists," as they are known in foreign-policy circles, were content to deal with the world as it was, in the stark light of national interest, even if this meant striking deals with Communists. The Soviet Union, they insisted, had interests too, and these were not always incompatible with our own. For the advocates of détente, led by Henry Kissinger, coexistence was the practical course, democratic revolution a potentially dangerous pipe dream.

After the fall of the Berlin Wall in 1989, the differences between neoconservatives and realists were brought into even starker relief. Though both camps supported the first Gulf War in 1990–91, they diverged sharply in their opinions of its conclusion. Neoconservatives were indignant over (the first) President Bush's decision to allow Saddam Hussein not just to remain in power but to suppress, with characteristic brutality, the Kurdish and Shiite revolts inspired by the American invasion. The Bush administration and its conservative defenders, for their part, explained the policy in classic realist fashion, expressing worries about the chaos that might ensue, in Iraq and perhaps throughout the Middle East, if Saddam's Baathist regime were toppled.

To this already volatile mix was added a long-dormant strain of conservative foreign-policy thought: isolationism. The Cold War had suppressed the instinctive desire of many American conservatives to stand apart from the seemingly distant, corrupting affairs of other nations, a position motivated in part by a belief in American exceptionalism but also by fears about the size and reach of the federal government. In the lead-up to the first Gulf War, this cause was resurrected by Patrick J. Buchanan, whose readiness to blame the conflict on Wall Street and Jewish supporters of Israel was reminiscent – to the distress of most other conservatives – of the antiwar rhetoric of the "America First" movement of the early 1940's.

By the mid-1990's, this isolationist impulse – what its advocates understandably prefer to call foreign-policy traditionalism or nationalism – had become more mainstream among Republicans, though not in the virulent form preached by Buchanan. On Capitol Hill in particular, many conservatives opposed the "humanitarian wars" waged by President Bill Clinton in Bosnia and Kosovo. In this, they were overwhelmingly seconded by conservative realists, who saw no vital American interests at stake in the Balkans. Neoconservatives thought it incumbent upon the U.S. to put an end to ethnic cleansing in the region and found themselves in a sometimes awkward alliance with liberals who, in other circumstances, were loudly critical of the exercise of American power.

The attacks of 9/11 brought an unusual degree of unity to the conservative foreign-policy establishment, as it did to the nation as a whole. Few on the right objected to the Bush administration's muscular response to the terrorists of al Qaeda and their Taliban patrons, even as many liberals counseled restraint and called for a more international approach. This conservative consensus dissolved quickly, however, once it became evident that the "war on terror" would not be confined to Afghanistan or to the groups directly responsible for the devastation of 9/11.

In his State of the Union address of January 2002, President Bush identified Iraq as one of the countries in a tripartite "axis of evil." His spokesmen soon made clear that the administration intended to confront Saddam Hussein and his Baathist regime. By the end of the year, Bush had secured authorization from Congress to use force against Iraq and had won a UN Security Council resolution demanding that the country disarm or "face serious consequences." On March 19, 2003, after months of fruitless diplomacy and inconclusive weapons inspections, Operation Iraqi Freedom began with air strikes on Baghdad by U.S. and coalition forces.

* * *

A number of important articles in the conservative debate on Iraq appeared in the period leading up to the war and in the first months of the occupation. In August 2002, for example, Brent Scowcroft, a leading realist and a key national-security adviser in previous Republican administrations, wrote an op-ed for the *Wall Street Journal* titled "Don't Attack Saddam," arguing that so massive and risky an undertaking would be a needless diversion from the war on terror. Once the war started, Robert Kagan and William Kristol took to the pages of the *Weekly Standard* to editorialize, with increasing indignation, about the inadequacy of postwar planning and the need for more troops. As it became apparent that no major caches of WMD's would be found in Iraq, conservative opinion-makers (like everyone else) began to ask pointed questions about the quality of prewar intelligence and the use to which it was put by the Bush administration.

All of these issues are touched upon in *The Right War?*, but only as they emerged in later discussions. For reasons of space and continuity, I have restricted the contents of the volume to articles that appeared in 2004–5, after these initial volleys of opinion. The chief advantage of this limited time frame is that it provides at least middling distance from the overheated polemical atmosphere in which the war began. As the American engagement in Iraq approached its first anniversary, conservative commentators started to step back from the conflict in an effort to gain a wider perspective. These reflections and second thoughts – arranged here in chronological order – were often occasioned by the news of the day (very depressing news, alas, for much of 2004), but all of them, I think, shed light on the large questions raised by America's most substantial foreign-policy commitment since the Vietnam War.

What does American history teach about the nature and limits of U.S. power? Are deterrence and containment still viable national-security doctrines in an age of suicide terrorism and weapons of mass destruction? What value should we attach to stability in parts of the world where the social and political status quo abets violent extremism? Should the U.S. – can the U.S. – be an agent for democratic change? Does such an agenda demand more cooperation with other nations, or less? Does the promotion of American principles serve American interests? If not, how should the two be reconciled?

The Right War? includes familiar clashes on these and other issues. Realists and neoconservatives take sharp aim at one another (and at assorted liberals), while traditionalists – preeminently Patrick J. Buchanan but also, to varying degrees, James Kurth, George F. Will, and Andrew J. Bacevich – decry the tragic consequences of it all. More surprising is the extent to which many of these writers turn a critical eye on their own camp or concede arguments to their antagonists. Among the neoconservatives, the contributions by David Brooks, Fouad Ajami, Francis Fukuyama, and Eliot A. Cohen are notable for their candid exploration of the failures of American policy in Iraq. As for the realists, the articles included here suggest an emerging split. Henry Kissinger and Fareed Zakaria contend that the (prudent, patient) promotion of democracy is now a necessary aspect of advancing American interests. On this point, Kissinger writes, the neoconservatives "have won their intellectual battle" – a concession that such old-school realists as Owen Harries, Robert F. Ellsworth, and Dimitri K. Simes are very far from granting.

The pessimism of many of these articles seems strangely off-key as I write this introduction in the spring of 2005. In the months since all but the last of them were published, Iraqis have voted in large and enthusiastic numbers, defying not only the terror campaign against their nascent democracy but also the dire predictions of the Bush administration's critics. The carnage has continued there, but so too have crucial, halting steps toward self-government. What's more, free elections have taken place in the Palestinian Authority, while in Lebanon, the "Cedar Revolution" has burst upon the scene, forcing an end to Syria's long domination of that country. Even Egypt and Saudi Arabia have given hints of democratic ferment.

The Middle East still has a great distance to go, and optimism, like pessimism, can be premature. But these events are enormously encouraging, especially for those of us who have supported the broad outlines (if not always the execution) of the Bush Doctrine and the transformation that it has wrought in American foreign policy – and in the world.

VICTOR DAVIS HANSON

1 Iraq's Future – and Ours

ON NOVEMBER 21, 2003, SOME MINOR ROCKET ATTACKS ON THE Iraqi oil ministry and on two hotels in Baghdad elicited an exceptional amount of attention in the global media. What drew the interest of journalists were the terrorists' mobile launchers: they were crude donkey carts.

This peculiar juxtaposition of 8th- and 21st-century technology was taken as emblematic of the entire American experience in Iraq – an increasingly hopeless clash between our overwhelming conventional strength and stealthy terrorists able to turn our own lethal means against us with cheap and ubiquitous native materials. How could we possibly win this contest, when an illiterate thug with a rusty RPG (rocket-propelled grenade) launcher could take down a West Point graduate along with his million-dollar Black Hawk helicopter while those upon whom we have been lavishing our aid cheered our deaths and ransacked the corpses?

In an extensive, on-the-ground account of the post-bellum chaos, George Packer in a recent issue of the *New Yorker* lists an array of missteps that brought us to this sorry pass. We put too much trust in exiled Iraqis; we allowed looters and fundamentalists to seize the initiative right after the war; we underestimated both the damage done to the infrastructure by Saddam Hussein and the pernicious and still insidious effects of his murderous, Soviet-style government hierarchy. Mark Danner, in the *New York Review of Books*, relates much the same story, emphasizing our tolerance of looting and our disbanding of the Iraqi army as factors contributing in tandem to the creation of the Iraqi resistance, now thriving on a combination of plentiful cash (from looting and prewar caches) and a surplus of weaponry and manpower (from the defunct army).

Reprinted from *Commentary*, January 2004, by permission; all rights reserved.

Both authors make good points, including about American naiveté and unpreparedness. But lacking in these bleak analyses of failures and setbacks are crucial and complicating elements, with the result that the overall picture they draw is both distorted as to the present and seriously misleading with regard to the future.

II

It is a genuine cause of lament that many American lives have been lost in what should have been an uncontested peace since the war ended in April. But let us begin by putting the matter in perspective. The reconstruction of Iraq is proceeding well: electrical power, oil production, everyday commerce, and schooling are all in better shape than they were under Saddam Hussein. More saliently, none of the biblical calamities confidently anticipated by critics of the March invasion has yet materialized. Those prophecies of Armageddon featured thousands of combatants killed, hundreds of oil wells set afire, mass starvation, millions festering in refugee camps, polluted waters in the Gulf, "moderate" Arab governments toppled, the "Arab street" in a rage, and a wave of 9/11-style terror loosed upon the United States.

We are an impatient people. In part, no doubt, our restlessness is a byproduct of our own unprecedented ease and affluence. Barbarians over the hills do not descend to kill us; no diseases wipe out our children by the millions; not starvation but obesity is more likely to do us in. Since we are so rich and so powerful, why is it, we naturally wonder, that we cannot simply and quickly call into being a secure, orderly, prosperous Iraq, a benign Islamic version of a New England township? What incompetence, or worse, lies behind our failure even to seize Osama bin Laden or Saddam Hussein?

But Iraq is not Middlebury or Amherst - and it will not be for another century. What is truly astonishing is not our inability in six months to create an Arab utopia, but the sheer audacity of our endeavor to send our liberating troops into the heart of an ancient and deeply chauvinistic culture that over the past decades had reduced itself to utter ruin. Saddam Hussein and his sons spent those decades gassing their own people, conducting maniacal wars against Iran and Kuwait, launching missiles into Israel and Saudi Arabia, despoiling the Mesopotamian wetlands and driving out the marsh people, and systematically murdering hundreds of thousands of innocents. Real progress would have meant anything even marginally better than this non-ending nightmare, let alone what we have already achieved in Iraq.

Nor did Saddam Hussein and his sons kill without help. After traveling 7,000 miles to dispose of him, we were confronted by his legacy - a society containing tens of thousands of Baathists with blood on their hands, 100,000 felons recently released from Saddam's prisons, and millions more who for decades took solace in a species of national pride founded on butchery and plunder. After a mere seven months, are we to be blamed for having failed magically to rehabilitate such people? Should we instead have imprisoned them en masse, tried them, shot them, exiled them?

Going into the heart of Mesopotamia, American troops passed Iraqi palaces with historic and often ominous names: Cunaxa, whence Xenophon's 10,000 began their arduous journey home; Gaugamela, where Alexander devastated the Persian imperial army; and, not far away in southeastern Turkey, Carrhae, where the Roman triumvir Crassus lost his 45,000-man army and his own head. Mesopotamia has long been a very dangerous place for Westerners. By any historical measure other than our own, it is nothing short of preposterous that, in less than a year's time, American troops would plunge into such a cauldron, topple the world's worst dictator, and then undertake to introduce the rudiments of a liberal society in the center of the ancient Islamic caliphate - all at a cost of a little over 400 lives.

Now, however, after one of the most miraculous victories in military history, we demand an almost instantaneous peace followed by the emergence of a sort of Iraqi Continental Congress. We demand the head of Saddam Hussein, forgetting that Adolf Eichmann disappeared for years in the post-Nazi archipelago abroad, and that neither Ratko Mladic nor Radovan Karadzic has yet been scooped from the swamp of the Balkans. Our journalists describe the chaos besetting a society allegedly traumatized by American war that in reality is struggling with the legacy of its own destructive past. In Iraq we are not trying to rebuild the equivalent of a flattened Hamburg or a Tokyo among the equivalents of shell-shocked and thoroughly confused Germans or Japanese. We are attempting something much more challenging: to impose a consensual system upon *spared* peoples, who in liberation did far more to destroy their own country (the losses to pillaging ran to about $12 billion) than we did in either the war or the ensuing occupation.

III

Most of the Baathists among our current enemies in Iraq chose to flee rather than stand and fight. The homes of Saddam's henchmen were not all bombed. Their friends were not killed. Their pride was only temporarily lost – to be regained, evidently, upon their discovery that it is easier and safer to murder an American who is building a school and operating under strict rules of engagement than to take on Abrams tanks barreling into Baghdad under a sky of F-16's.

Such are a few of the ironies entailed in our stunning military success, even if overlooked in analyses of the recent turmoil. And there are still more. Hard as it may be to accept, a rocky peace may well be the *result* of a spectacularly rapid victory. Imagine our war instead as a year-and-a-half continuum of active combat, stretching from the late-March 2003 invasion until the scheduled assumption of power of the Iraqi provisional government this coming July. Now suppose that over the course of this time frame, about 5,000 of Saddam's hardcore killers had either to be killed, captured, or routed from the country if there were ever to be any chance for real peace to emerge. Somehow, under conditions of full-scale combat, one suspects the job would have been much easier.

Of course, we must not wish the war would have lasted that long in order to allow us freely to destroy Saddam's remnants, but we must at least appreciate that short wars by their very nature often require messy clean-ups. After the shooting stops, the aid workers arrive; the hard-core, hypercritical journalists remain; and soldiers must build rather than shoot.

Here, too, a little historical perspective helps. The U.S. and its allies do not have a good record of achieving quick and easy peace after quick and easy victory. Recall our twelve-year, 350,000-sortie, $20-billion experience maintaining no-fly zones in the aftermath of the four-day ground phase of the Gulf war; the thousands of Europeans and Americans who are still in the Balkans after the seven-week victory over Milosevic; the ongoing international effort to pacify Afghanistan after the United States and its indigenous allies routed the Taliban in a mere six weeks. It is simply much more difficult for static and immobile peacekeepers under global scrutiny to deal with resurgent, unconquered, and itinerant enemies. If things are rough now in Iraq, it is because they were not so rough during March and April.

There are other, cultural aspects to our dilemma as well. Many Americans have come to believe that war is the worst thing that can happen to humans. It would probably not have been easy in 1991 to convince them of the need to prolong our "highway of death" in southern Iraq, even if doing so would have prevented Baathist troops from escaping to Basra and killing innocents; or of the need to bomb Serbians in Sbrenica in order to prevent them from killing women and children; or of the need to annihilate fleeing Taliban fighters to prevent them from drifting back into Kabul months later to shoot young Frenchwomen trying to feed the poor and hungry.

What such Americans have forgotten is that there *can* be much worse things than war. Stalin, Hitler, and Mao killed far more off the battlefield than all those lost in World War I and II; bloodbaths in Cambodia, Bosnia, and Rwanda transpired in "peacetime" precisely because there were no troops around to thwart the mass murderers. And then there is the lesson of General Patton's "unforgiving minute" – that brief window when the enemy collapses and flees and for that evanescent moment can be hit with impunity and made receptive to dictated terms. Whether out of exultation at our stunning success or from a misplaced sense of clemency, we chose to forfeit that rare opportunity.

What is more, in the immediate aftermath of the war we disbanded the Iraqi army, not out of oversight or folly but on the idealistic grounds that we wished to build a force untainted by Baathist officers and ideology. Not only did we thereby lose an opportunity to corral and systematically audit 400,000 soldiers in their barracks, but to the shame of wartime flight we added the greater ignominy of peacetime irrelevancy, soon to be exacerbated by shared unemployment and poverty.

If some of the constraints on our military conduct have been self-imposed, others are functions of (nonmilitary) reality. These days, our officers have adjusted to the fact that they operate in a topsy-turvy world, one where human-rights activists are capable of being largely silent about 80,000 Muslims killed in Chechnya but grow shrill when an occasional house of a killer in Tikrit is leveled or the family of a fugitive Baathist mass-murderer is interned. A William Tecumseh Sherman or a George Patton would have pointed out that the Sunni Triangle could be pacified only after the majority of its residents came to understand the hard way that they had much to lose and nothing to profit by indifference to or complicity with the Baathists. Their uncompromising and straightforward tactics are not thinkable today, when military officers are understandably more spooked by the prospect of media stories alleging American brutality than by the enemy.

IV

Not all of our problems are problems of perception, but at least a few are. What would have been the reaction of the *New Yorker* or the *New York Review of Books* had the coalition forces shot 500 looters to restore order and save the infrastructure of an entire people, or had we kept the Iraqi army intact to curb lawlessness, or had a no-nonsense provisional government of exiles ensured that the trains were to be running on time? Instead of hearing now about chaos and quagmire, we would be reading about poor families whose innocent teenage sons had been caught in crossfire, or about Baathists with dark pasts entrenched in the new military, or about the counterproductive American obsession with order rather than with pluralist democracy.

The reflexively critical gaze of the press operates all the way down to the tactical level, submitting every aspect of our military behavior to instantaneous and often hostile review. Partly in response to the biases of critics – but also in line with widespread utopian notions of leniency – we seek to mitigate the damage and death we inflict, thus inadvertently helping once again to render peace more deadly than war. Army interrogators who push or intimidate prisoners face court-martial or discharge, even though many of those prisoners have freely killed – and will again kill – hundreds of the weak and innocent. In the last days of combat, a few of our satellite-guided bombs were ingeniously laden with cement rather than explosives, in order admirably to curtail collateral damage.

But the more we seek to refine war by curbing the unpredictable and frightening nature of the violence that is the essence of that amoral enterprise, the more those inured to ferocity see our restraint not as magnanimity but as weakness or, worse still, a sort of decadence. (Our unwillingness to shoot looters was probably seen by most Iraqis not as a necessary indulgence but as fear of bloody confrontation – or as part of some farfetched conspiracy to induce Iraqis to run amok.) We have not lost confidence in our ability to conduct asymmetrical or unconventional warfare, but the task we have imposed on ourselves is no longer one of routing and eliminating terrorists and murderers; it is one of therapy. Confused by these mixed directives, our military is never quite sure whether it should be destroying or building; whether it should kill, be killed, or save; whether it should frown or smile. This can redound to the advantage of an armed and determined adversary with no such humanitarian obligations.

Post-bellum Iraq reminds us how much we are geared not to taking but rather to preserving lives – including, quite naturally, our own. Expensive communications, body armor, and redundancies in operational procedure are designed to protect soldiers from those who would blow themselves up to kill us. But the more money, time, and spiritual capital we quite properly invest in each of our soldiers, and the more precious each of them becomes to us, the more altered is the age-old and terrible calculus of the battlefield. One dead American causes far greater distress, not just among the American public but in the military itself, than the satisfaction prompted by the knowledge that dozens of Baathist murderers were killed in return.

No longer is our success in battle seen in a 10-to-1 kill ratio over the enemy, as at bloody Okinawa; or a 25-to-1 ratio, as during the 1968 Tet offensive; or the stunning 250-to-1 imbalance of the recent Afghan and Iraqi offensives, when perhaps as many as 10,000 Taliban and Iraqi soldiers in total were killed to our 450 or so combat deaths. Indeed, our military has rarely talked about the numbers of enemies killed or captured in Iraq, figuring, rightly or wrongly, that the public would either recoil from Vietnam-era nomenclature ("body counts") or yawn because its sole concern was that we not lose any of our own. As the size of our military continues to shrink, with fewer soldiers piloting fewer and ever more expensive planes and tanks, these trends will only continue.

Finally, as our government seeks – often successfully – to wage war with as little upheaval at home as possible, it never troubles to tap the inner reserves of the American people, who might well rise to the challenge of a long and difficult struggle against those who seek to kill us all. We are thus caught in yet another paradox: the more lethal and adroit an ever smaller number of American soldiers become, the more detached an ever greater number of Americans can be from the wars waged in their names. Our very prowess at arms has blinded us to what may yet be demanded of us by our current situation, namely, the need truly to mobilize ourselves as a nation in a deadly war.

V

What then are the lessons of this peace? We have been making major progress in both Afghanistan and Iraq, but both of these campaigns are better appreciated in the context of the wider war that started on September 11 – the worst attack on American shores in our history. That worldwide conflict is far from over.

Events in Iraq do not occur in isolation. In Afghanistan, Israel, Turkey, Bali, Pakistan, Morocco, and elsewhere, an identifiable enemy is killing Westerners or their supporters through shared methods of assassination and suicide bombings. These Islamic fascists eat, sleep, and use their ATM cards in real nation-states ruled and inhabited by real people, whose attitudes and activities either enhance or retard the killers in their midsts. A series of polls confirms that millions of these people, especially in the Middle East, were not all that unhappy about September 11, 2001. Dolls glorify Osama bin Laden; plastic Twin Towers with planes crashing into them are sold as toys in the West Bank. Roadside bombs take the lives of American civilians seeking to interview Palestinians as potential Fulbright fellows – and a gleeful populace stones the Americans' would-be rescuers. The Cairo papers print venom straight out of the mind of Joseph Goebbels. Our Saudi allies disseminate a more virulent hatred of America than do Iranians or Syrians.

All of this unmistakable enmity lends implicit support to the Baathist diehards who are now mining and shooting Americans in Iraq. And what message are we as a nation sending in return? That we give billions of dollars in aid to Jordanians, Egyptians, and Palestinians, that we have saved Muslims in Afghanistan, Kuwait, Somalia, Kosovo, and Bosnia, that we invite thousands of Muslims to emigrate to our shores to practice and proselytize their religion?

Yes, that is our message and our undeniable record. But the extremists and their passive supporters are already aware that the United States aids and saves millions of Muslims. They also grasp that we fear the bothersome mess of their terror and nihilism, and that historically our friendship has taken on the aspect of forbearance and then appeasement. While we publicly blame ourselves for our lack of sensitivity, they privately scoff that we are too sensitive. We talk of winning hearts and minds; they seethe not that Saddam was removed but that it was we who removed him.

If we are to be of service to the thousands of Americans whom we have asked to risk their lives in the alleys of Tikrit and on the peaks of Afghanistan, there is another, more deterrent message we might contemplate sending. It is that we ourselves are a bit unpredictable and now at last extremely angry, that without apology we can just as easily withdraw aid as extend it, expel visitors as welcome them, and become even worse enemies than we are good friends. Until we make clear to our adversaries the real consequences of their hatred, we will not be serving but subverting the accomplishments of our own soldiers.

What else might we do? To encourage triangulators like the Saudis and Yemenis to hunt down terrorists – as they have only recently begun to do, two years after September 11 – we should remind them that America is not a neutral power, and not necessarily an ally. During the cold war, we accepted that so long as all of Eastern Europe lay under the thrall of Communism, the possibility of free trade, easy travel, or large-scale immigration was precluded. Similarly, so long as there is not yet a single democracy in the Arab Middle East, so long as many governments there pander to a virulent and hateful ideology of anti-Americanism, and so long as millions either ignore or abet the killers of Americans and Jews, why should our relations with these countries not lie under threat of severance by a new iron curtain?

In such a policy, *everything* would be on the table - all foreign aid, travel, commerce, immigration. Our ties with a great number of Middle Eastern regimes should be contingent precisely on their efforts to stop the implicit or explicit help they give to our enemies. With Syria and Iran, in particular, we are already in a death race to put an end to their murderous autocracies faster than they can prevent consensual government from emerging in Iraq. That country will never be truly free as long as there are thousands of terrorists in nearby Damascus and Tehran - something that President Assad and the mullahs seem to grasp far better than we.

Above and beyond this, we must acknowledge the nature of the wider war against terrorism, and of the dark times we are in. We of the postmodern age will lose many more of our own in this struggle, and must kill far more of our premodern enemies to achieve victory. The alternative to that depressing prospect is not a brokered peace but abject defeat, punctuated by more September 11's.

Even apart from the toll in Israel and Iraq, *all* of the deadly terrorism since 9/11 - against the synagogue in Tunisia, against French naval personnel in Pakistan, Americans in Karachi, tourists in Bali, Israelis in Kenya, Russians in both Moscow and Chechnya, and foreigners in Saudi Arabia, the suicide car bombings in Morocco, the Marriott bombing in Indonesia, the mass murder in Bombay, the killings in Turkey, and so forth - has been perpetrated by Islamic fanatics and directed at Westerners, Christians, Hindus, Jews. In this respect, our efforts are better seen in comparison to World War II than by analogy to Panama or Serbia. Over 400 dead is a shocking figure if we are fighting a Noriega-type adversary; in a war to rid the world of the contemporary avatars of Nazism and Japanese militarism, it is proof of our competence so far but also, alas, only a down payment.

As for the Iraqis, it needs to be made clear to them that the country is theirs, but so is the responsibility to keep it theirs, and free. If, in years to come, they wish to avoid the embargos, no-fly zones, and periodic bombings of the past, then they must step forward now to establish a government that will preclude the emergence of a new Saddam Hussein or of Iranian-style mullahs.

How best to help them do this? In a perfect world, it might not be desirable, for example, to arm Shiites and Kurds to pacify the Sunni Triangle, but then many things in war are not desirable. Such militias might at least remind recalcitrant Baathists that thousands of Iraqis are angrier at them for what they did to their country than happy about what they are now trying to do to us.

It is another paradox, but inescapably true, that the more overwhelming our conventional battlefield superiority, the greater the need in the postwar period for different strategies to deal with killers and terrorists who recede when we bomb and blast only to reappear when we stop. Much of the hard military work that must be done in Afghanistan and Iraq should now pass from conventional soldiers to counter-insurgency units and Special Forces – numbering, let us hope, in the thousands rather than the hundreds. These, by means of intelligence-gathering and the creation of friendly cadres, are far better-equipped to perform the unenviable task of hunting down Taliban and Baathists, and to accomplish that task to the satisfaction rather than the chagrin of the local population.

This is not to deny the vital importance of maintaining daytime compounds from which American soldiers wearing Ray-Ban glasses, camouflage, and big boots can issue forth to exhibit strength and provide a bulwark for Iraqi police and militia. It is rather to recognize that there is necessarily something static and wholly against the American character in attempting to fight a defensive police action against paramilitary terrorists from fixed positions. The victory of last April will be largely preserved at night, by ingenious types who alone know how to win the hearts of local Iraqis as they kill the killers in their midst.

Contrary to myth, Americans can take casualties – but only if they know they are exacting a far greater toll on the enemy, and that they are on the offensive and on the way to overwhelming victory. This utter defeat of the Baathists and their terrorist supporters inside and outside the country is the task at hand. For good or ill, the peace in Iraq has been temporarily sidetracked from the political challenge of building a consensual society that will create the conditions inimical to both the ideology of political and religious extremism and its methodology of terror. But defeating Baathist diehards is no mere detour, and our efforts in that realm transcend the need to demonstrate to extremists and fanatics that they are in a war that they can only lose.

In an era of the greatest affluence and security in the history of civilization, the real question before us remains whether the United

States – indeed, whether any Western democracy – still possesses the moral clarity to identify evil as evil, and then the uncontested will to marshal every available resource to fight and eradicate it. In that sense, our willingness to use unremitting force to eliminate vast cadres of proven killers, in Iraq and elsewhere, is a referendum on modern democracy itself.

ROBERT KAGAN AND WILLIAM KRISTOL

2 The Right War for the Right Reasons

WITH ALL THE TURMOIL SURROUNDING DAVID KAY'S COMMENTS on the failure to find stockpiles of biological and chemical weapons in Iraq, it is time to return to first principles, and to ask the question: Was it right to go to war?

Critics of the war, and of the Bush administration, have seized on the failure to find stockpiles of weapons of mass destruction in Iraq. But while his weapons were a key part of the case for removing Saddam, that case was always broader. Saddam's pursuit of weapons of mass destruction was inextricably intertwined with the nature of his tyrannical rule, his serial aggression, his defiance of international obligations, and his undeniable ties to a variety of terrorists, from Abu Nidal to al Qaeda (a topic we will not cover in detail here, rather referring readers to Stephen F. Hayes's reporting in this magazine over the past year). Together, this pattern of behavior made the removal of Saddam desirable and necessary, in the judgment of both the Clinton and Bush administrations. That judgment was and remains correct.

I

It is fashionable to sneer at the moral case for liberating an Iraqi people long brutalized by Saddam's rule. Critics insist mere oppression was not sufficient reason for war, and in any case that it was not Bush's reason. In fact, of course, it was one of Bush's reasons, and the moral and humanitarian purpose provided a compelling reason for a war to remove Saddam. It should certainly have been compelling to those (like us) who supported the war on Slobodan Milosevic a few years ago. In our view – and here we disagree with what Paul Wolfowitz said to *Vanity Fair* a few months ago – liberating the Iraqi people from Saddam's brutal, totalitarian dictatorship would by itself have been sufficient reason to remove Saddam.

Such a rationale is not "merely" moral. As is so often the case in international affairs, there was no separating the nature of Saddam's rule at home from the kinds of policies he conducted abroad. Saddam's regime terrorized his own people, but it also posed a threat to the region, and to us. The moral case for war was linked to strategic considerations related to the peace and security of the Middle East.

Saddam was not a "madman." He was a predator and an aggressor. He achieved through brute force total dominance at home, and it was through force and the threat of force that he sought dominance in his region, as well. He waged war against Iran throughout the 1980's. He invaded Kuwait in 1990. He spent tens of billions of dollars on weapons, both conventional and unconventional. His clear and unwavering ambition, an ambition nurtured and acted upon across three decades, was to dominate the Middle East, both economically and militarily, by attempting to acquire the lion's share of the region's oil and by intimidating or destroying anyone who stood in his way. This, too, was a sufficient reason to remove him from power.

The last time we restated the case for war in Iraq (in October 2003), we quoted extensively from a speech delivered by President Clinton in February 1998. This time we quote extensively from another speech, delivered ten months later, in December 1998, by President Clinton's national security adviser, Sandy Berger. Like President Clinton, Berger did a masterful job of laying out the case for removing Saddam Hussein. And Berger's argument extended beyond the issue of weapons.

Yes, Berger acknowledged, America's "most vital national interest in dealing with Iraq" was to "prevent Saddam from rebuilding his military capability, including weapons of mass destruction, and from using that arsenal to move against his neighbors or his own people." But the threat Saddam posed, by his "continued reign of terror inside Iraq and intimidation outside Iraq," was broader than that. The future course of the Middle East and the Arab world was at stake in Iraq.

"The future of Iraq," Berger argued, "will affect the way in which the Middle East and the Arab world in particular evolve in the next decade and beyond." Those peoples were engaged in a "struggle between two broad visions of the future." One vision was of "political pluralism" and "economic openness." The other vision fed on discontent and fear; it stood for "violent opposition to liberalizing forces." So long as Saddam remained "in power and in confrontation with the world," Berger argued, Iraq would remain "a source of potential conflict in the region," and perhaps more important, "a source of inspiration for those who equate violence with power and compromise with surrender."

In the end, Berger explained, containment of Saddam would not be enough. The "immediate military threat" might be held at bay for the moment. "But even a contained Saddam" was "harmful to stability and to positive change in the region." And in fact, containment was probably not "sustainable over the long run." It was "a costly policy, in economic and strategic terms." The pattern of the previous years – "Iraqi defiance, followed by force mobilization on our part, followed by Iraqi capitulation" – had left "the international community vulnerable to manipulation by Saddam." The longer the standoff continued, Berger warned, "the harder it will be to maintain" international support. Nor was there any question what Saddam would do if and when containment collapsed. "Saddam's history of aggression, and his recent record of deception and defiance, leave no doubt that he would resume his drive for regional domination if he had the chance. Year after year, in conflict after conflict, Saddam has proven that he seeks weapons, including weapons of mass destruction, in order to use them."

For this reason, Berger continued, the Clinton administration had concluded it would be necessary at some point to move beyond containment to regime change. At stake was "our ability to fight terror, avert regional conflict, promote peace, and protect the security of our friends and allies." Quoting President Clinton, Berger suggested "the best way to address the challenge Iraq poses is 'through a government in Baghdad – a new government – that is committed to represent and respect its people, not repress them; that is committed to peace in the region.' "

We made substantially the same argument in a January 1998 letter to President Clinton, a letter whose signatories included Donald Rumsfeld, Paul Wolfowitz, Richard Armitage, and Robert Zoellick. In our letter, we argued that

> The policy of "containment" of Saddam Hussein has been steadily eroding over the past several months. As recent events have demonstrated, we can no longer depend on our partners in the Gulf War coalition to continue to uphold the sanctions or to punish Saddam when he blocks or evades U.N. inspections. Our ability to ensure that Saddam Hussein is not producing weapons of mass destruction, therefore, has substantially diminished. Even

> if full inspections were eventually to resume, which now seems highly unlikely, experience has shown that it is difficult if not impossible to monitor Iraq's chemical and biological weapons production. The lengthy period during which the inspectors will have been unable to enter many Iraqi facilities has made it even less likely that they will be able to uncover all of Saddam's secrets. As a result, in the not-too-distant future we will be unable to determine with any reasonable level of confidence whether Iraq does or does not possess such weapons.

That last prediction turned out to be better than we knew at the time. But we did note that uncertainty itself was a danger, because it meant that the United States would have difficulty knowing whether or how fast the risk from Saddam was increasing. The uncertainty of the situation would, we argued, "have a seriously destabilizing effect on the entire Middle East." It now appears that this uncertainty about Iraq's actual capabilities was perhaps what Saddam aimed to achieve.

II

So the threat of Saddam's weapons of mass destruction was related to the overall political and strategic threat his regime posed to the Middle East. Still, there is no question that Saddam's history with and interest in weapons of mass destruction made his threat distinctive. The danger was not, however, that Iraq would present a direct threat to the physical security of the United States or, in the current popular phrase, pose an "imminent" threat to the American homeland. Our chief concern in 1998, like Berger's, was the threat Saddam posed to regional security and stability, the maintenance of which was in large part the responsibility of the United States. If Saddam "does acquire the capability to deliver weapons of mass destruction," we argued, which eventually he was "almost certain to do if we continue along the present course," American troops in the region, American allies, the stability of the Middle East, and the world's supply of oil would all be put at risk. The threat to the United States was that we would be compelled to defend our allies and our interests in circumstances made much more difficult and dangerous by Saddam's increasingly lethal arsenal.

That was why Saddam's weapons of mass destruction programs, both what we knew about them and what we did not know about them, gave the situation a special urgency. It was urgent in 1998, and it was urgent four years later. There was no doubt in 1998 – and there is no doubt today, based on David Kay's findings – that Saddam was seeking both to pursue WMD programs and to conceal his efforts from U.N. weapons inspectors. After 1995, when the defection of Saddam Hussein's son-in-law and chief organizer of the weapons programs, Hussein Kamal, produced a wealth of new information about Iraqi weapons programs and stockpiles – information the Iraqis were forced to acknowledge was accurate – the U.N. weapons inspections process had become an elaborate cat-and-mouse game. As President Clinton recalled in his speech three years later, Kamal had "revealed that Iraq was continuing to conceal weapons and missiles and the capacity to build many more." The inspectors intensified their search. And they must have been having some success, for as they drew closer to uncovering what the Iraqis were hiding, Saddam grew less and less cooperative and began to block their access to certain facilities.

Finally, there was the famous confrontation over the so-called "presidential palaces" – actually vast complexes of buildings and warehouses that Saddam simply declared off-limits to inspectors. Clinton intelligence officials observed the Iraqis moving equipment that could be used to manufacture weapons out of the range of video cameras that had been installed by U.N. inspectors. By the end of 1997, the *New York Times* reported, the U.N. inspection team could "no longer verify that Iraq is not making weapons of mass destruction" and specifically could not monitor "equipment that could grow seed stocks of biological agents in a matter of hours."

President Clinton declared in early 1998 that Saddam was clearly attempting "to protect whatever remains of his capacity to produce weapons of mass destruction, the missiles to deliver them, and the feed stocks necessary to produce them." The U.N. inspectors believed, Clinton continued, that "Iraq still has stockpiles of chemical and biological munitions . . . and the capacity to restart quickly its production program and build many, many more weapons." Meanwhile, a February 13, 1998, U.S. government White Paper on Iraq's weapons of mass destruction stated that "in the absence of UNSCOM inspectors, Iraq could restart limited mustard agent production within a few weeks, full production of sarin within a few months, and pre-Gulf War production levels – including VX – within two or three years."

It was President Clinton who, in February 1998, posed the critical question: "What if [Saddam] fails to comply and we fail to act, or we take some ambiguous third route, which gives him yet more opportunities to develop this program of weapons of mass destruction. . . . Well, he will conclude that the international community has lost its will. He will then conclude that he can go right on and do more to rebuild an arsenal of devastating destruction. And some day, some way, I guarantee you he'll use this arsenal." "In the next century," Clinton predicted, "the community of nations may see more and more of the very kind of threat Iraq poses now – a rogue state with weapons of mass destruction, ready to use them or provide them to terrorists . . . who travel the world among us unnoticed."

Over the course of 1998, the U.N. inspections process collapsed. Attempts to break the stalemate with Saddam and allow the U.N. inspectors access to the prohibited sites came to naught. About a week after Berger gave his speech warning of the limitations of containment, the Clinton administration launched Operation Desert Fox, a four-day missile and bombing strike on Iraq aimed at destroying as much of Saddam's weapons capabilities as possible. Based on American intelligence, the Clinton administration targeted suspected weapons production facilities throughout Iraq. The Air Force and intelligence agencies believed the bombing had destroyed or degraded a number of Iraqi weapons of mass destruction facilities, but they never knew the extent of the damage, because, of course, there were no inspectors left to investigate.

Saddam expelled the U.N. inspectors in response to the attack, and they did not return until November 2002. As Clinton this past summer recalled, "We might have gotten it all; we might have gotten half of it; we might have gotten none of it. But we didn't know." Clinton went on to say about President Bush's actions in the fall of 2002, "So I thought it was prudent for the president to go to the U.N. and for the U.N. to say you got to let these inspectors in, and this time if you don't cooperate the penalty could be regime change, not just continued sanctions."

The situation as it stood at the beginning of 1999 was troubling to all concerned, and not just to American officials. A report to the U.N. Security Council in January 1999 by Richard Butler, head of the U.N. weapons inspections team, warned that much was not known about the Iraqi program but that there was ample reason to believe a significant weapons of mass destruction program still existed in Iraq. Butler recounted a seven-year history of Iraqi deception and concealment of proscribed weapons and activities. During the first four years of inspections, Butler noted, the inspectors "had been very substantially misled by Iraq both in terms of its understanding of Iraq's proscribed weapons programs and the continuation of prohibited activities, even under the [U.N.'s] monitoring." Only the defection of Hussein Kamal had revealed that the inspectors had been wrong in their "positive conclusions on Iraq's compliance." But even after Kamal's defection, the Iraqis had continued to conceal programs and mislead the inspectors. The Iraqis were caught lying about whether they had ever put VX nerve agent in so-called "special warheads." Scientific examinations proved that they had.

The Iraqis were also caught lying about their biological weapons program. First they denied having one; then, when that falsehood was exposed, they denied weaponizing their biological weapons agents. Eventually they were forced to admit that they "had weaponized BW agents and deployed biological weapons for combat use." The U.N. inspectors reported that hundreds of shells filled with mustard agent had been declared "lost" by Iraq and remained unaccounted for. There were some 6,000 aerial bombs filled with chemical agent that were unaccounted for. There were also some "special warheads" with biological weapons agent unaccounted for. Butler's report concluded that, in addition, "it needs to be recognized that Iraq possesses an industrial capacity and knowledge base, through which biological warfare agents could be produced quickly and in volume, if the Government of Iraq decided to do so."

The inspectors left, and for the next four years, Saddam's activities were shrouded in darkness. After all, many prohibited Iraqi activities had escaped detection even while the inspectors were trying to monitor them. Without the inspectors, the task of keeping track of Saddam's programs was well-nigh impossible.

III

When the Bush administration came to office, therefore, it had no less reason to worry about Saddam's potential capabilities than the Clinton administration. And it had no more reason to believe that containment would be sustainable. In the early months of the administration, Bush officials began to contemplate some increased support for Iraqi opposition forces, pursuant to legislation passed overwhelmingly in 1998, which was supported by the Clinton administration. (The Iraq Liberation Act chronicled Saddam's use of chemical weapons and declared that Iraq "has persisted in a pattern of deception and concealment regarding the history of its weapons of mass destruction programs." It continued: "It should be the policy of the United States to support efforts to remove the regime headed by Saddam Hussein from power in Iraq and to promote the emergence of a democratic government to replace that regime.") Meanwhile, Secretary of State Colin Powell was trying to prevent the collapse of the international sanctions regime and to staunch the hemorrhaging of consensus at the U.N. Security Council by instituting a more streamlined effort, the so-called "smart sanctions."

Then came the terrorist attacks of September 11, 2001. September 11 shocked the nation, and it shocked the president. Its effect was to make many both inside and outside the administration take a closer look at international threats, because it was clear that all of us had been too sanguine about such threats prior to September 11. Nor was it in the least surprising that the issue of Iraq arose immediately. True, neither candidate in the 2000 election had talked much about Iraq. But that was not because anyone believed it had ceased to be an urgent and growing problem. The Clinton administration didn't want to talk about it because it felt it had run out of options. The Bush campaign didn't talk about it because Bush was running a campaign, ironic in retrospect, which promised a less active, more restrained American role in the world. But that did not mean the Iraq issue had gone away, and after September 11, it returned to the fore. After all, we had a decade-long history of confrontation with Iraq, we were flying military missions in Iraqi air space, President Clinton had declared Saddam the greatest threat to our security in the 21st century, Clinton officials like Sandy Berger and Madeleine Albright had concluded that Saddam must eventually be removed, and U.N. weapons inspectors had written one alarming report after another about Saddam's current and potential weapons capabilities.

So the Bush administration concluded that it had to remove the Saddam Hussein regime once and for all, just as Clinton and Berger had suggested might someday be necessary. For all the reasons that Berger had outlined, Saddam's regime itself was the problem, above and beyond his weapons capabilities. It was an obstacle to progress in the Middle East and the Arab world. It was a threat to the Iraqi people and to Iraq's neighbors. But a big part of the threat involved Saddam's absolute determination to arm himself with both conventional and unconventional weapons.

September 11 had added new dimensions to the danger. For as Bush and many others argued, what if Saddam allowed his weapons capabilities to be shared with terrorists? What if, someday in the future, terrorists like those who crashed airplanes into the World Trade Center and the Pentagon had nuclear, chemical, or biological weapons? Would they hesitate to use them? The possible nexus between terrorism and Iraq's weapons program made Iraq an even more urgent issue. Was this concern far-fetched? If so, it was exactly the same far-fetched concern that had preoccupied President Clinton in 1998, when he warned, in his speech on Iraq, about a "rogue state with weapons of mass destruction, ready to use them or provide them to terrorists," and when he had spoken of an "unholy axis" of international terrorists and outlaw states as one of the greatest threats Americans faced.

Nor was it surprising that as President Bush began to move toward war with Iraq in the fall and winter of 2002, he mustered substantial support among Democrats as well as Republicans. A majority of Democratic senators – including, of course, John Kerry and John Edwards – voted for the resolution authorizing the president to use force against Iraq. And why not? The Bush administration's approach to Iraq was fundamentally in keeping with that of the Clinton administration, except that after September 11, inaction seemed even less acceptable. The majority of the Democratic party foreign policy establishment supported the war, and not because they were misled by the Bush administration's rhetorical hype leading up to the war. (Its hype was appreciably less than that of Clinton secretary of defense William Cohen, who appeared on national television in late 1997 holding a bag of sugar and noting that the same amount of anthrax "would destroy at least half the population" of Washington, D.C. At a Pentagon press briefing on Iraq's WMD, Cohen also noted that if Saddam had "as much VX in storage as the U.N. suspects," he would "be able to kill every human being on the face of the planet.") Nor did they support the war because they were fundamentally misled by American intelligence about the nature and extent of Saddam's weapons programs. Most of what they and everyone else knew about those programs we had learned from the U.N. inspectors, not from U.S. intelligence.

IV

Some of that intelligence has now turned out to be wrong. Some of it has turned out to be right. And it is simply too soon to tell about the rest. The press has focused attention almost entirely on David Kay's assertion that there were no stockpiles of chemical and biological weapons when the United States and its allies invaded Iraq last March. We'll address that assertion in a moment. But what about the rest of Kay's testimony?

The key question for more than a decade, for both the Clinton and the Bush administrations, was not only what weapons Saddam had but what weapons he was trying to obtain, and how long it might be before containment failed and he was able to obtain them. The goal of American policy, and indeed of the U.N. Security Council over the course of the dozen years after the end of the Gulf War in 1991, was not primarily to find Saddam's existing stockpiles. That was subsidiary to the larger goal, which was to achieve Iraq's disarmament, including the elimination not only of existing prohibited weapons but of all such weapons programs, to ensure that Iraq would not possess weapons of mass destruction now or in the future. As

Richard Butler and other weapons inspectors have argued, this task proved all but impossible once it became clear that Saddam was determined to acquire such weapons at some point. As Butler repeated time and again in his reports to the Security Council, the whole inspections regime was premised on Saddam's cooperation. But Saddam never cooperated, not in the 1990's and not in 2003.

It is important to recall that the primary purpose of Security Council Resolution 1441, passed on November 8, 2002, was not to discover whether Saddam had weapons and programs. There was little doubt that Saddam had them. The real question was whether he was ready to make a clean breast of everything and give up not only his forbidden weapons but also his efforts to acquire them once and for all. The purpose was to give Saddam "one final chance" to change his stripes, to offer full cooperation by revealing and dismantling all his programs and to forswear all such efforts in the future.

After all, what would be accomplished if Saddam turned over stockpiles and dismantled programs, only to restart them the minute the international community turned its back? Saddam might be slowed, but he would not be stopped. This was the logic that had led the Clinton administration to conclude that someday, somehow, the only answer to the problem would be Saddam's removal from power. Not surprisingly, the Bush administration was even more convinced that Saddam's removal was the only answer. That the administration went along with the inspections process embodied in Resolution 1441 was a concession to international and domestic pressure. No senior official, including Secretary Powell, believed there was any but the smallest chance Saddam would comply with the terms of Resolution 1441.

Resolution 1441 demanded that, within 30 days, Iraq provide "a currently accurate, full, and complete declaration of all aspects of its programs to develop chemical, biological, and nuclear weapons, ballistic missiles, and other delivery systems such as unmanned aerial vehicles and dispersal systems designed for use on aircraft, including any holdings and precise locations of such weapons, components, sub-components, stocks of agents, and related material and equipment, the locations and work of its research, development and production facilities, as well as all other chemical, biological, and nuclear programs, including any which it claims are for purposes not related to weapon production or material." Administration officials doubted Saddam would do this. They hoped only that, once Saddam's noncompliance became clear, they would win unanimous support for war at the U.N. Security Council.

And it was pretty clear at the time that Saddam was not complying. In his May 30, 2003, report to the Security Council, Hans Blix reported that the declared stocks of anthrax and VX remained unaccounted for. And he elaborated: "Little progress was made in the solution of outstanding issues. . . . The long list of proscribed items unaccounted for and as such resulting in unresolved disarmament issues was not shortened either by the inspections or by Iraqi declarations and documentation."

Now, of course, we know more definitively that Saddam did not comply with Resolution 1441. That is a part of Kay's testimony that has been widely ignored. What Kay discovered in the course of his eight-month-long investigation was that Iraq had failed to answer outstanding questions about its arsenal and programs. Indeed, it had continued to engage in an elaborate campaign of deception and concealment of weapons activities throughout the time when Hans Blix and the UNMOVIC inspectors were in the country, and right up until the day of the invasion, and beyond.

As Kay told the Senate Armed Services Committee last month, the Iraq Survey Group "discovered hundreds of cases, based on both documents, physical evidence, and the testimony of Iraqis, of activities that were prohibited under the initial U.N. Resolution 687 and that should have been reported under 1441, with Iraqi testimony that not only did they not tell the U.N. about this, they were instructed not to do it and they hid material." Kay reported, "We have had a number of Iraqis who have come forward and said, 'We did not tell the U.N. about what we were hiding, nor would we have told the U.N.,' " because the risks were too great. And what were the Iraqis hiding? As Kay reports, "They maintained programs and activities, and they certainly had the intentions at a point to resume their programs. So there was a lot they wanted to hide because it showed what they were doing was illegal." As Kay reported last October, his survey team uncovered "dozens of WMD-related program activities and significant amounts of equipment that Iraq concealed from the U.N. during the inspections that began in late 2002." Specifically, Kay reported:

- A clandestine network of laboratories and safehouses within the Iraqi Intelligence Service that contained equipment suitable for research in the production of chemical and biological weapons. This kind of equipment was explicitly mentioned in Hans Blix's requests for information, but was instead concealed from Blix throughout his investigations.
- A prison laboratory complex, which may have been used in human testing of biological weapons agents. Iraqi officials working to

prepare for U.N. inspections in 2002 and 2003 were explicitly ordered not to acknowledge the existence of the prison complex.

- So-called "reference strains" of biological organisms, which can be used to produce biological weapons. The strains were found in a scientist's home.
- New research on agents applicable to biological weapons, including Congo Crimean Hemorrhagic Fever, and continuing research on ricin and aflatoxin – all of which was, again, concealed from Hans Blix despite his specific request for any such information.
- Plans and advanced design work on new missiles with ranges up to at least 1,000 kilometers – well beyond the 150-kilometer limit imposed on Iraq by the U.N. Security Council. These missiles would have allowed Saddam to threaten targets from Ankara to Cairo.

Last month Kay also reported that Iraq "was in the early stages of renovating the [nuclear] program, building new buildings."

As Kay has testified repeatedly, Iraq was "in clear material violation of 1441." So if the world had known in February 2003 what Kay says we know now – that there were no large stockpiles of weapons, but that Iraq continued to pursue weapons of mass destruction programs and to deceive and conceal these efforts from the U.N. inspectors led by Blix during the time allocated by Resolution 1441 – wouldn't there have been at least as much, and probably more, support for the war? For Saddam would have been in flagrant violation of yet another set of commitments to disarm. He would have demonstrated once again that he was unwilling to abandon these programs, that he was unwilling to avail himself of this "last chance" and disarm once and for all. Had the world discovered unambiguously in February 2003 that Saddam was cheating on its commitments in Resolution 1441, surely even the French would have found it difficult to block a U.N. resolution authorizing war. As Dominique de Villepin acknowledged in the contentious months before the war, "We all realize that success in the inspections presupposes that we get full and complete cooperation from Iraq." What if it were as clear then as it is now that Saddam was engaged in another round of deceit and concealment?

If Kay is right, Saddam had learned a lesson at some point in the 1990's, perhaps after the Kamal defection, perhaps before or after Operation Desert Fox in 1998. But it was not the lesson the United States or the rest of the world wanted him to learn. At some point, Saddam may have decided that instead of building up large stockpiles of weapons, the safer thing would be to advance his covert programs for producing weapons but wait until the pressure was off to produce the weapons themselves. By the time inspectors returned to Iraq in 2002, Saddam was ready to be a little more forthcoming, because he had rejiggered his program to withstand somewhat greater scrutiny. He had scaled back to a skeletal program, awaiting the moment when he could breathe life back into it. Nevertheless, even then he could not let the inspectors see everything. Undoubtedly he hoped that if he could get through that last round, he would be home free, eventually without sanctions or further inspections. We now know that in early 2003, Saddam assumed that the United States would once again launch a bombing campaign, but not a full scale invasion. So he figured he would survive, and, as Kay concluded, "They maintained programs and activities, and they certainly had the intentions at a point to resume their programs."

Was this a satisfactory outcome? If this much had been accomplished, if we had succeeded in getting Saddam to scale back his programs in the hope of eventually turning them on again, was that a reason not to go to war? Kay does not believe so. Nor do we. If the United States had pulled back last year, we would have placed ourselves in the trap that Berger had warned about five years earlier. We would have returned to the old pattern of "Iraqi defiance, followed by force mobilization on our part, followed by Iraqi capitulation," followed by a new round of Iraqi defiance - and the wearing down of both the international community and the United States.

There was an argument against going to war last year. But let's remember what that argument was. It had nothing to do with whether or not Saddam had weapons of mass destruction and WMD programs. Everyone from Howard Dean to the *New York Times* editorial board to Dominique de Villepin and Jacques Chirac assumed that he had both. Most of the arguments against the war concerned timing. The most frequent complaint was that Bush was rushing to war. Why not give Blix and his inspectors another three months or six months?

We now know, however, that giving Blix a few more months would not have made a difference. Last month Kay was asked what would have happened if Blix and his team had been allowed to continue their mission. Kay responded, "All I can say is that among an extensive body of Iraqi scientists who are talking to us, they have said: The U.N. interviewed us; we did not tell them the truth, we did not show them this equipment, we did not talk about these programs; we couldn't do it as long as Saddam was in power. I suspect regardless of how long they had stayed, that attitude would have been the same." Given the "terror regime of Saddam," Kay concluded, he and his team learned things after the war "that no U.N. inspector would have ever learned" while Saddam was still in power.

So it is very unlikely that, given another three months or six months, the Blix team would have come to any definitive conclusion one way or another. Nor, therefore, would there have been a much greater probability of winning a unanimous vote at the Security Council for war once those additional six months had passed. Whether the United States could have kept 200,000 troops on a permanent war footing in the Persian Gulf for another six months is even more doubtful.

V

Did the administration claim the Iraqi threat was imminent, in the sense that Iraq possessed weapons that were about to be used against the United States? That is the big charge leveled by the Bush administration's critics these days. It is rather surprising, given the certainty with which this charge is thrown around, how little the critics have in the way of quotations from administration officials to back it up. Saying that action is urgent is not the same thing as saying the threat is imminent. In fact, the president said the threat was not imminent, and that we had to act (urgently) before the threat became imminent. This was well understood. As Senate Democratic leader Tom Daschle said on October 10, 2002, explaining his support for the legislation authorizing the president to go to war, "The threat posed by Saddam Hussein may not be imminent, but it is real, it is growing, and it cannot be ignored."

One reason critics have been insisting that the administration claimed the threat from Iraq was imminent, we believe, is that it is fairly easy to prove that the danger to the United States was not imminent. But the central thesis of the antiwar argument as it was advanced before the war asserted that the threat from Iraq would not have been imminent even if Saddam had possessed every conceivable weapon in his arsenal. Remember, the vast majority of arguments against the war assumed that he did have these weapons. But those weapons, it was argued, did not pose an imminent threat to the nation because Saddam, like the Soviet Union, could be deterred. Indeed, the fact that he had the weapons, some argued, was all the more reason why the United States should not go to war. After all, it was argued, the likeliest scenario for Saddam's actually using the weapons he had was in the event of an American invasion. The current debate over "imminence" is an ex post facto attempt to relitigate the old argument over the war. The non-discovery of weapons stockpiles has not changed the contours of that debate.

VI

On "Meet the Press" on February 8, Tim Russert asked the president whether the war in Iraq was "a war of choice or a war of necessity." The president paused before responding, asking Russert to elaborate, as if unwilling to accept the dichotomy. He was right.

After all, fighting a "war of choice" sounds problematic. But how many of our wars have been, strictly speaking, wars of necessity? How often did the country face immediate peril and destruction unless war was launched? Was World War I a war of necessity? Was World War II before the attack on Pearl Harbor, or afterwards with respect to fighting Germany in Europe? Was the Spanish-American War a war of necessity? Was the Korean War? Never mind Vietnam, the Dominican Republic, Grenada, Panama, Somalia, Haiti, Bosnia, and Kosovo. And what about the first Gulf War? Many argued that Saddam could be (indeed, was) contained in Kuwait, and that he could eventually have been forced to retreat by economic sanctions.

In some sense all of these wars were wars of choice. But when viewed in the context of history and international circumstances, they were all based on judgments about the costs of inaction, the benefits of action, and on strategic calculations that action then would be far preferable to action later in less favorable circumstances. In other words, war was necessary to our national interest, if not absolutely necessary to the immediate protection of the homeland.

In this case, we believe that war would have come eventually because of the trajectory that Saddam was on – assuming the United States intended to continue to play its role as guarantor of peace and security in the Middle East. The question was whether it was safer to act sooner or later. The president argued, convincingly, that it was safer – it was necessary – to act sooner. Sanctions could not have been maintained; containment, already dubious, was far less persuasive after September 11; and so the war to remove Saddam was, in the broad strategic sense, in the sense relevant to serious international politics, necessary. This is of course a legitimate subject of debate – but it would be almost as much so even if large stockpiles of weapons had already been recovered.

VII

So what about those stockpiles? The failure to find them, and now David Kay's claim that they did not exist at the time of the invasion last year (a claim reported by an astonishing number of journalists as meaning they never existed at all), has led many to maintain that the entire war was fought on false pretenses. We have addressed that claim. But we also want to address Kay's assertion.

We are prepared to believe that the large stockpiles of anthrax, ricin, VX, and other biological and chemical weapons that once existed were at some point destroyed by the Iraqis. But we do not understand why Kay is so confident he knows what happened to those stockpiles, or to other parts of Saddam's weapons programs that have not been found.

According to Kay's testimony before the Senate (and since he has provided no written report and no documentation to support his recent claims, this is all anyone has to go on), Kay and his team "went after this not in the way of trying to find where the weapons are hidden." When the Survey Group did not find the weapons in "the obvious places," presumably meaning the places that had been identified by intelligence and other sources, Kay explains, he tried other means of discovering the truth. His principal method appears to have been interviews with scientists who would have known what was produced and where it might be stored, as well as a search through a portion of the documents uncovered after the war. Kay acknowledges that stockpiles may, in fact, still be hidden somewhere. But he does not believe they are.

Under questioning from the senators, however, Kay admitted a few areas of uncertainty. The first concerns his interviews with Iraqi scientists. On some occasions Kay has claimed that, with Saddam out of power, it could be assumed that scientists once fearful of telling the truth would now be willing to speak. Therefore, their testimony that no weapons stockpiles exist could be trusted. But when asked whether people involved in Iraqi weapons programs might now fear prosecution for war crimes, Kay said, "Absolutely. And a number of those in custody are worried about that greatly," which is "one reason they're not talking." So it turns out there are scientists who are not talking. This produces, Kay suggests, "a level of unresolvable ambiguity" about Saddam's weapons programs. But is the ambiguity truly "unresolvable," or was it just unresolvable within the limited time of Kay's investigation? Is it possible that when all the scientists feel safe enough to talk, we may learn more?

The same question might be asked about the physical searches Kay did not conduct. When Kay delivered his interim report in October 2003, he noted that there were approximately 130 ammunition storage areas in Iraq, some of them spanning an area of about 50 square miles, and including some 600,000 tons of artillery shells, rockets, aviation bombs, and other ordnance. In the 1990's, U.N. inspectors learned that the Iraqi military stored chemical ordnance at the same ammunition depots where the conventional rounds were stored. As of October, only 10 of these ammunition depots had been searched by U.S. teams. Kay has not said how many were searched in the succeeding four months, but one suspects a great many still have not been examined. Surely this creates another level of ambiguity, which, in time, may be resolved.

Finally there is the question of Iraqi documents. We understand that thousands of pages of documents seized at the end of the war have still not been read. During the 1990's, U.N. inspectors frequently opened treasure troves of information simply with the discovery of a single document in a mountain of paper. Is it possible that some of the unread documents contain useful information? In addition, according to Kay's October report and his most recent testimony, Iraqi officials undertook a massive effort to destroy evidence, burning documents and destroying computer hard-drives. The result, Kay acknowledged, is that "we're really not going to be able to prove . . . some of the positive conclusions that we're going to come to." Yet another level of ambiguity.

The truth is, neither Kay nor anyone else knows what happened to the weapons stockpiles that we know Iraq once had – because the Iraqis admitted having them. Again, we are willing to be persuaded that Saddam had no weapons stockpiles last year when the war began. But it is too soon, we believe, to come firmly to that conclusion. Nor do we find particularly persuasive the argument that Saddam was only pretending to have weapons of mass destruction, or that he was delusional and being deceived by all around him. These hypotheses are possible. It is also possible we will find stockpiles of weapons, or evidence of their destruction or removal just before the war.

Kay, oddly, has himself suggested in one press interview that the stockpiles or some portion of them may have been transferred to Syria before the war. If that were true, then it would not be the case, pace Kay, that "we were all wrong." This past week, moreover, another U.S. government report concerning Iraq's weapons surfaced in the press. Although widely misreported as confirming Kay's claim regarding the stockpiles, in fact the report casts doubt on it. In December 2002, according to *USA Today*, a team of U.S. intelligence analysts predicted it would be extremely difficult to find weapons of mass destruction in the aftermath of an invasion. The study had "considered but rejected the possibility that Iraq had no banned weapons." But it predicted that "locating a program that . . . has been driven by denial and deception imperatives is no small task." Efforts to find the arms after the war would be like "trying to find multiple needles in a haystack . . . against the background of not knowing how many needles may have been hidden."

It remains possible that new evidence will be found. We understand why some now want to declare the search over. But we can hardly see how it benefits the people of the United States or the world to declare it over prematurely.

VIII

Whatever the results of that search, it will continue to be the case that the war was worth fighting, and that it was necessary. For the people of Iraq, the war put an end to three decades of terror and suffering. The mass graves uncovered since the end of the war are alone sufficient justification for it. Assuming the United States remains committed to helping establish a democratic government in Iraq, that will be a blessing both to the Iraqi people and to their neighbors. As for those neighbors, the threat of Saddam's aggression, which hung over the region for more than two decades, has finally been eliminated. The prospects for war in the region have been substantially diminished by our action.

It is also becoming clear that the battle of Iraq has been an important victory in the broader war in which we are engaged, a war against terror, against weapons proliferation, and for a new Middle East. Already, other terror-implicated regimes in the region that were developing weapons of mass destruction are feeling pressure, and some are beginning to move in the right direction. Libya has given up its weapons of mass destruction program. Iran has at least gestured toward opening its nuclear program to inspection. The clandestine international network organized by Pakistan's A. Q. Khan that has been so central to nuclear proliferation to rogue states has been exposed. From Iran to Saudi Arabia, liberal forces seem to have been encouraged. We are paying a real price in blood and treasure in Iraq. But we believe that it is already clear – as clear as such things get in the real world – that the price of the liberation of Iraq has been worth it.

JAMES KURTH

3 Iraq: Losing the American Way

THE IRAQ WAR HAS BEEN UNDERWAY FOR LESS THAN A YEAR, BUT IT has already lasted long enough for us to get some sense of its place in American history and particularly in the grand narrative of America's role in the world. The war has a complex relation with the major dimensions of American foreign policy – particularly the diplomatic, military, and political – but it is increasingly evident that the war policy of the Bush administration represents a radical abandonment of traditional American ways of dealing with the world, ways that overall have served the United States very well.

First, the way that the administration prepared for the war – disregarding the objections of every international organization and most of America's traditional allies – was a sharp departure from the long-standing U.S. diplomatic practice of obtaining some form of international approval and legitimization for our wars and military interventions. The Iraq War represents a repudiation of the traditional American way of diplomacy. Second, the way that the administration has fought the war – deploying military forces unusually few in number and now stretched far too thin – has been a sharp departure from the long-standing U.S. military practice of using overwhelming mass not only to defeat an enemy but also to deter any renewed resistance later. The Iraq War represents a repudiation of the traditional American way of war. Finally, the way that the administration has tried to establish stability and peace – promoting liberal democracy while imposing military occupation – is in some senses an extension of the historic U.S. practice with democratization projects,

Reprinted from the *American Conservative*, March 15, 2004, by permission.

but it is one carried to such an unrealistic and impractical extreme that the prospects for success are bleak. The Iraq War represents a perversion of the traditional American way of democratization. In sum, the war is a three-dimensional assault on the American way in international affairs. It is reasonable to expect that it will cause serious harm to America's role in the world.

The diplomatic damage has already been much discussed by policy analysts. Certainly, the arrogant posturing and unilateral actions of the Bush administration as it went to war alienated most of our traditional European allies and provoked suspicion, resentment, and even anger in many. However, unexpected difficulties and experienced incapacities can teach even abrasive officials that help from others - even inferior others - can be a good thing. By now, almost one year into the war, the administration has been driven by its hardships in Iraq to solicit the assistance of the very nations, and the United Nations, that it held in such contempt at the beginning of the war. And remarkably, but realistically, these nations and the United Nations are beginning to respond positively and to heal their breach with the United States. Most of the diplomatic damage from the war is likely to prove self-correcting and short-lived, perhaps like the quarrels of Russia and China with the United States regarding the Kosovo War five years ago.

The Iraq War is likely, however, to cause more grave and long-term injury to the U.S. military and to U.S. efforts to promote democracy abroad. This is because of its violations of the traditional American way of war and way of democratization.

The American Way of War

Military strategists and historians have discerned in some nations a distinctive strategic culture or way of war. In the last third of the 20th century, there was a widespread understanding among these professionals that there was a distinctive American way of war and that it was characterized by a reliance upon such advantages as (1) overwhelming mass (a pronounced advantage in men and materiel), (2) wide-ranging mobility (a pronounced advantage in transportation and communication), (3) high-technology weapons systems, and, underlying and sustaining them all, (4) high public support for the war effort. The purest expression of this American way of war was, of course, World War II. Another excellent example was the Persian Gulf War. However, the origins of the American way of war lie in the greatest

American conflict of all, the Civil War. The use of overwhelming mass was crucial to the final victory of the North; it was exemplified by the strategy of Ulysses S. Grant. Conversely, the use of wide-ranging mobility was critical to the initial victories of the South; it was exemplified by the strategy of Robert E. Lee.

The classical American way of war was a product of the distinctive geographical and economic features of the United States. The U.S. possessed a vast continental territory, which was endowed with ample natural resources and with a population larger than that of most European powers. Thus the United States almost always had a pronounced advantage in men and materiel. Only the Soviet Union could surpass the U.S. in this respect. In turn, mass geography and widespread population created a need for a correspondingly extensive transportation and communication network, and the large industry and advanced technology of the U.S. economy provided the means with which to build it. Furthermore, the United States was bordered by two oceans; it was not only a continent but also a continental island. This also created demand for a transportation and communication network that extended to other continents. This meant that the United States always had a pronounced advantage in the rapid movement of people and products in peace and of men and materiel in war. No power has ever surpassed the U.S. in this respect. The conjunction of a pronounced advantage in both mass and mobility made the United States the most successful military power of the 20th century, and thereby made the 20th century the American century. No other military power could excel in both dimensions.

On the rare but important occasions when the United States could not deploy its advantages in both mass and mobility, the U.S. military faced serious problems. Both the Korean War and the Vietnam War degenerated into wars of attrition in which the U.S. military had the advantage in mass firepower but no obvious advantage in the mobility of its ground combat forces. In the last two years of the Korean War, both the U.S. Army and the communist armies were trapped in a static war of position near the 38th Parallel, and the end result was a stalemate. In the Vietnam War, the communist guerrilla forces had the advantage in mobility, and this contributed greatly to the U.S. defeat. Indeed, it is the nature of any guerrilla war that the insurgent forces have the advantage of mobility, and the counterinsurgency forces have the advantage of mass. It seems that the classical American way of war has no obvious answer if the military challenge comes from guerrillas and insurgents.

In the aftermath of its Vietnam debacle, the U.S. Army painfully examined the lessons of that war, and it largely concluded that the classical American way of war was really the only right way of war for the Army. The lessons learned were institutionalized in the curriculum of the Army War College, as well as several other military schools, and in the strategic doctrine, bureaucratic organization, and weapons procurement of the Army itself. Many of the lessons learned were crystallized in what became known as the Weinberger/Powell Doctrine (after Caspar Weinberger, secretary of defense in the Reagan administration and Gen. Colin Powell, chairman of the Joint Chiefs of Staff in the first Bush administration). Central to the classical American way of war and its recapitulation in the Weinberger/Powell Doctrine was the idea that when the United States goes to war, it should do so as a nation defending its vital national interests against another nation, and when the U.S. Army goes to war, it should do so as an army fighting another army. Wars to advance peripheral, imperial interests and wars against insurgent forces were violations of the American way of war.

The Rumsfeld Transformation Project

From the beginning of the second Bush administration, Secretary of Defense Donald Rumsfeld has worked vigorously and systematically to overthrow the classical American way of war and the Weinberger/Powell Doctrine and to replace them with a new program of military "transformation" and a new doctrine of preemptive (really preventive) war. He has moved to reduce the role of heavy weapons systems (armor and artillery) and large combat divisions in the U.S. Army and to increase the role of lighter and smaller forces (airborne and special operations); in effect, he seeks to reduce the role of mass and to accentuate the role of mobility. To implement his transformation project, he has canceled the Crusader heavy-artillery system, and he has appointed a retired Special Forces general to be the new Army Chief of Staff. Most importantly, however, Rumsfeld has seen the Iraq War as the pilot plant and exemplary case of his grand project of transformation. If the U.S. could win a war in Iraq with a transformed military and a transformed doctrine, it would also be a decisive victory in Washington for the thoroughly new American way of war in its bureaucratic struggles with the old one.

The Rumsfeld transformation project gains credibility because there are indeed some serious problems with the classical American way of war – particularly with the idea that the U.S. Army should only fight another army. The most obvious difficulty is that there no longer seems to be any other real army to fight. Indeed, neither the Army, the Navy, nor the Air Force has any equivalent force or "peer competitor" to fight. Although the Chinese nation might become a peer competitor to the American nation in a couple of decades, that is far in the future, and the last peer competitor – the Soviet military – is now far in the past.

The United States still has enemies, however, most obviously in transnational networks of Islamic terrorists but also in rogue states, such as North Korea. These enemies will seek to attack the United States not with conventional military forces or an American-style way of war but with asymmetrical warfare. At the upper end of the war spectrum, this will mean weapons of mass destruction, particularly nuclear ones in the case of North Korea. At the lower end of the spectrum will be terrorist operations like al-Qaeda and guerrilla warfare, with the Iraqi insurgents now becoming the exemplar. Of course, the most ominous threat comes from a diabolical synthesis of the upper end and the lower end – weapons of mass destruction in the hands of transnational terrorist networks.

The Rumsfeld transformation program and preemptive doctrine do not really address the challenge of rogue states that have already acquired nuclear weapons. Hypothetically, some combination of highly accurate intelligence and highly effective weapons, such as nuclear bunker bombs, could destroy an enemy's stock of WMD. However, the failure to find any significant stock of such weapons in Iraq certainly casts doubt on the accuracy of U.S. intelligence. And even highly effective weapons systems would have a hard time destroying widely dispersed stocks of biological weapons. The only way that the Rumsfeld transformation project can deal with the WMD threat is when a rogue state has not yet acquired these weapons and a U.S. military operation can destroy the rogue regime before it does so. But this would really be a preventive war, not a preemptive one. This was the case with Iraq and conceivably could become the case with Iran.

Nor does the Rumsfeld transformation project really address the challenge of transnational terrorist networks, such as al-Qaeda. This threat is better dealt with by a multidimensional array of agencies and instruments (intelligence, security, and financial) working with their counterparts in other countries that face similar threats, particularly those in Europe. The war in Iraq certainly has not helped to enhance these counterterrorist capabilities, and it may have made more difficult the necessary international trust and cooperation.

The Rumsfeld Army and Counterinsurgency War

The only task that the new Rumsfeld Army, with its lighter, more mobile configuration, can perform better than the old classical Army, with its heavy armor and artillery configuration, will be operations against an enemy that is even more light and mobile, such as guerrillas and insurgents. And here, several ironies are immediately apparent. First, the origins of the Weinberger/Powell Doctrine lie in the lessons learned from the Vietnam War, and its basic impetus was "no more Vietnams." Among other things, this meant that the regular units of the U.S. Army would fight no more counterinsurgency wars. The Rumsfeld transformation project amounts to a radical overthrow of the Weinberger/Powell Doctrine, and it seeks to return the Army to the period at the beginning of the Vietnam War – the era when Secretary of Defense Robert McNamara was engaged in his own radical program of military transformation and when other political appointees of the Kennedy and Johnson administrations were enthusiastic advocates of some major combination of high-technology and counterinsurgency. More fundamentally, the Rumsfeld project seeks to transform the U.S. Army into an instrument which will fight for peripheral, imperial interests, and not just for vital national ones. As such, the new way of war can be seen as the neoconservative way of war.

Second, it was not until the United States invaded Iraq and imposed a military occupation that the U.S. faced any guerrilla threat that needed to be dealt with by regular U.S. military forces. (Almost everyone agreed that the guerrilla forces in Afghanistan and in Colombia would be better handled by a combination of U.S. Special Forces and local military forces.) The U.S. occupation of Iraq has created, for the first time since the Vietnam War, the very problem that the Rumsfeld transformation project was supposed to solve.

Third, even before Rumsfeld began his construction of his new Army and his deconstruction of the old one, the United States already had a long established, lighter, and more mobile ground force. That was the U.S. Marines. During the first half of the 20th century, the Marines had far more experience and success with light and mobile operations than did the Army. This included operations against insurgents in the Caribbean basin and in Central America. With only minor modifications, and perhaps some expansion, the Marines could perform virtually all of the tasks that Rumsfeld's lighter, more mobile, transformed Army is supposed to perform. But his new Army may not be able to perform some of the tasks that the old army could perform so well, such as quickly overwhelming another peer competitor army, if one should ever come into being and pose a threat to the vital national interests of the United States.

The American Way of Democratization

The 20th century witnessed numerous attempts to bring democracy to countries that hitherto had been ruled by dictatorial or authoritarian regimes. Most of these efforts were promoted by the United States, and many of them were backed by U.S. military intervention and occupation. Because the 20th century was the American century, it was also the century of democratization. Indeed, the century began with the United States engaged in two separate military occupations to bring democracy (albeit of a distinctively American sort and in a somewhat distant future) to colonies of the former Spanish empire, one in the Philippines and one in Cuba; the Philippine occupation and successful repression of the insurgents there was especially bloody and costly. A decade later, President Woodrow Wilson defined the essence of this new century - which indeed might be seen also as the Wilsonian century - when he first sent the U.S. Marines into several Latin American countries and declared that he was going to "teach the South Americans to elect good men," and then sent the entire U.S. military into Europe and declared that the United States was going "to make the world safe for democracy."

The U.S. attempt at the beginning of the 21st century to use military conquest and occupation to bring democracy to Iraq and, by a process vaguely defined, perhaps to its neighbors as well (particularly Syria, Iran, and Saudi Arabia) is thus the latest chapter in a grand American narrative that has been underway for more than a hundred years. By now, many countries know what it means to be, in the words of Jean-Jacques Rousseau, "forced to be free."

Indeed, there have been four great theaters where the United States has performed its epic drama of political democratization through military occupation, of ballots through bullets, over the decades. These were (1) the Caribbean basin and Central America from the 1900's–1930's (Cuba, the Dominican Republic, Haiti, and Nicaragua) and again from the 1960's–1990's (the Dominican Republic and Haiti again and also Grenada and Panama); (2) Central Europe from the 1940's–1950's (West Germany, Austria, and Italy); (3) Northeast Asia from the 1940's–1950's (Japan and South Korea); and (4) Southeast Asia from the 1960's–1970's (particularly South Vietnam).

Together, these add up to more than a dozen cases in which the United States has used military occupation to bring about political democratization. They provide useful precedents and lessons for the current efforts in Iraq. (The Bush administration and neoconservative writers have repeatedly cited the U.S. successes in West Germany and Japan, but they have been notably silent about the large numbers of failures or disappointments elsewhere, particularly in the Caribbean basin and Central America.)

In addition, the 1990's were the decade of numerous attempts to bring democracy to the countries of the former Soviet Union and communist Eastern Europe. With the exception of Bosnia and Kosovo, these democratization projects did not involve military occupation by U.S. forces. However, as we will see, these ex-communist countries (almost two dozen in number) also provide plenty of evidence and lessons relevant to the prospects for democratization in Iraq.

The Bush administration and the neoconservatives promoted the Iraq War and accompanying regime change as the first phase in a grand project that would bring democracy to Iraq's neighbors and perhaps even to the Middle East more generally. Whenever they had to present an historical precedent to show that this kind of radical and ambitious project had succeeded in the past, they pointed to West Germany and Japan.

They never mentioned the many other U.S. efforts to use military force to democratize countries in Latin America, and of course they never mentioned the epic U.S. failure in South Vietnam. (The one exception is Max Boot, especially in his important book, *The Savage Wars of Peace: Small Wars and the Rise of American Power*.) Nor did they mention the most recent, wide-ranging, and numerous efforts with democratization among the countries of the former Soviet Union and communist Eastern Europe. If any honest discussion about the prospects for democratization in Iraq and other countries of the Middle East had included any analysis of a few of these three dozen cases, the discussion would have ended with a general consensus that the prospects were surely bleak.

The German and Japanese Exceptions

The cases of West Germany and Japan certainly demonstrate that military conquest and occupation can bring about a successful and permanent democratization. The U.S. achievement in these countries was all the more impressive since, in the 1940's, the leading American area specialists and professional experts frequently argued that the peculiar features of German and Japanese history and culture made democracy an alien and unlikely system for these nations. When, in the early 2000's, the leading American area specialists and professional experts have made similar arguments about Arab or Muslim history and culture, one can understand why the promoters of the democratization project for the Middle East could dismiss these arguments and why they might do so in good faith. It is important, however, to look at the circumstances of the German and Japanese cases in more detail. There were three crucial ways in which these circumstances differed from those of today's Iraq.

A prior liberal-democratic experience. First, Germany and Japan (as well as Austria and Italy) actually had considerable experience with some version of liberal democracy only a couple of decades before, during the 1920's between the First World War and the Great Depression. The Weimar Republic, with its grand drama of blighted hopes and dark tragedy, is especially well known, but Japan also experienced liberalization and even democratization in the 1920's. Austria had a political system similar to the Weimar Republic. And Italy had had a functioning liberal democracy for more than two decades before Mussolini put an end to it in 1922. For a time, each of these countries had developed liberal, democratic, and even social-democratic parties. Although these parties were repressed by the later totalitarian or authoritarian regimes, in the late 1940's the experience was still in the memories of substantial portions of the population. Indeed, some of the prominent leaders of the liberal-democratic period were still there - Konrad Adenauer in Germany, Karl Renner in Austria, Alcide de Gasperi in Italy, and Shigeru Yoshida in Japan - and the U.S. occupation authorities soon drew upon them to assume leadership in the new (really re-newed) liberal-democratic systems.

With regard to this feature of prior historical experience, the contrast between West Germany and Japan in the late 1940's and Iraq (as well as Iran, Syria, and Saudi Arabia) today could not be greater. These latter countries have never been liberal democracies. Further, the most liberal (but hardly democratic) regime in Iraqi history was the monarchy of King Faisal II, but that was violently overthrown in 1958, almost half a century ago. In Iraq, there is no historical base whatsoever for the American democratization project.

To get some sense of how successful externally imposed democratization would be in the absence of internally developed historical experience, one would have to look instead at the U.S. efforts to impose democracy upon such countries as Cuba, the Dominican Republic, Haiti, Nicaragua, and Panama. Here, the only cases that can be said to be successful were the slow establishment of a liberal-democratic system in the Dominican Republic during the decade or so after the U.S. military intervention and occupation in 1965–1966 and the quick establishment of such a system in Panama after the U.S. intervention and occupation of 1989–1990. In contrast, each of the U.S. democratization projects of the 1900's–1930's ended in failure, with the liberal-democratic system overthrown and replaced by some kind of dictatorial regime.

A greater foreign threat. Second, and probably more important, West Germany and Japan in the late 1940's each perceived a foreign threat that was even greater than the one posed by the U.S. occupation. As oppressive as the military forces of the United States might have seemed to the West Germans and Japanese, there was the fear of something that would be even worse: the military forces of the Soviet Union. The threat from the Soviet military was especially obvious to the West Germans, who had ample evidence of the reign of pillage, rape, and murder that the Red Army inflicted upon Germans in the East and could be expected to inflict upon Germans in the West, if they ever got the chance. Even the Japanese feared a possible conquest by the Soviet military and revolution by the Japanese communists, particularly after they saw what the Soviets did to the Japanese colonists and soldiers they captured in Manchuria. As bad as the reality of the American occupation was for both nations, the specter of a Soviet occupation was a good deal worse. And it soon became clear to many West Germans and Japanese that only the American military stood in the way of that specter being realized.

With regard to this second feature, that of perceived foreign threat, there is again a great contrast between West Germany and Japan then and Iraq now. Of course, given the memory of the Iran-Iraq War of the 1980's and the close relations between the Shi'ite regime in Iran and the Shi'ite majority in Iraq, Iran would appear to pose a potential threat to Iraq. And given the long-standing hostility of the Turks to the Kurds, Turkey might also appear to pose a potential threat to Iraq.

But Iraqis perceive these hypothetical threats in the context of the ethnic hostilities within Iraq itself. For now, the Iraqi Shi'ites fear and loathe the Iraqi Sunnis more than they do the Iranian Shi'ites, and it even seems that for now the Iraqi Kurds fear and loathe the Iraqi Sunni Arabs more than they do the Turks. And it is increasingly evident that both the Sunnis and the Shi'ites loathe the American occupation as much or more.

Again, to get some sense of how acceptable a U.S. military occupation would be in the absence of a still-greater foreign military threat, one would have to look not at West Germany and Japan but instead at the U.S. occupations in Cuba, the Dominican Republic, Haiti, Nicaragua, and Panama. In the cases where the occupation was prolonged beyond a couple of years, there developed substantial local resentment and even resistance. And in the two most successful cases (the Dominican Republic in 1965–1966 and Panama in 1989–1990), the United States withdrew its military forces and ended its occupation in less than a year.

An ethnically homogenous population. Third, and probably most important, West Germany and Japan (and also Austria and Italy) were among the most ethnically homogeneous nations in the world. There were no significant ethnic minorities – they formed less than two percent of the populations – and there were no significant secession movements. Democratization did bring all sorts of political conflicts and cleavages – particularly around issues of economic class – but no ethnic group or territory voted to separate itself from the rest of the nation.

With regard to this third feature, the ethnic homogeneity prevalent in Germany and Japan is manifestly lacking in Iraq. As is well known, Iraq has never been ethnically homogeneous; from its creation in 1920, it has always been divided into three ethnic parts, the Sunni Arabs, the Shi'ite Arabs, and the Kurds (who are Sunni, but non-Arab), with the Sunni minority imposing an authoritarian and usually brutal regime upon the Shi'ite majority and the Kurdish minority. Moreover, the three ethnic parts have roughly corresponded to three territorial parts, with the Sunni Arabs in the center, the Shi'ite Arabs in the south, and the Kurds in the north (with mixed populations in major cities). Iraq was always an unstable equilibrium, a partition waiting to happen, artificially held together by the iron bonds of an authoritarian and brutal regime. In such circumstances, "regime change" would inevitably result in state change or even country change; in particular, democratization would mean that one or more of the three ethnic and territorial parts of Iraq would vote to separate itself from the others. One could have an Iraq, but without democracy. Alternatively, one could have democracy, but without an Iraq. But one could not have both.

To get some sense of how successful democratization would be with such pronounced ethnic heterogeneity, one would have to look not at West Germany and Japan in the late 1940's but instead at the recent and very extensive experience of democratization in the former communist countries. Certainly, one would have to look especially at the Balkans, which were once called the Near East and which is not that far geographically and sociologically from the contemporary Middle East.

Here the evidence is unambiguous. In virtually every country in the communist world where there was ethnic heterogeneity, democratization – which included free elections – was followed immediately by secession and partition. This was largely peaceful in the case of the Slavic and the Baltic republics of the Soviet Union and in the case of the "velvet divorce" between the Czech Republic and the Slovak Republic. It was violent and even genocidal in the Caucasian republics of the Soviet Union and in several of the republics of Yugoslavia. But be the process peaceful or violent, the democratization of multiethnic societies almost always issued in secession and partition. Given these results of democratization in multiethnic countries of the communist world in the 1990's – especially the violent results in the Caucasus and the Balkans, which are so proximate to Iraq both geographically and historically – it is almost incredible that anyone could seriously argue that the most relevant comparisons to Iraq were the homogeneous nations of West Germany and Japan in the 1940's.

The Coming Failure

In summary, ample historical experience with a wide variety of democratization projects predicts that the U.S. effort to bring democracy to Iraq will end in failure. That effort may fail because the Iraqi people do not have the cultural values, social conditions, or historical experience with which to construct a democracy. Or it may fail because the Iraqi people come to associate democracy with the U.S. occupation and with all the disruptions and humiliations that a military administration inevitably brings. Or it may fail because there is actually no Iraqi people at all, only three peoples who will use democracy to break away from each other – at best, this would result in three democracies, rather than one; at worst, it would result in three states engaged in a new war of their very own. Or it may fail because of all of the above. With all these paths leading straight to failure, it will take a miracle for the U.S. democratization project in Iraq to succeed.

The failure of democratization in Iraq will discredit similar U.S. efforts elsewhere. The damage will be greatest in the Middle East and in the Muslim world more broadly, where Islamism will be left as the only valid ideology and Islamization as the only vital political and social project. Elsewhere, the harm will not be as profound, but for a few years at least, other countries will dismiss any U.S. proclamations and promotions of democratization as just another preposterous, feckless, and tiresome American conceit.

The United States might be able to absorb and eventually recover from this failure in Iraq, rather like it absorbed and eventually recovered from its epic failure in Vietnam three decades ago. Indeed, 30 years from now, Islamism might itself be discredited in the Middle East, rather like communism is discredited in Southeast Asia today. But like that earlier war, at the end of the day virtually all honest and reasonable people will agree that it would have been best if the United States had never gone to war at all.

HENRY A. KISSINGER

4 Intervention With a Vision

WHAT MARKS THIS CENTURY AS ONE OF UNPRECEDENTED upheaval is not primarily the emergence of new centers of power such as China or India; that has happened before, though not on this global scale. Nor is it the fact that significant states are losing control over all or part of their territory. The unique aspect is that when state power weakens, non-state terrorist groups fill the vacuum for the purpose of threatening the state system itself. The challenge is not simply to reestablish an international system but to prevent vacuums that suck into themselves the nihilistic elements trying to destroy order altogether.

At least since Woodrow Wilson, the United States has had its own definition of international order: the idea that wars are caused less by clashing interests than by unrepresentative domestic institutions. In the Wilsonian view, foreign policy based on national interest and state power prevails when democratic institutions have failed. Since democracies settle their disputes by reason, not by war, the spreading of democracy is, to this school of thought, America's ultimate mission, and regime change its ultimate sanction.

The belief that compatible domestic structures are the ultimate foundations of international peace is not new. It was the basis of the Holy Alliance after the Napoleonic wars. The opposite of democratic, it asserted that monarchical systems were the best guarantee of international stability because they were impervious to the fickleness of public opinion. And dynastic leaders were said to be more peaceful because they did not require conquests to remain in office. Though these propositions would not have been sustained by an objective examination of the record

Reprinted from the *Washington Post*, April 11, 2004, by permission.

of 18th-century diplomacy, they led to interventions to produce regime change in Naples in 1821 and in Spain in 1823. The effort to universalize autocratic governance ultimately failed because the national interests of two members of the Holy Alliance - Austria and Russia - clashed in the Balkans and because Great Britain rejected the claimed right of universal intervention.

The current doctrine of global democratic interventionism faces comparable obstacles. It postulates without much evidence - because there have never been enough democracies to test it - the essential harmony of democracies. Europe's current pacifism is in part the result of exhaustion from wars of the 20th century. It deals with how to achieve order between states, but not with the prevention of challenges born from chaos.

Yet for America, the belief in the moral significance of democracy has been a fundamental theme of a society settled by immigrants. America must stand for democratic values if its foreign policy is to have any long-term support among its people. The issue is how to apply them.

Nor would a policy based on national interest defined largely in security terms prove practical. Power is an amalgam of capability and will, making it perhaps the most elusive component of international relations to assess precisely. A policy based on interest alone requires perfect flexibility and an instant readiness to adjust to changed circumstance. This was difficult at all times and is increasingly so in the face of the combination of bureaucratic complexities, contradictory public pressures, and the growing role of non-state actors, both benign and hostile.

But having said this, what does support for democracy mean for the practical conduct of foreign policy? How does the United States promote such a diplomacy in the face of widespread international criticism that charges us at the same time with hegemonic power and missionary crusading spirit?

America is engaged in a wide range of activities in the name of democracy and human rights. It publishes annual reports on the human rights record of every country in the world; it expresses public opinions on the democratic and human rights shortcomings of even permanent U.N. Security Council members; it applies congressionally mandated sanctions; it has gone to war in Bosnia and Kosovo over essentially human rights issues; it invaded Iraq in part to bring about regime change.

No other country has treated human rights and the support of democracy as so central or has permitted so direct a role to so many elements of its public opinion in the implementation of a specific aspect of its foreign policy. All these initiatives promote the checks-and-balances system of the

American constitutional experience, without modification on the basis of history or circumstance.

Does the United States have the capacity to achieve its lofty goals, and if so, how quickly? Democracy in the Western world evolved over centuries. The Catholic Church, though hardly democratic in its internal practices, contributed to the eventual emergence of democracy by insisting on the separation of authority between God and Caesar. This represented a first tentative, but essential, step toward a pluralistic perception of governance. Centuries later, the Reformation institutionalized religious, and hence eventually political, pluralism by emphasizing the importance of the individual conscience. The Enlightenment took the next step in its insistence on analysis based on reason. The Age of Discovery stretched horizons. Capitalism made individual initiative the engine of successful economies. The concepts of representative institutions, separation of power, and checks and balances evolved over centuries from a rich tradition.

No other culture has produced a comparable evolution. Islamic societies have rarely separated church and state and never have acknowledged pluralistic interpretations of justice. In most Confucian societies, neither religious nor nongovernmental organizations have had the autonomy or the legitimacy to challenge governmental authority except by outright rebellion.

To say that democracy has cultural prerequisites does not deny it ultimate applicability to other societies but only takes note of the fact that compressing the evolution of centuries into an inappropriate time frame risks huge unintended consequences. Where societies are divided by faith or ethnicity, our practices run the risk of ratifying a permanent distribution of power based precisely on those ethnic divisions. Where the minority has no prospect of becoming a majority, elections may often result in civil war or chaos - the very breeding ground for militant terrorist organizations.

Because democracy must be rooted in domestic factors, it will thrive only where it reflects cultural, historical, and institutional backgrounds. This is why the attempt to impose Western institutions elsewhere rarely succeeds without protracted Western tutelage. In the Balkans, it has produced three protectorates - in Bosnia, Kosovo, and Macedonia - entirely dependent on outside forces and showing little tendency toward self-sustaining political evolution; in Kosovo, a self-sustaining internal evolution would likely run counter to American values and interests in the region. And in its essence, the reconstruction of Iraq involves an extended period of an American protectorate. These operations were necessary, but they define their own limits. Regime change is a special case; it cannot be the primary exercise of American military power. Priorities must be established, at least with respect to the availability of military force for the process of democratization.

A foreign policy to promote democracy needs to be adapted to local or regional realities, or it will fail. In the pursuit of democracy, policy - as in other realms - is the art of the possible. Diplomacy on behalf of democracy needs to reflect a political and strategic design rather than ad hoc bows to bureaucratic or public constituencies.

This proposition is often strenuously resisted by those who want to treat democratization as an end in itself. But slogans do not create a foreign policy. When the United States plays a major role in the destruction of existing institutions, as in the transition in Iran in 1979 and in Indonesia in 1998 and, even more, when it goes to war to bring about regime change, it must do so in the name of some operational definition of democracy and its evolution. It is important to remember that the most successful building of democracy in the last half-century occurred when non-democratic regimes in places like Korea, Taiwan, and Turkey fostered an economic growth that produced middle classes, which in turn, and with some American help, insisted on representative institutions and checks and balances. When democratization is pushed in a conceptual and political vacuum, the outcome is likely to be chaos or regimes inimical to our values and perhaps our security. America needs urgently to develop a concept of political evolution that combines the authority required for economic progress with the human rights required for a democratic evolution. Though it is often argued that, for example, the hostility of the Iranian ayatollahs toward the United States was caused by America's previous support of non-democratic regimes, reality is far more complex. Critics who urge the United States to help bring them into power will not necessarily follow policies compatible with either our security or our values.

Iraq is turning into the test case. Regime change was impelled by strategic imperatives together with moral convictions. But the reconstruction of Iraq was in no way comparable to the occupations of Germany and Japan. In those countries, the populations were supportive; there was no alternative to democratic reform - indeed, reform and cooperation with the occupation were the sole means of regaining legitimacy and control over the national destiny. In Iraq these conditions are nearly reversed. The ethnic and religious divisions are so deep that in its early stages, democratization threatens to become a form of communalism. The creation of a governing authority on July 1 is the first small step on a long road toward a stability from which a secular middle class can emerge strong enough to insist on full representative government. An extended period of American involvement is required and some degree of internationalization. But whatever the process, its prerequisite is America's willingness to see it through. Success is the only exit strategy. And as in Iraq, we must navigate in the rest of the Middle East between the imperative of reform and the danger of generating more chaos.

As the United States enters its national debate and – one hopes – a period of reconciliation afterward, no challenge is more important than to define a direction of foreign policy integrating our values and our interests. We paralyze ourselves when we treat these categories as absolutes and opposites. The advocates of "interest" must recognize that support for democracy is a fundamental goal that has to be built into American policy. The proponents of a value-based foreign policy need to understand that their challenge is no longer to establish their principle but to implement it, and that down their road beckons not only democracy but ungovernable vacuums. The advocates of the important role of a commitment to democracy in American foreign policy have won their intellectual battle. But institution-building requires not only doctrine but a vision recognizing cultural and historical circumstance. Such humility is not an abdication of American values; it is the only way to implement these values effectively.

THE EDITORS OF NATIONAL REVIEW

5 An End to Illusion

IRAQ SEEMS TO HAVE RETURNED TO RELATIVE STABILITY FOR the moment. The militia of Moqtada al-Sadr has withdrawn from cities in the south. The power play by the radical cleric did not herald the broad Shiite uprising that many feared, and that was played up by the American press. But his mini-putsch gave the U.S. a glimpse at the abyss in Iraq.

Since the conclusion of the war, the Bush administration has shown a dismaying capacity to believe its own public relations. The post-war looting was explained away as the natural and understandable exuberance of a newly-liberated people. (Now some Coalition officials suggest that a crackdown would have sped the reconstruction.) Secretary of Defense Donald Rumsfeld denied the obvious reality of a guerrilla resistance and compared it to urban street crime in the United States. Every piece of good news has been hailed as turning the corner, even as the insurgency has remained stubbornly strong.

It is easy now to pick at what seem to have been errors in the occupation. There probably weren't enough troops. The administration probably wasn't determined enough to get international help, even on its own terms - although this would have had to happen in an environment poisoned by U.N. fecklessness and French bad faith in the run-up to the war. The administration clearly wasn't ready for the magnitude of the task that rebuilding and occupying Iraq would present.

Even if the administration had avoided these mistakes and made all moves correctly, it is still possible Iraq would be very messy. But this

Reprinted from *National Review*, May 3, 2004 (posted online April 16, 2004), by permission.

concession points to an intellectual mistake made prior to the occupation: an underestimation in general of the difficulty of implanting democracy in alien soil, and an overestimation in particular of the sophistication of what is fundamentally still a tribal society and one devastated by decades of tyranny. This was largely, if not entirely, a Wilsonian mistake. The Wilsonian tendency has grown stronger in conservative foreign-policy thought in recent years, with both benefits (idealism *should* occupy an important place in American foreign policy, and almost always has) and drawbacks (as we have seen in Iraq, the world isn't as malleable as some Wilsonians would have it).

But Iraq was not a Wilsonian - or a "neoconservative" - war. It was broadly supported by the Right as a war of national interest. The primary purpose of the war was always to protect U.S. national security, by removing a destabilizing and radical influence in the strategically crucial Persian Gulf and eliminating a potential threat to the United States. President Bush deserves great credit for grasping this nettle. The current task in Iraq is also driven by national-security concerns. Getting chased from Iraq would make it open season on U.S. interests throughout the Middle East. Allowing radicals to prevail there would be a sharp setback in the War on Terror. And forging a non-fascist, non-radical, non-hostile government in Iraq could affect the entire region's geopolitics for the better. Success in post-war Iraq therefore is necessary primarily to serve U.S. interests, secondarily to assist Iraqis.

In light of recent events, however, we should downplay expectations. If we leave Iraq in some sort of orderly condition, with some sort of legitimate non-dictatorial government and a roughly working economy, we will be doing very well. The first step toward that goal is dealing harshly with our enemies. We must re-establish the prestige and authority that were badly frayed when we watched a crowd of thugs desecrate American bodies in Fallujah. Just as important is the political process. Part of what is happening in Iraq now is a nationalist reaction to being governed by a foreign occupying force. We should do our best to stick to the June 30th deadline for a handover of power. The Governing Council, which appears to lack a deep well of legitimacy, should be dissolved and the "loya jirga option" - the selection of a broadly representative assembly that can in turn elect a cabinet - pursued.

Ultimately, even if our choices now can help or hurt, it is Iraqis who have to save Iraq. It is their country, not ours. In coming weeks and months, we will have to defer to the authorities we hope will eventually take control, in the process endorsing compromises that we will consider less than ideal. But it is time for reality to drive our Iraq policy, unhindered by illusions or wishful thinking. We should do what we can to give Iraqis a chance at a better future, then pray that they take it.

ANDREW SULLIVAN

6 Quitters

THE WAR TO DEPOSE SADDAM WAS ALWAYS AN UNLIKELY WAR FOR conservatives. Traditional conservatives tend to view most attempts at radically altering society with a good degree of skepticism. They tend to view war primarily as a means for the narrow advancement of national interest, leavened occasionally with a dollop of *enlightened* national self-interest. In the internal politics of the last world empire – the British one – the Tories tended to warn against the attempt to impart liberal values to "restless natives," while the Liberals took up what was seen as the "White Man's Burden."

Within American conservatism, there has always been an isolationist strain and a realist one balancing any liberal aspirations in foreign policy for the GOP. In retrospect, it's peculiar that such strains were so weakened in the run-up to the Iraq war. Op-ed mutterings from Brent Scowcroft were muted by his star pupil's insistence (I refer to Condi Rice) that Saddam remained a gathering threat to the United States. The far right – represented by Patrick Buchanan and the proudly protectionist and isolationist *American Conservative* magazine – seemed marginal at best. But there was, perhaps, always a moment when conservatism was bound to begin to resist more aggressively what is, indisputably, a liberal project of nation-building in Iraq.

Perhaps that moment has now arrived with *National Review*'s latest Tory editorial, which makes all the right noises about seeing the conflict in Iraq through to a democratic conclusion, while laying the groundwork for a conservative argument to cut and run at the first opportunity. For some

Reprinted from the *New Republic Online*, posted April 20, 2004, by permission.

reason, this editorial isn't available online for the blogosphere to have at it. So here I reprint it, with my comments.

> An End to Illusion

Ah, the set-up. What illusion? I have great difficulty remembering any serious conservative supporter of the war who believed that democracy would flourish immediately upon our invasion of a crumbling and unstable totalitarian state. Sure, the administration in retrospect underestimated the mistrust the Shia still harbored after the betrayal by the previous President Bush in 1991. Sure, they painted too rosy a picture of the post-war world in Iraq. But it would be more accurate to say that they painted almost no picture of the post-war environment in Iraq. It was less a function of rose-colored glasses than of forgetting to put the glasses on at all.

> Iraq seems to have returned to relative stability for the moment. The militia of Moqtada al-Sadr has withdrawn from cities in the south. The power play by the radical cleric did not herald the broad Shiite uprising that many feared, and that was played up by the American press. But his mini-putsch gave the U.S. a glimpse at the abyss in Iraq.

Abyss? Again, what is a perfectly sensible summary of events – the retreat of al-Sadr in the face of certain military defeat, the lack of broad Shia support for him across Iraq, and the beginnings of a (still tentative) calming process in Falluja – then suddenly becomes an "abyss." What could such an "abyss" mean? An entire national uprising against the U.S. military? So far, there seems little reason to believe that will happen – and many reasons to believe that, however much Iraqis rightly want to live in a country without 130,000 foreign troops, they don't want a return to either dictatorship or the chaos of civil war. The only thing preventing that now is American power. There is no abyss beckoning here, except the abyss that would undoubtedly occur if America were to lose nerve and retreat.

> Since the conclusion of the war, the Bush administration has shown a dismaying capacity to believe its own public relations. The post-war looting was explained away as the natural and understandable exuberance of a newly liberated people. (Now some Coalition officials suggest that a crackdown would have sped the reconstruction.) Secretary of Defense Donald Rumsfeld denied the obvious reality of a guerrilla resistance and compared it to urban street crime in the United States. Every piece of good news has been hailed as turning the corner, even as the insurgency has remained stubbornly strong.

That's not what was said. Rumsfeld didn't broadly conflate the looting with the spontaneous demonstrations of new freedom. He simply lamely tried to dismiss what anyone could see: that there were far too few troops for post-war order, even if there had been plenty for military success. Again, there are plenty of reasons to criticize Rumsfeld. He bears great responsibility for the sometimes shambolic post-war military under-staffing. But he has generally described the insurgents as far worse than mere street criminals. He has identified them as remnants of the Baathist regime, combined with some foreign terrorist elements. His reference to street crime was a petty effort in the immediate wake of invasion to downplay some of the lawlessness that resulted from his inadequate troop staffing, not a general description of the resistance to foreign occupation.

It's also unclear how "stubbornly strong" the "insurgency" actually is. The U.S. and coalition forces have a very delicate task of keeping order while winning "hearts and minds." Until this past month, when al-Sadr played his cards, military casualties had been falling quite fast. There is no concerted insurgency in the Kurdish north; and resistance throughout the Shia south has been sporadic. In fact, the reason why the news from the last two weeks appeared to be so dramatic was precisely the contrast between that violence and the slow military and reconstruction progress that had been made before then. I'm not minimizing the dangers here. I'm just saying that the notion of a continuous "insurgency" since the invasion – an insurgency that remains "stubbornly strong" – is far too crude an assessment of the twists and turns of Iraqi opinion and guerrilla warfare in the last twelve months.

> It is easy now to pick at what seem to have been errors in the occupation. There probably weren't enough troops. The administration probably wasn't determined enough to get international help, even on its own terms – although this would have had to happen in an environment poisoned by U.N. fecklessness and French bad faith in the run-up to the war. The administration clearly wasn't ready for the magnitude of the task that rebuilding and occupying Iraq would present.
>
> Even if the administration had avoided these mistakes and made all moves correctly, it is still possible Iraq would be very messy. But this concession points to an intellectual mistake made prior to the occupation: an underestimation in general of the difficulty of implanting democracy in alien soil, and an overestimation in particular of the sophistication of what is fundamentally still a tribal society and one devastated by decades of tyranny. This was largely, if not entirely, a Wilsonian mistake. The Wilsonian tendency has grown stronger in conservative foreign-policy thought in recent years, with

> both benefits (idealism *should* occupy an important place in American foreign policy, and almost always has) and drawbacks (as we have seen in Iraq, the world isn't as malleable as some Wilsonians would have it).

Again, this is too crude. The administration always argued that the construction of democracy in Iraq would be a tough job. Sure, before the war, it didn't emphasize this enough to the American people - something for which the White House is now paying in the opinion polls. But I know of no neoconservative optimist in the White House who believed that a viable, peaceful democracy in Iraq would be within reach a mere year after the invasion. Yes, many did underestimate the astonishing damage done to civil society by decades of the most brutal dictatorship imaginable, the devastation of sanctions on the Iraqi infrastructure, and the psychological damage done to the communal psyche after living in a collective torture chamber for years on end.

But again, what are the standards of success here? Many neoconservatives believed, as I did, that the very immunity of the Arab world to democratic change was a major reason for worrying about the potential success of military intervention in defense of democracy and pluralism. But the perceived difficulty of that transition - and the immense dangers of trying to achieve it - were outweighed by the gathering national security threat that surging Islamo-fascism, al Qaeda-style terrorism, and weapons of mass destruction could pose to the West as a whole. None of our options, in other words, were pretty. But we had learned on September 11 that mere observation and pin-prick attempts to stymie discrete terrorist operations could not shield us from devastating attack. In that context, the Iraq gamble - and it was a gamble - was regarded as one worth taking. A mere year later, after a couple of weeks of violence, it is absurdly premature to judge this enterprise as doomed.

> But Iraq was not a Wilsonian - or a "neoconservative" - war. It was broadly supported by the Right as a war of national interest. The primary purpose of the war was always to protect U.S. national security, by removing a destabilizing and radical influence in the strategically crucial Persian Gulf and eliminating a potential threat to the United States. President Bush deserves great credit for grasping this nettle. The current task in Iraq is also driven by national-security concerns. Getting chased from Iraq would make it open season on U.S. interests throughout the Middle East. Allowing radicals to prevail there would be a sharp setback in the War on Terror. And forging a non-fascist, non-radical, non-hostile government in Iraq could affect the entire region's geopolitics for the better. Success in post-war Iraq therefore is necessary primarily to serve U.S. interests, secondarily to assist Iraqis.

Yes and no. If you read the many addresses that President Bush gave before the war, you will find all these strains of argument. But you will also find a clear strand of democratic internationalism that has more in common with the optimism of cold war liberals than the skepticism of realist conservatives. That's why so many in the realist camp opposed the war; and it's why many in the libertarian camp also opposed it. The constituency for war against Saddam was not primarily made up of conservative realists. They were there - but their realism was tempered by the view that without radically altering the culture of the Islamicized Middle East, realism would be defunct as an option. There are times when ideological movements have to be confronted ideologically - and Islamo-fascism was and is just such a movement. This recognition doesn't junk realist conservative thought; but it provides an essential complement. Blind realism is no realism at all. In some ways, neoconservatism is currently a hyper-realist doctrine because it has incorporated the role of ideas into the need to be vigilant against threats to national security.

> In light of recent events, however, we should downplay expectations. If we leave Iraq in some sort of orderly condition, with some sort of legitimate non-dictatorial government and a roughly working economy, we will be doing very well. The first step toward that goal is dealing harshly with our enemies. We must re-establish the prestige and authority that were badly frayed when we watched a crowd of thugs desecrate American bodies in Fallujah. Just as important is the political process. Part of what is happening in Iraq now is a nationalist reaction to being governed by a foreign occupying force. We should do our best to stick to the June 30th deadline for a handover of power. The Governing Council, which appears to lack a deep well of legitimacy, should be dissolved and the "loya jirga option" - the selection of a broadly representative assembly that can in turn elect a cabinet - pursued.
>
> Ultimately, even if our choices now can help or hurt, it is Iraqis who have to save Iraq. It is their country, not ours. In coming weeks and months, we will have to defer to the authorities we hope will eventually take control, in the process endorsing compromises that we will consider less than ideal. But it is time for reality to drive our Iraq policy, unhindered by illusions or wishful thinking. We should do what we can to give Iraqis a chance at a better future, then pray that they take it.

It is hard to disagree with much of this. It's sensible and pragmatic - except for its obvious avoidance of the need for U.N. involvement to help achieve our objectives. (Good luck hoping for some positive mention of the United Nations in *National Review*.) It would be foolish to let the perfect be the enemy of the good, and much of what has happened in the last twelve months in Iraq has shown the slow acceptance by the CPA of that truism. But there is something contradictory in the tone and premise of these paragraphs. If you accept the conservative case that changing culture is and will always be difficult, and if you accept the fact that the United States now does truly "own" Iraq as a geopolitical problem, then the notion of "leaving it" as soon as we can makes no sense. There is no exit strategy because we need to reassure Iraqis yearning for a new future that we will be there with them for the long haul. Not in the shape of 130,000 troops forever. But certainly with tens of thousands for the foreseeable future, with investment, with cross-cultural exchanges, with hard and soft power for however long it takes to make a success of this new frontier. I see no way we can make a success of Iraq without a minimum commitment of a decade at least.

To have supported the invasion of Iraq only now to support as quick an exit as possible is to give us the worst of both worlds. The kind of skepticism and realism *National Review*'s editors are now flirting with should have demanded no intervention in the first place – as the Buchanan brigades averred. The kind of idealism and honest realism also at work in these paragraphs requires us in the wake of invasion to commit not to this kind of second-guessing and the soft bigotry of low expectations for the developing world. It requires us to pledge a renewed commitment to making this necessary experiment work, to making the loss of life worth something deep and lasting, to make the removal of evil the ground-clearing for the patient, tough, and intractable task of creating something good. And that good is not just for the people of Iraq, but for the people of the Arab world – and, ultimately, the security of America as well.

DAVID BROOKS

7 A More Humble Hawk

I DIDN'T GET THIS JOB BECAUSE I WAS SELF-EFFACING, BUT TODAY I'M really going to beg for your indulgence. I thought it might be useful to describe the doubts and thoughts going through the mind of one ardent war supporter - me - during these traumatically bloody weeks in Iraq.

The first thing to say is that I never thought it would be this bad. I knew it would be bad. On the third day of the U.S. invasion, I wrote an essay for *The Atlantic* called "Building Democracy Out of What?" I pointed out that we should expect that the Iraqis would have been traumatized by a generation of totalitarianism. That society would have been brutally atomized. And that many would have developed a taste for sadism and an addiction to violence. On April 11, 2003, I predicted on "The NewsHour" on PBS that we and the Iraqis would be forced to climb a "wall of quagmires."

Nonetheless, I didn't expect that a year after liberation, hostile militias would be taking over cities or that it would be unsafe to walk around Baghdad. Most of all, I misunderstood how normal Iraqis would react to our occupation. I knew they'd resent us. But I thought they would see that our interests and their interests are aligned. We both want to establish democracy and get the U.S. out.

I did not appreciate how our very presence in Iraq would overshadow democratization. Now I get the sense that while the Iraqis don't want us to fail, since our failure would mean their failure, many don't want to see us succeed either. They want to see us bleed, to get taken down a notch, to suffer for their chaos and suffering. A democratic Iraq is an abstraction they want for the future; the humiliation of America is a pleasure they can savor today.

Second, let me describe my attitude toward the Bush administration. Despite all that's happened, I was still stirred by yesterday's Bush/Blair statements about democracy in the Middle East. Nonetheless, over the past two years many conservatives have grown increasingly exasperated with the administration's inability to execute its policies semicompetently.

When I worked at *The Weekly Standard*, we argued ad nauseam that the U.S. should pour men and materiel into Iraq – that such an occupation could not be accomplished by a light, lean, "transformed" military. The administration was impervious to the growing evidence about that. The failure to establish order was the prime mistake, from which all other problems flow.

On July 21, 2002, my colleague Robert Kagan wrote the first of several essays lamenting the administration's alarming lack of preparation for post-Saddam Iraq. Yet the administration seemed content to try nation-building on the cheap.

Many of us also assumed, wrongly, that the administration would launch a fresh postwar initiative to globalize the reconstruction effort. My friends at the Project for the New American Century urged the U.S. to go to the U.N. for a reconstruction resolution, to build a broad coalition to aid rebuilding, and to establish a NATO-led security force. That never happened.

Despite all this – and maybe it's pure defensiveness – I still believe that in 20 years, no one will doubt that Bush did the right thing. To his enormous credit, the president has been ruthlessly flexible over the past months and absolutely committed to seeing this through. He is acknowledging the need for more troops. He is absolutely right to embrace Lakhdar Brahimi's plan to dissolve the Governing Council and set up an interim government. This might take attention away from the U.S., and change the atmosphere in the country.

It's also inspiring to see the Iraqi center working so hard to keep political conflict under control, especially during these horrible weeks. Every time they get a chance to vote, Iraqi citizens show they are ready for democracy. A young diplomat, Tobin Bradley, is going around the country organizing local elections. In almost every case, the parties that do best are professional and practical, emphasizing the people's concrete needs.

This time, unlike 1920, say, Iraqis can see a panoply of new and thriving democracies. They have witnessed Iran's horrible experience with theocracy. Once the political process moves ahead, nationalism will work in our favor, as Iraqis seek to become the leading reformers in the Arab world.

We hawks were wrong about many things. But in opening up the possibility for a slow trudge toward democracy, we were still right about the big thing.

Crisis of Confidence

IT'S PRETTY CLEAR WE'RE PASSING THROUGH ANOTHER PIVOT POINT in American foreign policy. A year ago, we were the dominant nation in a unipolar world. Today, we're a shellshocked hegemon.

We still face a world of threats, but we're much less confident about our own power. We still know we can roll over hostile armies, but we cannot roll over problems. We get dragged down into them. We can topple tyrants, but we don't seem to be very good at administering nations. Our intelligence agencies have made horrible mistakes. Our diplomacy vis-a-vis Western Europe has been inept. We have a military filled with heroes, but the atrocities of a few have eclipsed the nobility of the many.

In short, we are on the verge of a crisis of confidence.

Yesterday, members of the administration were once again called to Capitol Hill to testify about a gruesome mistake. Once again investigations were begun and commissions were formed. Once again those of us who support this war and this administration were hard pressed to excuse what had just happened. Once again, baffling questions arose. Whose bright idea was it to keep Saddam's gulag open as a U.S. prison, anyway?

It's hard not to be impressed with the way the military crisply opened criminal investigations into the depravity at Abu Ghraib. It's hard not to be appalled by the Pentagon's blindness to the psychological catastrophe these photos were bound to create. Even yesterday, months after the atrocities were first known, Rumsfeld and company were incapable of answering the most elemental questions from John McCain, Lindsey Graham, and others about who was in charge of the prison, and why the photos weren't immediately seen as weapons of mass morale destruction. If Rumsfeld had held a conference and pre-emptively presented these photos to the world, with his response already set, things would not look nearly as bad as they do now.

Believe me, we've got even bigger problems than whether Rumsfeld keeps his job. We've got the problem of defining America's role in the world from here on out, because we are certainly not going to put ourselves through another year like this anytime soon. No matter how Iraq turns out, no president in the near future is going to want to send American troops into any global hot spot. This experience has been too searing.

Unfortunately, states will still fail, and world-threatening chaos will still ensue. Tyrants will still aid terrorists. Genocide will still occur. What are we going to do then? Who is going to tackle the future Milosevics, the future Talibans? If you were one of those people who thought the world was dangerous with an overreaching hyperpower, wait until you get a load of the age of the global power vacuum.

In this climate of self-doubt, the "realists" of right and left are bound to re-emerge. They're going to dwell on the limits of our power. They'll advise us to learn to tolerate the existence of terrorist groups, since we don't really have the means to take them on. They're going to tell us to lower our sights, to accept autocratic stability, since democratic revolution is too messy and utopian.

That's a recipe for disaster. It was U.S. inaction against al Qaeda that got us into this mess in the first place. It was our tolerance of Arab autocracies that contributed to the madness in the Middle East.

To conserve our strategy, we have to fundamentally alter our tactics. To shore up public confidence, the U.S. has to make it clear that it is considering fresh approaches.

We've got to acknowledge first that the old debates are obsolete. I wish the U.S could still go off, after Iraq, at the head of "coalitions of the willing" to spread democracy around the world. But the brutal fact is that the events of the past year have discredited that approach. Nor is the U.N. a viable alternative. A body dominated by dictatorships is never going to promote democratic values. For decades, the U.N. has failed as an effective world power.

We've got to reboot. We've got to come up with a global alliance of democracies to embody democratic ideals, harness U.S. military power, and house a permanent nation-building apparatus, filled with people who actually possess expertise on how to do this job.

From the looting of the Iraqi National Museum to Abu Ghraib, this has been a horrible year. The cause is still just, but to keep it moving forward, we have to reinvent the enterprise.

GEORGE F. WILL

8 Time for Bush to See the Realities of Iraq

OH? WHO?

Appearing Friday in the Rose Garden with Canada's prime minister, President Bush was answering a reporter's question about Canada's role in Iraq when suddenly he swerved into this extraneous thought:

> There's a lot of people in the world who don't believe that people whose skin color may not be the same as ours can be free and self-govern. I reject that. I reject that strongly. I believe that people who practice the Muslim faith can self-govern. I believe that people whose skins aren't necessarily - are a different color than white can self-govern.

What does such careless talk say about the mind of this administration? Note that the clearly implied antecedent of the pronoun "ours" is "Americans." So the president seemed to be saying that white is, and brown is not, the color of Americans' skin. He does not mean that. But that is the sort of swamp one wanders into when trying to deflect doubts about policy by caricaturing and discrediting the doubters.

Scott McClellan, the president's press secretary, later said the president meant only that "there are some in the world that think that some people can't be free" or "can't live in freedom." The president meant that "some Middle Eastern countries - that the people in those Middle Eastern countries cannot be free."

Perhaps that, which is problematic enough, is what the president meant. But what he suggested was: Some persons - perhaps many persons; no names being named, the smear remained tantalizingly vague - doubt his nation-building project because they are racists.

That is one way to respond to questions about the wisdom of thinking America can transform the entire Middle East by constructing a liberal democracy in Iraq. But if any Americans want to be governed by politicians who short-circuit complex discussions by recklessly imputing racism to those who differ with them, such Americans do not usually turn to the Republican choice in our two-party system.

This administration cannot be trusted to govern if it cannot be counted on to think and, having thought, to have second thoughts. Thinking is not the reiteration of bromides about how "all people yearn to live in freedom" (McClellan). And about how it is "cultural condescension" to doubt that some cultures have the requisite aptitudes for democracy (Bush). And about how it is a "myth" that "our attachment to freedom is a product of our culture" because "ours are not Western values; they are the universal values of the human spirit" (Tony Blair).

Speaking of culture, as neoconservative nation-builders would be well-advised to avoid doing, Pat Moynihan said: "The central conservative truth is that it is culture, not politics, that determines the success of a society. The central liberal truth is that politics can change a culture and save it from itself." Here we reach the real issue about Iraq, as distinct from unpleasant musings about who believes what about skin color.

The issue is the second half of Moynihan's formulation – our ability to wield political power to produce the requisite cultural change in a place such as Iraq. Time was, this question would have separated conservatives from liberals. Nowadays it separates conservatives from neoconservatives.

Condoleezza Rice, a political scientist, believes there is scholarly evidence that democratic institutions do not merely spring from a hospitable culture, but that they also can help create such a culture. She is correct; they *can*. They did so in the young American republic. But it would be reassuring to see more evidence that the administration is being empirical, believing that this *can* happen in some places, as opposed to ideological, believing that it *must* happen everywhere it is tried.

Being steadfast in defense of carefully considered convictions is a virtue. Being blankly incapable of distinguishing cherished hopes from disappointing facts, or of reassessing comforting doctrines in face of contrary evidence, is a crippling political vice.

In "On Liberty" (1859), John Stuart Mill said, "It is, perhaps, hardly necessary to say" that the doctrine of limited, democratic government "is meant to apply only to human beings in the maturity of their faculties." One hundred forty-five years later it obviously is necessary to say that.

Ron Chernow's magnificent new biography of Alexander Hamilton begins with these of his subject's words: "I have thought it my duty to exhibit things as they are, not as they ought to be." That is the core of conservatism.

Traditional conservatism. Nothing "neo" about it. This administration needs a dose of conservatism without the prefix.

FOUAD AJAMI

9 Iraq May Survive, but the Dream Is Dead

IT WAS HIGH TIME PRESIDENT BUSH SPOKE TO THE NATION OF THE war in Iraq. A year or so ago, it was our war, and we claimed it proudly. To be sure, there was a minority that never bought into the expedition and genuinely believed that it would come to grief. But most of us recognized that a culture of terror had taken root in the Arab world. We struck, first at Afghanistan and then at the Iraqi regime, out of a broader determination to purge Arab radicalism.

No wonder President Bush, in the most intensely felt passage of Monday night's speech, returned to Sept. 11 and its terrors. "In the last 32 months, history has placed great demands on our country," he said. "We did not seek this war on terror. But this is the world as we find it." Instinctively, an embattled leader fell back on a time of relative national consensus.

But gone is the hubris. Let's face it: Iraq is not going to be America's showcase in the Arab-Muslim world. The president's insistence that he had sent American troops to Iraq to make its people free, "not to make them American" is now – painfully – beside the point. The unspoken message of the speech was that no great American project is being hatched in Iraq. If some of the war's planners had thought that Iraq would be an ideal base for American primacy in the Persian Gulf, a beacon from which to spread democracy and reason throughout the Arab world, that notion has clearly been set aside.

We are strangers in Iraq, and we didn't know the place. We had struggled against radical Shiism in Iran and Lebanon in recent decades, but we expected a fairly secular society in Iraq (I myself wrote in that vein at the time). Yet it turned out that the radical faith – among the Sunnis as well as the Shiites – rose to fill the void left by the collapse of the old despotism.

In the decade that preceded the Iraq expedition, we had had our fill with the Arab anger in the streets of Ramallah and Cairo and Amman. We had wearied of the willful anti-Americanism. Now we find that anger, at even greater intensity, in the streets of Falluja. Iraqis had been muzzled for more than three decades. Suddenly they found themselves, dangerously and radically, free. Meanwhile, behind concrete walls and concertina wire, American soldiers and administrators hunkered down in an increasingly hostile land.

Back in the time of our triumph – that of swift movement and of pulling down the dictator's statues – we had let the victory speak for itself. There was no need to even threaten the Syrians, the Iranians, and the Libyans with a fate similar to the one that befell the Iraqi despotism. Some of that deterrent power no doubt still holds. But our enemies have taken our measure; they have taken stock of our national discord over the war. We shall not chase the Syrian dictator to a spider hole, nor will we sack the Iranian theocracy.

Once the administration talked of a "Greater Middle East" where the "deficits" of freedom, knowledge, and women's empowerment would be tackled, where our power would be used to erode the entrenched despotisms in the Arab-Muslim world. As of Monday night, we have grown more sober about the ways of the Arabs.

It seems that we have returned to our accommodation with the established order of power in the Arab world. The young Jordanian monarch, Abdullah II, has even stepped forward to offer the age-old Arab recipe for the mayhem in Iraq's streets: a man on horseback, an Iraqi "with a military background who has experience of being a tough guy who could hold Iraq together for the next year." No foreign sword, however swift and mighty, could cut through the Gordian knot of a tangled Arab history.

In their fashion, Iraqis had come to see their recent history as a passage from the rule of the tyrant to the rule of the foreigners. We had occupied the ruler's palaces and the ruler's prisons. It was logistics and necessity, of course – but that sort of shift in their world acquitted the Iraqi people, absolved them of the burden of their own history, left them on the sidelines as foreign soldiers and technicians and pollsters and advocates of "civic society" took control of their country.

And now, in a familiar twist, President Bush proposes – with the approval of a sovereign Iraqi government, of course – the demolition of the Abu Ghraib prison. We would cleanse their shame – and ours. Iraqis had not stormed their own Bastille, as it were; their liberty remains an American gift. And no surprise, they shall see through the deed, and discount it. If and when our bulldozers go to work at Abu Ghraib, it will be just another episode in which the Iraqis are spectators to their own history.

Back in our time of confidence, we had (rightly in my view) despaired of the United Nations and its machinery and its diplomatic-speak. But we now seek a way out, and an Algerian-born envoy, Lakhdar Brahimi, is the instrument of our deliverance. So we are all multilateralists now, and the envoy of a world organization entangled in its own scandal in Iraq – the oil-for-food program it administered and is now investigating – will show us the way.

Iraq is treacherous territory, but Mr. Brahimi gives us a promise of precision. The Iraqis shall have a president, two vice presidents, a prime minister, and 26 ministers who will run the country. We take our victories where we can. In Falluja, the purveyors of terrorism – nowadays they go by the honored name of mujahedeen – are applying the whip in public to vendors of wine and liquor and pornographic videos. (A measure of justice, it could be said, has finally come to Falluja.) But there is the consolation lamely offered by our president: Iraq today has an observer who attends the meetings of the World Trade Organization!

Imperial expeditions in distant, difficult lands are never easy. And an Arab-Islamic world loaded with deadly means of destruction was destined to test our souls and our patience. This is not "Bush's War." It is – by accident or design, it doesn't matter now – our biggest undertaking in the foreign world since Vietnam. We as a nation pay dearly every day. We fight under the gaze of multitudes in the Arab world who wish us ill, who believe that we are getting our comeuppance.

The gains already accomplished in Iraq, and the gains yet to be secured, are increasingly abstract and hard to pin down. The costs are visible to us, and heartbreaking. The subdued, somber tone with which the war is now described is the beginning of wisdom. In its modern history, Iraq has not been kind or gentle to its people. Perhaps it was folly to think that it was under any obligation to be kinder to strangers.

OWEN HARRIES

10 The Perils of Hegemony

A DISTINGUISHED ANALYST OF INTERNATIONAL POLITICS, MARTIN Wight, once laid it down as a fundamental truth of international politics that "Great Power status is lost, as it is won, by violence. A Great Power does not die in its bed." But 12 years ago, the Soviet Union, a state not exactly averse to violence, confounded all expectations by doing just that. It sickened and quietly expired, without war or bloodshed.

When the communist superpower ceased to exist, it did more than bring the Cold War to an end. It also altered fundamentally the structure of the international political system. For the first time in its history, that system became unipolar. The United States became a global hegemon. While there have often been local or regional hegemonies - the Soviet Union in Eastern Europe, for example, or the United States in the Caribbean, and later in the Atlantic Alliance - there has never before been one that dominated the whole system.

How fundamental a change this is is indicated by the fact that one of the main themes in the history of the state system has been the repeated and determined efforts of alliances of states to prevent any of their number from achieving systemic hegemony, even at the cost of long and bloody wars. Phillip II of Spain in the 16th century, Louis XIV in the 17th and early 18th centuries, Napoleon at the beginning of the 19th century, the Emperor Wilhelm II of Germany and Hitler in the 20th century each tried for domination; all were eventually thwarted. And millions were killed in the process.

Britain played a prominent part in forming coalitions to balance and oppose the would-be dominant power, changing its allies as the challengers changed. Then, in the 19th century, Britain itself became very powerful. It dominated the world industrially, commercially, and financially. Its navy ruled the seas. It had a vast empire and established a Pax Britannica in large areas of the world. All this has led some to claim that in the middle of the 19th century Britain had indeed achieved global hegemony. But it is not a convincing claim. For Britain never achieved or sought to achieve dominance in continental Europe, which was the heart of the state system, where things were finally decided. It never acquired the formidable land army that would have been necessary to exert such dominance. Indeed the German chancellor, Bismarck, used to say derisively that if the British army was to land on the North German coast, he would send a policeman to arrest it.

During the time of their greatest power, the British followed a prudent policy of "Splendid Isolation," keeping their distance from matters that did not affect them seriously and not taking too assertive a role in European affairs. They played the role of offshore balancer, aiming not at achieving hegemony but at preventing any other states from doing so, while Britain itself dominated much of the rest of the world. So, no, Britain in the Victorian era was not a true global hegemon.

Stronger states have typically joined together against the prospective hegemon – as England, Austria, Holland, and Russia allied against the France of Louis XIV, or as France, England, and Russia joined together to balance a very powerful and assertive Germany before 1914. On the other hand, weaker and more vulnerable states, or those that for some reason – ethnic, cultural, or ideological affinity; a history of past friendly association – have hopes that they may receive favorable treatment at the hands of the ambitious state, may opt to become its associates or accomplices. Balancing or bandwagoning is basically the choice for all those caught in the scope of the hegemon's ambition.

But how can they know in advance the scope of that ambition? The answer is that they cannot know, but as a matter of prudence they must assume. That is, they must assume that in a system of independent states coexisting in a state of anarchy, without any superior authority to restrain them or common loyalty to bind them, those who have the capacity to do so will dominate others who are weaker. As a wit summed it up: When there is no agreement as to which suit is trumps, clubs are always trumps.

This view may seem unduly cynical, an example of the kind of self-fulfilling fear that characterizes Realpolitik and the Hobbesian view of international politics. And it may be that. But it is an interpretation of the motives and behaviors of states that has a long pedigree. It is to be found, for example, in the first great work on interstate politics, Thucydides's *History of the Peloponnesian War*, written some two and a half thousand years before Henry Kissinger put pen to paper.

When Thucydides comes to discuss the causes of that war, he says that he will begin by giving an account of the specific complaints and disagreements that Athens and Sparta had with each other. But he advises that these in themselves will provide an inadequate and misleading explanation of the conflict. In an often quoted sentence, he gives what he considers the real, the fundamental, cause: "What made war inevitable was the growth of Athenian power and the fear which this caused in the Spartans."

Why the fear? Because, as he puts it, "the strong do what they can and the weak suffer what they must." What they can, note, not what they might originally have intended to do. For unchecked power creates its own motives and sets its own agenda. As Alexander Hamilton put it in another classic political text, the *Federalist Papers*:

> To presume a want of motives for such contests, as an argument against their existence, would be to forget that men are ambitious, vindictive, and rapacious. To look for a continuation of harmony between a number of independent, unconnected sovereignties situated in the same neighborhood would be to disregard the uniform course of human events, and set at defiance the accumulated experience of ages.

Indeed, the Founding Fathers of the United States had such a fear of uncontained power, even in the hands of their elected fellow countrymen, that they made the separation and balancing of powers the outstanding feature of their constitution.

The policy conclusion that follows from such an analysis was most succinctly put by another Greek historian, Polybius, in the form of a maxim: "It is never right to help a power to acquire a predominance that will render it irresistible" - never right, that is, if a state values its own independence. If it should value order or peace above all else, there might be a case for submitting to the prospective hegemon. But that would be at the cost of one's independence and freedom of action.

* * *

America's emergence as a hegemonic power came not by deliberate effort, but inadvertently, by the default of the Soviet Union. One moment the United States was part of a bipolar balance, the next it was left as the one superpower in a unipolar world. It had not changed its policies or mode of behavior to bring this about. The speed with which things changed meant that American hegemony was an accomplished fact before anyone had time to react to it or attempt to prevent it.

And the process drew little attention to itself: most eyes were fixed on Moscow. For these reasons, the usual historical process of determined opposition to an aspiring hegemon did not take place.

Indeed, it took America herself some time to realize what had happened and how dominant she now was. When the Soviet system collapsed, the American people, far from enjoying an unalloyed sense of triumph, were experiencing their own crisis of confidence. In the late 1980's, it was widely believed, especially by American opinion leaders and intellectuals, that America was in decline and suffering from what historian Paul Kennedy had recently labeled "imperial overstretch." The American economy was experiencing a long bad spell. Japan and Germany were coming up fast, and it was widely believed that the former would soon displace the United States as the number one economic power in the world.

Apart from all that, the country was suffering from serious social ills, and opinion polls were making it clear that the American people were tired of the burdens of foreign policy and wanted a re-ordering of priorities. Jeane Kirkpatrick, who had herself been a dedicated cold warrior, was expressing a widely held view when she wrote in 1990:

> The United States performed heroically in a time when heroism was required; altruistically during the long years when freedom was endangered. The time when Americans should bear such unusual burdens is past. With a return to "normal" times, we can again become a normal nation - and take care of pressing problems of education, family, industry, and technology. It is time to give up the dubious benefits of superpower status and become again an open American republic.

It was widely believed, both in the United States and elsewhere, that this was a unipolar moment, not a unipolar era. For the general assumption was that the end of the Cold War signaled a return to normality, and in international politics normality had always meant multipolarity. As late as 1994, Henry Kissinger was predicting the gradual military decline of the United States, the emergence of "at least six major powers."

All these factors combined to obscure and disguise what should have been obvious both to Americans and the rest of the world: that the United States now had hegemonic power. Whatever problems the U.S. economy had, it still accounted for well over a quarter of the world's gross domestic product. And soon it was to recover and enjoy a long boom fuelled by the so-called New Economy of information technology. In the 1990's, the United States economy was to grow nearly twice as fast as the European Union and three times as fast as Japan.

The United States also dominated what we have now been instructed to think of as "soft power," cultural and intellectual influence represented by everything from Harvard to Hollywood, CNN to McDonald's, popular music to computer software to jeans. Joseph Nye of Harvard, who coined the term, argues that these mold the tastes and thoughts of others, making them want what Americans want - and thus, without any co-ordinated intent, constitutes a kind of cultural hegemony. I have my doubts as to whether all this constitutes "power" in any real sense. After all, many Americans, far from approving of many aspects of their popular culture, are appalled that it represents America in the minds of millions of foreigners. And far from desiring all aspects of American culture, many foreigners see its manifestations as symbolizing all that they reject in America and resent in their own countries.

Last, but certainly not least, the United States possessed in unprecedented measure a form of power about which there is no ambiguity: military power. Until the Cold War, Americans had always been suspicious of professional armies. After all, the country had come into existence in the 18th century as the result of the exertions of citizen-soldiers against a British professional army. In his Farewell Address to the nation in 1796, George Washington, himself the country's greatest soldier, urged future generations to "avoid the necessity of those overgrown military establishments, which under any form of government are inauspicious to liberty."

His advice was followed. For nearly two centuries, the country never maintained a large peacetime army. Whenever a crisis occurred, it quickly raised forces of citizen-soldiers to meet it. Once the crisis was over - after the Civil War, after World Wars I and II - these forces were promptly disbanded. Soldiering was a low-prestige occupation, the army marginal to the life of the country. Until the beginning of the Cold War in the late 1940's, the United States did not have a Defense Department. It did not have a National Security Council. It did not have a Central Intelligence Agency. All these were only created in 1947, just as the Cold War was getting underway.

Four and a half decades later, the condition of the U.S. military, and its significance in American life, had experienced a monumental transformation. The Pentagon had become the most powerful department in American government. It sustained a huge defense industry of vital importance to the U.S. economy. Its officers were no longer languishing in the boondocks, but were an influential part of the Washington scene. A network of institutions, colleges, think-tanks, and journals sustained a sophisticated military culture. Given all this, it is not surprising that at the end of the Cold War there was not an immediate demobilization and drastic scaling down of the military establishment. It had become too powerful, too deeply embedded, for that to happen.

In politics, the relationship between ends and means is not all one-way. The capacity to do something contributes – sometimes substantially – to the attractiveness of doing it. Given that the United States had far and away the most powerful military machine in the post-Cold War world, it is not really surprising then that before long Madeleine Albright was asking an astonished Colin Powell: What is the use of having such a powerful military force if you are not prepared to use it?

* * *

According to Charles Krauthammer, from the end of the Cold War until the terrorist attack of Sept. 11, 2001, the United States took a ten-year "holiday from history." On the face of it, this seems a strange way to characterize American behavior during the decade. United States military forces were more active during these years than at any time since the Vietnam War – in the Gulf and Iraq, in Somalia, in Haiti, in Bosnia, in Afghanistan, in Sudan, in Colombia, and in Kosovo. The American economy enjoyed a sustained six-year boom. On Washington's initiative, NATO expanded eastward towards the Russian border. The North American Free Trade Agreement was negotiated and the World Trade Organization established.

Far from thinking that the United States was on vacation during these years, other countries were increasingly aware of its dominant presence. During the Clinton administration, German Chancellor Gerhard Schroeder expressed the view, "That there is danger of unilateralism, not by just anybody but by the United States, is undeniable." The French Foreign Minister, Hubert Vedrine, reflected, "American globalism dominates everything. Not in a harsh, repressive, military form, but in people's heads."

Closer to home, by the mid-1990's as sound and patriotic a judge as James Schlesinger was detecting a "growing hubris" in the conduct of American foreign policy, and "a naive belief that assertiveness is now cost-free and does not entail serious consequences." In what sense, then, could it be thought that the United States was taking a "holiday from history"?

What Krauthammer meant, I believe, was that during these years, the United States, having become the sole remaining superpower and an authentic global hegemon, had failed to activate a grand purpose commensurate with that status. Most countries might not feel the need for such a thing. But Americans do. They have a great taste for doctrines that set out the objectives that are to determine policy, as in the Monroe Doctrine, the Truman Doctrine, and the Reagan Doctrine.

No such thing was evident during the last decade of the 20th century. George Bush senior confessed that he wasn't very good at "the vision thing," and his concept of a "new world order" was stillborn. His successor, William Clinton, was an improviser with little taste for doctrines or vision. A connoisseur of opinion polls and focus groups, he knew that Americans consistently gave foreign policy a very low priority, so he acted accordingly, taking a limited interest in foreign policy. When he did, he lived largely by improvisation.

In January 2001, George W. Bush succeeded Clinton. How the Bush administration's foreign policy would have developed in the absence of the Sept. 11 attack, we shall never know. But in an instant the terrorists gave the country the clear purpose that it had previously lacked. That organizing principle came under the name of a "war on terrorism." It was adopted not as a result of cool calculation or choice, but out of necessity and in a mood of understandable outrage at the unprecedented violation that had been visited on the United States.

Now the concept of a War on Terror is general enough to support more than one meaning. It can be interpreted precisely, in terms of destroying the organizations and instruments of terror and protecting the homeland against their efforts. But it can also be defined broadly to encompass changing the conditions that give rise to terrorism, and the creation of an international order that would be inimical to its existence - not only "draining the swamp," as the phrase goes, but creating a fertile liberal and democratic pasture in its place.

Initially, the stress was on the former. But there were many in Washington's foreign-policy establishment who saw things in much more sweeping terms, and Sept. 11 shifted the balance in their favor - away from prudence and moderation toward conceptual boldness and an ambitious use of American power. Within a year, the War on Terror had metastasized into something much grander and more radical; something that would give full expression to one of the strongest strands in the history of the

American people: the profound belief that they and their country are destined to reshape the world. America's "cause is the cause of all mankind," said Benjamin Franklin; "We have the power to begin the world over again," insisted Tom Paine; "God has predestined, mankind expects, great things from our race. . . . We are pioneers of the world," said Herman Melville. Abraham Lincoln declared America to be "the world's last best hope." And so on and on.

Many in and around the Bush administration shared this sense of America's destiny and saw in 9/11 not merely a disaster to be revenged but an opportunity to reawaken and redirect America to its true historic mission.

This is what Robert Kagan means when he insists that "America did not change on Sept. 11. It only became more itself." As he explains, the national ideology has always insisted that "The proof of the transcendent importance of the American experiment would be found not only in the continual perfection of American institutions at home but also the spread of American influence in the world. . . . That is why it was always so easy for so many Americans to believe, as so many still believe today, that by advancing their own interests, they advance the interests of humanity."

In the aftermath of Sept. 11 those who thought in these terms came into their own. The result became fully evident a year after the terrorist attack with the publication of a 31-page statement by the president titled "The National Security Strategy of the United States of America."

For a document concerned with strategy, it puts an extremely heavy emphasis on ideology in defining America's purpose. In its first three pages alone, it uses the words "liberty" and "freedom," or some variation of them, 25 times, while the word "interest" occurs only twice. The document declares that the national strategy will be based on "a distinctly American internationalism." It will "use this moment of opportunity to extend the benefits of freedom across the globe . . . will actively work to bring the hope of democracy, development, free markets, and free trade to every corner of the world." To that end, the United States will seek "to create a balance of power that favors human freedom: conditions in which all nations and all societies can choose for themselves the rewards and challenges of political and economic liberty." Note that the assumption is that, given a free choice, these are the values that all people will choose.

As well as reordering the internal conditions of countries in this way, the United States will reorder relations among states, for, as the document asserts, "the international community has the best chance since the rise of the nation-state in the seventeenth century to build a world where great powers compete in peace instead of continually prepare for war."

The president ends his introduction by declaring, "The United States has responsibility to lead this great mission." It is made unambiguously clear that the United States military will be an indispensable instrument for the creation of a new order and that the United States intends to maintain indefinitely the enormous military superiority it now enjoys. It is time, the president says,

> [T]o reaffirm the essential role of American military strength. We must build and maintain our defenses beyond challenge. . . . Our forces will be strong enough to discourage potential adversaries from pursuing a military build-up in hopes of surpassing, or equalizing, the power of the United States.

The military will be used actively and assertively, deployed even more widely than it was during the Cold War as a kind of global gendarmerie maintaining order.

And this strategy intends to maintain, if not increase, America's military power as it discourages others from building up theirs. Thus, two pages before it declares the essential role of American military strength, it advises the Chinese that:

> In pursuing advanced military capabilities that can threaten its neighbors in the Asia-Pacific region, China is following an outdated path that, in the end, will hamper its own pursuit of national greatness.

This might seem a clear example of double standards. The defenders of the new doctrine do not deny this but justify it in terms of the special responsibilities of the United States for world order. As Robert Kagan puts it, because of those responsibilities, America "must refuse to abide by certain international conventions that may constrain its ability to fight effectively. . . . It must support arms control, but not always for itself. It must live by a double standard." Which, of course, raises the important question of whether other countries will ever be willing to accept that double standard. The whole history of international politics suggests that they will not.

Also key to the new doctrine is its abandonment of deterrence, which was effective in dealing with a rational and cautious adversary like the Soviet Union, but is less so in dealing with risk-taking rogue states. Instead, a greatly extended policy of pre-emptive action must now be adopted:

> The greater the threat, the greater is the risk of inaction – and the more compelling the case for taking anticipatory action to defend ourselves, even if uncertainty remains as to the time and place of the enemy's attack. To

forestall or prevent such hostile acts by our adversaries, the United States will, if necessary, act preemptively.

Another feature of the Bush doctrine is its unilateralism. ("We will not hesitate to act alone, if necessary.") In a sense, the very genesis of the document testifies to this, since its intention to alter the international system fundamentally was announced with little or no consultation with other states. What can one say about this strategic doctrine? The first thing to be emphasized is its breathtaking scope and huge ambition to do no less than to effect a transformation of the political universe - according to some of its language, to stamp out evil and war between states, to create a benign world. Students of the realist school tend to see such goals as beyond even the reach of a country with the enormous power of the United States. While America has enough strength to defeat all other adversaries and rivals, it remains to be seen whether she can conquer Utopia.

In insisting upon the dominant role of the United States and the assertive use of American power, the doctrine makes very questionable assumptions about what the other states will accept. They are asked to take good intentions on trust, but states have never been prepared to do this with other would-be hegemons.

Will the United States be the exception? Does the fact that it is a democratic and liberal state make a decisive difference? Will other states accept the concept of a benign hegemon or regard it as a contradiction in terms? Bearing in mind the distrust of unbalanced and concentrated power that is manifest in the United States' own constitution, Americans should not be surprised if others are skeptical.

The thrust and tone of the doctrine reject the advice given by most pundits on the best way to play a hegemonic role: to be restrained and prudent in the use of power, to disguise it, to strive to act as far as possible by persuasion and consensus. In the 1940's, when the United States was already the dominant power within the Western Alliance, it acted on this advice. It went out of its way to act multilaterally, to create a network of rule-making institutions - the UN, IMF, World Bank, and GATT - that allowed it to act co-operatively with others, as *primus inter pares* - the first among equals. There is little of this to be found in the current doctrine. The prevailing view in Washington, as famously enunciated by Secretary of Defense Rumsfeld, has been, "the worst thing you can do is allow a coalition to determine what your mission is."

The Bush doctrine should be taken seriously and not dismissed as rhetoric. It has already been put into effect in Iraq: the use of American military force as the main instrument; pre-emptive action; a clear indication that the United States was prepared to act without a Great Power consensus, and unilaterally if necessary; and the avowed intention to replace a tyrannical regime with a liberal representative government. That is why the Iraq commitment has an importance that goes way beyond the fate of Iraq itself. If, in the end, it turns out successfully, it is likely that the mishaps that have occurred since the end of the heavy fighting will be seen as part of a learning experience, a breaking-in period for a new, revolutionary, strategic doctrine. If, on the other hand, it fails at the first hurdle – if, that is, the United States finds that bringing about a decent political order is beyond its capacity – then not only will there have to be a reconsideration of the whole global strategy, but the limits of the United States' capacity will have been made evident, and the inclination to resist it greatly strengthened.

* * *

To the critics, the belief that democratic institutions, behavior, and ways of thought can be exported and transplanted to societies that have no experience of them is profoundly mistaken. While the United States can provide an example to emulate, democracy is not a commodity that can be exported, or a gift that can be bestowed. To be viable, political institutions and political cultures require a long, organic, indigenous growth, and to attempt from without a sudden dislocation of what exists is more likely to produce unintended consequences than intended ones.

Supporters of the policy tend to regard all this as defeatist, an elaborate rationalization for doing nothing. Liberty, they assert, is a universal value, every society and culture desires it. To work for its realization through democratic institutions is not to impose anything, but merely to remove impediments and to render assistance in a learning process.

In terms of achievability, the trump cards in the hands of those who favor the policy and usually the first cards played are the examples of post-World War II Germany and Japan. But neither is particularly valid or relevant. The German and Japanese peoples were utterly defeated and crushed at the end of that conflict, and there were no surviving institutions or centers of opposition. In Iraq today the population is considered liberated, not defeated and deprived of rights. Second, Germany and Japan in 1945 were genuine nation states with homogenous populations and a strong sense of identity. This is true of few of the possible candidates for democratization today. Most of the states of the Middle East are artificial creations, arbitrarily carved out by Western powers. Third, and most important, before falling into the hands of extremist regimes, both Germany and Japan had considerable experience of the rule of law and civil society, as well as some significant experience of democratic practice. They had well-educated populations and substantial middle classes. Again, none of this is true of most of the targeted states today.

Another American experience seems much more relevant. Long before the United States became a global hegemon, it was a regional hegemon in the Caribbean. From the end of the 19th century it dominated the region and intervened as it saw fit. It occupied Haiti for 19 years, Nicaragua for even longer. Yet to this day the region has not produced one genuine, stable democracy. Nor was the United States to lay the foundations for a viable democracy during the three decades that it ruled the Philippines.

Some social scientists believe that the most reliable indicator of a country's chances of achieving a viable democratic system is its economic performance. More precisely, a mean per capita income of around $6,000 makes the chance of a successful democratic transition very high. There are exceptions. The correlation does not apply to states with high incomes derived, not from effort, but solely from the luck of sitting on vast reserves of oil. But the correlation is a strong one, and the reasons are fairly evident. A developed economy requires, among other things, a reasonable education system, a developed middle class, significant access to information, a legal system that enforces rules of commerce in a way that foreign investors and traders find acceptable.

What implications does this have for the policy of promoting democracy? First, in many cases the most efficient way of proceeding initially may not be the direct one of focusing on political reform but the indirect one of developing strong economic institutions. Second, the greater effort should be directed at those countries that are approaching the transition stage with incomes that are not derived from oil or mineral wealth.

Even if the goal of promoting democracy is achievable, is it desirable? This may seem a strange question, for we are all in favor of "democracy," aren't we? Yes, we are, but when we speak of democracy, we almost invariably mean liberal democracy: a combination of democracy as a way of selecting government by competitive election and liberalism as a set of values and institutions, including the rule of law, an independent judiciary, an honest and impartial civil service, a strong respect for human rights and private property. While we are accustomed to the two being linked together, it is worth considering whether there is a necessary connection between them.

Liberalism has in the past thrived in countries that were not democratic, as it did, for example, in Britain in the late 18th and early 19th centuries.

Democracy can be, and often is, installed in countries that are not liberal. Democratic governments can assume intrusive and oppressive power – regarding property, for example, or religious practice, or the starting of businesses – while still observing the basic democratic requirements. In his recent book *The Future of Freedom*, Fareed Zakaria argues that illiberal democracy is an increasingly prevalent phenomenon. It would, he believes, be a healthier state of affairs if the evolution toward an orderly rule of law and liberal civil society by some kind of enlightened elite were to precede the installation of a democratic order, as was the case with most stable Western democracies. He argues that in considering the interrelationship between liberalism and democracy, we should recognize that the former is the precondition of a successful implementation of the latter, rather than vice versa. This may be particularly sound advice in dealing with the Middle East, for many of those who know the region well believe that if democracy were to be introduced under the prevailing conditions, the immediate result would be the installation of governments that would be even more militantly Islamist, repressive, and anti-Western than those that now exist.

There is one other important respect in which democracy figures in the discussion of international relations in the post-Cold War era. It is claimed that the increasing spread of democracy across the globe will greatly reduce the incidence of warfare and create an extended zone of peace. For, it is maintained, the historical evidence shows that democracies rarely, if ever, go to war with each other.

One can, of course, argue about definitions and particular cases, but it is generally true that liberal democracies have managed to get along with each other without war. Britain and the United States have not fought a war since 1812. Britain and France, bitter and violent rivals in their pre-democratic days, have been at peace since 1815. America and Canada can live with a common border that is thousands of miles long, without any fortifications on it. Why is this? One answer was given by Immanuel Kant. He maintained that in a republican state, as opposed to an authoritarian one, there would be a presumption against war. Citizens "would be very cautious in . . . decreeing for themselves all the calamities of war." For it would be they who would have to fight the wars, pay for them, and repair the devastation that would result.

In an important sense Kant claims too much, for all the reasons he gives for liberal democracies not fighting each other would also apply to liberal democracies not fighting other non-democratic states as well. But in fact, democracies have gone to war with non-democratic states and peoples very frequently, and for a variety of reasons: imperial expansion, ideology, territorial rivalry, to secure markets, to punish, to restore or impose order. More often than not, these wars have been enthusiastically supported by citizens.

Whatever the explanation, it is certainly true that war between liberal democracies in today's world seems utterly improbable. Whether the same would hold true for other democracies - between, say, an increasingly illiberal India and a Pakistan in which a corrupt and venal version of democracy had been restored - is an open question.

Some years ago, when enthusiasm for exporting democracy was building up in Washington, as the end of the Cold War approached, I wrote,

> Americans of all political persuasions believe profoundly that it is their right and duty - indeed their destiny - to promote freedom and democracy in the world. It is a noble and powerful impulse, one not casually to be ridiculed or dismissed. But acting on it - if one is concerned to be effective and not merely to feel virtuous - is a complicated and delicate business, and the dangers are many. Success requires that this impulse be balanced against, and where necessary, circumscribed by, other interests that the United States must necessarily pursue, more mundane ones like security, order, and prosperity. For these represent not merely legitimate competing claims but the preconditions for a lasting extension of democracy.

Success requires, too, an awareness of the intractability of a world that does not exist merely in order to satisfy American expectations - a world that, for the most part, cannot satisfy those expectations in the foreseeable future. While determination and purposefulness are important ingredients in any effective policy, the attempt to force history in the direction of democracy by an exercise of will is likely to produce more unintended than intended consequences. The successful promotion of democracy calls for restraint and patience, a sense of limits and an appreciation of the wisdom of indirection, a profound understanding of the particularity of circumstances. As Thomas Carlyle once put it, "I don't pretend to understand the Universe - it's a great deal bigger than I am.... People ought to be modester."

This still reflects my views on the subject.

FAREED ZAKARIA

11 Like It's 1999: How We Could Have Done It Right

FOREIGN POLICY IS NOT THEOLOGY. THE ONLY WAY TO MAKE sensible choices in this realm is to weigh costs and benefits. A policy that might have been wise crumbles if the costs become prohibitive. For example, protecting South Vietnam from a communist invasion from the north was a worthwhile goal. The horrendous costs of doing so, however, made it a bad policy. For those of us who supported the war in Iraq, the question is simple - have the costs risen so high that they outweigh any benefit? It's a fair question, since the manner in which Iraq has been handled over the past 18 months has racked up enormous costs. Still, I think the intervention has the potential to be a success if we learn the lessons - the right lessons - of this last year and a half.

I was not one of those who had been urging another war against Iraq ever since the first Gulf war. Through the 1990's, I thought the strategy pursued by the first Bush and Clinton administrations - sanctions and containment - was a reasonable solution to a difficult problem. But, by the late 90's, this strategy was falling apart. In the isolated atmosphere created by sanctions, Saddam Hussein's grip on power had tightened. He had found ways to manipulate the sanctions system by cheating and smuggling (the best estimate of his take is $10 billion). Yet, the sanctions were pushing hundreds of thousands of Iraqis into poverty every year, a reality that was televised across the Arab world daily.

Keeping Saddam "in his box" meant air attacks almost weekly on Iraqi military facilities. It also meant the United States had to maintain a garrison in Saudi Arabia, something that was creating enormous regional

Reprinted from the *New Republic*, June 28, 2004, by permission.

instability. Recall that Osama bin Laden's infamous 1996 fatwa is titled "Declaration of War Against the Americans Occupying the Land of the Two Holy Places." Bin Laden's main complaints against the United States were that it was "occupying" Saudi Arabia and starving the Iraqi people. Palestine came in a distant third. Being a man gifted with a great sense of mass appeal, bin Laden had calculated that these were the causes most likely to galvanize Arabs and Muslims.

I did not believe Saddam had a lethal arsenal of chemical, biological, and nuclear weapons, and I wrote as much in the months before the war (though, like everyone who is being honest, I am utterly astonished by what appears to be the lack of *any* weapons). But Saddam was an erratic, unpredictable leader who had been actively working against the United States and its interests - and peace in the region - for two decades. That meant he was a looming threat. Given the collapsing sanctions regime, at some point the United States would have to decide to move in one direction or the other. It could either welcome Saddam back into the community of nations and let him do what he would as a free agent. Or it could gather an international coalition to replace him. I wish that this latter policy had been pursued slowly and deliberately, with a genuine effort to forge a broad coalition and get the United Nations behind it. But, in the end, you have to decide whether to support the policy the president is pursuing - not the variation of it you wish he were pursuing. And I decided that, while timing and circumstances were not perfect, getting rid of one of the most ghastly regimes in the world, one that was a continued threat to U.S. interests, was worth supporting. Morality and realpolitik came together in the case against Saddam.

Given what's happened in Iraq over the last year, was all this wrong? It is becoming conventional wisdom to speak of Iraq as an unmanageable crisis that no policy can untangle. "[Not] every problem has a solution," wrote Peter Galbraith in the *New York Review of Books*. But is that really the lesson of the last year? That nation-building is impossible in Iraq? That the Iraqis are savages who cannot govern themselves? That America is bound to fail in such endeavors?

If that is the case, then how to make sense of East Timor, Kosovo, and Bosnia (not to mention Japan, Germany, South Korea, and a host of other cases)? Over the last five years, the United States has helped these societies overcome terrible odds, maintain peace, and begin to build more decent governments. They are still far from perfect (Kosovo is, in fact, a mess), but they're a lot better off than they were. All of these places are quite different from Iraq, but, in some ways, the problems they posed were far more challenging. If, in Iraq, you face a potential civil war, in Bosnia you had an actual one, lasting for years, that had created deep scars. If Iraqi nationalism seems fierce, Serbian and Croatian nationalism was by any measure more violent and internecine. If – to take the unspoken assumption – Muslims are the problem, Bosnia and Kosovo have lots of them.

The real lesson of the last year is that the Bush administration's inept version of nation-building failed. The administration's strategists used Iraq as a laboratory to prove various deeply held prejudices: for example, that the Clinton administration's nation-building was fat and slow, that the United Nations was irrelevant, that the United States faced no problem of legitimacy in Iraq, that Ahmed Chalabi would become a Mesopotamian Charles de Gaulle. In almost every case, facts on the ground quickly disconfirmed these theories. But, so committed were these government officials to their ideology – and so powerful within the administration – that it took 14 months for policy to adjust to these failures. In the last month, the United States has finally reversed course, sending more troops, scaling back de-Baathification, dumping Chalabi, bringing in the United Nations, and listening to Iraqis on the ground. This shift in policy is already making a difference, easing the anti-Americanism and the sense of international isolation that has plagued the Iraq mission. If they keep up the reversals, Iraq still has a chance.

Compare Iraq with Afghanistan. Looked at in the abstract, Afghanistan is potentially far more chaotic than Iraq. It's a country riven with tribes and warlords that hasn't had a functioning state for 30 years – and perhaps not for three centuries. Yet, America's nation-building there has been more successful than in Iraq – with far less money spent on it. Many problems remain, but the country is unquestionably better off than it was under the Taliban. The simplest statistic to prove the point is that, since the fall of Kabul, two million Afghan refugees have returned to their country.

Why has Afghanistan been more successful than Iraq? In Afghanistan, the Bush administration adopted a version of postwar policies developed over the 90's. After the war, it handed the political process over to the United Nations and directed its military efforts through NATO. The United Nations was able to structure a political process (the *loya jirga*) that had legitimacy within Afghanistan as well as internationally. With some massaging, it produced a pro-Western liberal as president. Making the military efforts multinational has meant that today, the European Union spends about as much on Afghanistan as the United States and that the new Afghan army is being trained jointly by the United States and . . . France.

The biggest mistake I made on Iraq was to believe that the Bush administration would want to get Iraq right more than it wanted to prove its own prejudices right. I knew the administration went into Iraq with some crackpot ideas, but I also believed that, above all else, it would want success on the ground. I reasoned that it would drop its pet theories once it was clear they were not working. I still don't understand why the Bush team proved so self-defeatingly stubborn. Perhaps its initial success in Afghanistan emboldened it to move forward unconstrained. Perhaps its prejudices about Iraq had developed over decades and were deeply held. Perhaps the administration was far more divided and dysfunctional than I had recognized, making rational policy impossible.

But, since we are listing mistakes, the biggest one many opponents of the war are making is to claim that Iraq is a total distraction from the war on terrorism. In fact, Iraq is central to that conflict. I don't mean this in the deceptive and dishonest sense that many in the Bush administration have claimed. There is no connection between Saddam's regime and the *terrorists* of September 11. But there is a deep connection between his regime and the *terrorism* of September 11. The root causes of Islamic terrorism lie in the dysfunctional politics of the Middle East, where failure and repression have produced fundamentalism and violence. Political Islam grew in stature as a mystical alternative to the wretched reality - secular dictatorships - that have dominated the Arab world. A new Iraq provides an opportunity to break this perverse cycle. The country is unlikely to become a liberal democracy any time soon. But it might turn out to be a pluralistic state that gives minorities limited protections, allows for some political participation, and has a reasonably open society. That would be a revolution in the Arab world.

The right lesson of Iraq so far is not that nation-building must fail, but rather that President Bush's approach to it, unless corrected, will fail. The right lesson is not that U.S. military intervention always ruptures alliances and creates an enraged international public, but rather that this particular intervention did. Most important, it is not that American power aggressively employed does more harm than good. Rather, the right lesson is that American power, because it is so overweening, must be used with extraordinary care and wisdom. Most of the world's problems - from AIDS to the Israeli-Palestinian issue - would be better served with more American intervention, not less. But, because of the blunders in Iraq, it is possible that most of the world, and far too many Americans, will draw the wrong lesson on this final point as well.

MAX BOOT

12 Reality Check – This Is War

THE PANIC GRIPPING WASHINGTON OVER THE STATE OF IRAQ MAKES it clear we have been spoiled by the seemingly easy, apparently bloodless victories of the last decade. From the Persian Gulf War of 1991 to the Afghanistan war of 2001, we got used to winning largely through air power. There were casualties, of course, but few of them were on our side. In Kosovo, we managed to prevail without losing a single person. We forgot what real war looks like. Iraq is providing an unwelcome reminder of how messy and costly it can be.

By comparison with the wars of the last decade, what's happening in Iraq appears to be a terrible failure. Things look a little different if you compare it with earlier conflicts.

Look at three key indicators:

- *Casualties.* As of Wednesday, we've lost 800 service people in Iraq (666 of them from hostile fire), and more than 4,500 have been wounded (of whom 1,769 returned to duty within 72 hours). At least 200,000 soldiers and Marines have served in Iraq – including many who have since left – so that amounts to a total casualty rate of about 2.5%. If you add Air Force, Navy, and logistics personnel supporting Operation Iraqi Freedom (at least 150,000), the casualty rate drops to 1.5%.

  How does that compare with previous U.S. wars? By my calculation, using data from Information Please and the Oxford Companion to American Military History, the losses we've suffered in Iraq are so far among the lowest of any of our major conflicts. Comparing the number of U.S. wounded and dead with the size of the force deployed, in Vietnam the casualty rate was 6.2%; in World War I and

Reprinted from the *Los Angeles Times*, May 27, 2004, and July 15, 2004, by permission.

World War II, just above 6.5%. On D-day, June 6, 1944, more than three times as many servicemen were lost as died in Iraq in the past year.

The Iraq war rate seems high only because our unstated benchmark is the 1991 Gulf War (total casualty rate: 0.14%). This is not meant to deprecate the sacrifices of our soldiers; for friends and family members, no statistics can assuage their grief. But, from a historical vantage point, what's remarkable is how few casualties we've suffered, not how many.

- *Nation-building.* No, we haven't established a liberal democracy in Iraq. But it's only been a year. We occupied West Germany for four years after 1945, Japan for seven years. We occupied the Philippines for almost half a century after the Spanish-American War. More recently, Bosnia is still occupied by the international community nine years after the end of hostilities, as is Kosovo five years later.

  It takes a long time to bring order out of chaos. The most successful examples of nation-building, such as the British in India, required hundreds of years. No one is suggesting that the United States should occupy Iraq nearly that long, of course, but it's unrealistic to expect too much in only a year. The fact that an interim Iraqi government will be established June 30, and elections held by Jan. 30, is actually pretty speedy by historical norms.
- *Abuses.* I make no excuses for the sadistic creeps at Abu Ghraib whose misconduct deserves the harshest possible punishment. But let's be serious. For all the media's coverage, this is no My Lai (1968) or No Gun Ri (1950) – both instances in which innocent civilians were gunned down by U.S. troops. Nor is this comparable to the abuses that occurred during the Philippine War (1899–1903), when Brig. Gen. Jacob Smith instructed his men to turn the island of Samar into "a howling wilderness" and kill "all persons . . . who are capable of bearing arms."

  In Iraq, there is no evidence of the kind of systematic torture employed by the French in Algeria (1954–62) or the kind of "concentration camps" invented by the British in the Boer War (1899–1902). U.S. troops haven't simply leveled whole towns, as the Russians did in Chechnya (1994–95) or the Syrians in Hama (1982). Even in World War II – the "good war" – there were numerous instances of Americans shooting enemy soldiers trying to surrender, to say nothing of the carpet-bombing of German and Japanese civilians.

On the historical scale of abuses, the misconduct of a few soldiers in Iraq ranks pretty low. Most soldiers and Marines actually have exhibited great restraint in the face of an enemy that hides behind civilians and fires from mosques.

I don't mean to imply that everything is going great in Iraq. There are huge problems, especially the lack of security, and the Bush administration has badly bungled many aspects of the occupation. All I'm suggesting is that we keep a sense of perspective: Mistakes and setbacks occur in every war. At least in every war before the 1990's.

In Modern Imperialism, U.S. Needs to Walk Softly

WITH THE COALITION PROVISIONAL AUTHORITY DISBANDED AND L. Paul Bremer III back at home, it's time to ponder the future of American imperialism. Many, of course, will huffily reply that U.S. imperialism has no future, and they will point to all the troubles we've encountered in Iraq during the last year as evidence.

But whatever happens in Iraq, there will continue to be strong demand for U.S. interventions around the world. Failed states and rogue states constitute the biggest threats to world peace in the foreseeable future, and only the United States has the will and the resources to do anything about them. Even many of those who detested the invasion of Iraq plead for the U.S. to bring order to places like Darfur, a province in Sudan where genocide is occurring. The U.S. cannot shrug off the burden of global leadership, at least not without catastrophic cost to the entire world, but it can exercise its power more wisely than it did in Iraq over the past year.

One of Bremer's chief failings was that he tried to act the part of an imperial proconsul. He and his spokesmen hogged the media spotlight, which only exacerbated Iraqis' tendency to blame them for everything that went wrong, from too many car bombings to not enough electricity. It was almost as if Bremer were Lord Curzon, the notoriously vain viceroy of India from 1898 to 1905, who delighted in pomp and circumstance, such as the grandiose festival he staged in 1903 to mark Edward VII's coronation as king of Britain and emperor of India. For obvious reasons – the rise of nationalism, the fall of traditional European empires – that approach doesn't work well today. No one is going to crown George II emperor of Mesopotamia.

Yet the infinitely adaptable British had different ways of ruling different parts of their empire, and some of them are applicable today. There was, for instance, Lord Cromer (born Evelyn Baring), who effectively ruled Egypt from 1883 to 1907 with the modest titles of British agent and consul general.

The British came to dominate Egypt in 1879 when they, along with the French, imposed financial controls to ensure that foreign bond-holders would be repaid by a bankrupt government. (Shades of the International Monetary Fund!) The British occupied the country on their own in 1882 after a nationalist revolt. But they refrained from formally annexing it, which would only have stirred up nationalist sentiment.

The Ottoman rulers, styled as khedives, were kept in office while Cromer pulled the strings from behind the scenes. This became known as the "veiled protectorate," and it essentially continued even after Egypt was granted full independence and proclaimed a constitutional monarchy in 1922. The system worked until 1952, when a group of army officers led by Col. Gamal Abdel Nasser deposed the king and seized power for themselves. The Nasserite coup showed that the British approach had run its course, but it had allowed Britain to dominate the biggest nation in the Middle East for more than 70 years. It wasn't a bad deal for Egypt, either, which enjoyed more freedom and better government than it received from Nasser and his dictatorial successors.

The U.S. today doesn't need the same level of control in Iraq that the British had in Egypt, and it needs to be much more serious about promoting democracy than the British were. Formal empire isn't our destiny. But, while fostering self-rule, the U.S. must also ensure that Iraq will not dissolve into civil war or become a haven for terrorists or weapons proliferators. This will require a long-term U.S. presence – a presence that will be much more palatable to Iraqis now that the U.S. has moved to its own form of a "veiled protectorate," with an Iraqi president and prime minister playing highly visible roles and the new U.S. envoy, John Negroponte, fading into the background.

The only wonder is that it took so long. In Afghanistan, the U.S. wisely settled on the indirect approach from the start with the appointment of Hamid Karzai as president. U.S. Ambassador Zalmay Khalilzad exercises a lot of influence, but he does so quietly, without generating the backlash that would occur if he proclaimed himself the administrator of Afghanistan.

Another successful model of modern-day imperialism can be found in Bosnia and Kosovo, which the U.S. and its allies run through an international protectorate similar to the one that Britain and France imposed on Egypt in 1879. The blessing of the United Nations confers welcome legitimacy.

Whether we like it or not, liberal imperialism is needed today to deal with the most troubled regions of the planet. But if we are going to be effective imperialists, we need to follow the Cromer, not the Curzon, model.

ANDREW J. BACEVICH

13 A Time for Reckoning

REALITY HAS NOT DEALT KINDLY WITH THE HOPES AND EXPECTATIONS conjured up to justify Operation Iraqi Freedom. Although the war may not be lost, it cannot be won, at least not as the Bush administration once defined winning. What then are we to make of this experience?

The question may strike some as premature. Whether President Bush (or President Kerry) "stays the course" or cuts American losses, difficult days lie ahead. The bill yet to be levied for this misadventure promises to be steep. More Americans and even larger numbers of Iraqis will lose their lives. Combat operations and the black hole of "nation-building" will consume additional billions of dollars, adding to the ocean of red ink that is the federal budget. Yet even as events wind their way toward what promises to be a deeply unsatisfactory denouement, the argument over what it all means must necessarily be joined. Common sense dictates that we apply to future U.S. policy what we have learned in Iraq, and the future will not wait.

With an eye toward that future – and with no claim that any of what follows qualifies as definitive – herewith a first cut at identifying the war's operative lessons.

First, ideology makes a poor substitute for strategy. With the invasion of Iraq, it became impossible to deny that in the heady aftermath of the Cold War American grand strategy became uncoupled from reality. Certain that history had spoken and that Americans were uniquely able to interpret its meaning, policymakers both Democratic and Republican uncorked old vials of Wilsonian illusion and breathed deeply. As a consequence, zealotry supplanted calculations of power and interest as a determinant of U.S. policy.

Bill Clinton entertained visions of globalization, creating a world without borders in which all nations would be sure to enjoy the blessings of peace, prosperity, and democracy. George W. Bush topped Clinton, vowing after 9/11 not only to eliminate terror (an impossibility) but also to put an end to evil. But mixing utopianism and politics is a recipe for miscalculation and an invitation to strategic bankruptcy - as the Iraq War has painfully reminded us.

It is the tradition of George Washington rather than the tradition of Woodrow Wilson that best serves American interests. The nation's first president - and successors like Lincoln, both Roosevelts, Truman, and Eisenhower - understood not only the uses but also the limits of power. That balanced sensibility, anchored to considerations of prudence, has vanished from the current foreign-policy elite. There is an urgent need to restore it.

Second, wars leave loose ends. In a political sense, decisive victory - meaning military success that makes a clean sweep of the complaints giving rise to war in the first place - is a pipe dream.

Operation Iraqi Freedom was supposed to finish the job that Bush's father had left undone in 1991. Oust Saddam Hussein, the war's supporters promised, and all sorts of good things were sure to follow. War would transform Iraq into the first Arab democracy, usher the Middle East into an era of lasting peace, and nudge Islam toward moderation and modernity. Today, the Ba'athist regime is gone, but none of the predicted benefits seems likely to materialize. Instead the United States has exchanged the limited burdens of containment for the far more onerous burdens of occupation. We have overthrown a tin-pot dictator posing no immediate threat to the United States and thereby energized and encouraged far more dangerous enemies. Rather than persuading Muslims to see America as liberator and friend, we have cemented our image as Great Satan.

War is like a highly toxic drug: with the cure come side effects. And Iraq reminds us that the side effects can prove worse than the disease.

Third, allies have choices – and will exercise them. Across a decade of hyping the United States as "sole superpower" and "indispensable nation," too many policymakers persuaded themselves that America's traditional allies had no alternative but to accede to U.S. "global leadership." Both the Persian Gulf War of 1990–1991 and the Kosovo conflict of 1999 seemed to show that when Washington called, others clamored to board the bandwagon. To opt out was to be left out and left behind: from Washington's perspective, this was a risk that few "friends" were likely to take.

Iraq demolished such fantasies. Allies are not vassals. When interests diverge sufficiently, "friendship" counts for little. The Iraq experience has, time and again, affirmed this fundamental principle: when "old Europe" chose to sit out the war altogether; when Turkey rejected Washington's request to allow U.S. troops to cross its territory; when Spanish voters concluded that occupying Iraq was exacerbating rather than reducing the threat of terror. At every step of the way, as key allies stiffed us, the costs borne by the United States have necessarily risen.

Even before Iraq, the bonds that once joined what was called "the West" had already (and perhaps inevitably) begun to fray. Thanks to its insistence on preventive war, the Bush administration has hastened the West along the path toward oblivion. Nations whose support we once assumed to be a given now question the acceptability of the *Pax Americana* and may yet muster the collective will to proffer an alternative. Before launching on more crusades, we have diplomatic fences to mend.

Fourth, Israel's war is not our war. President Bush's undifferentiated "global war on terror" has encouraged the government of Ariel Sharon to assert that Israel's enemies and America's enemies are one and the same. But they are not. Indeed, Sharon's misguided effort to crush resistance to Israel's occupation of the West Bank and Gaza through brute force serves only to complicate and exacerbate our own problems. Sharon's policy will not work, and as Israel's chief supporter we get tagged with much of the blame.

Resolving the Israeli-Palestinian dispute will not itself alleviate Muslim antagonism toward the United States. But absent such a resolution, that antagonism will fester, thereby providing fertile ground for Osama bin Laden and other Islamic radicals to enlist new recruits.

We should not deceive ourselves about the prospects of bringing real peace to the Holy Land. Something like partition is probably the best outcome one can hope for. But brokering and if necessary enforcing such a partition rather than vainly attempting to democratize the Arab world at the point of a sword ought to form the centerpiece of U.S. policy in the Middle East. Further deference to Israeli hardliners like Sharon, who know nothing but force, is contrary to American interests. True friends of the Jewish state will see it as contrary to Israel's interests as well.

Fifth, "shock and awe" gets you only so far. More than a decade ago, the previous U.S. war against Iraq brought to full flower the American romance with high-tech warfare. Operation Iraqi Freedom has offered the fullest illustration to date of what this new American way of war can and cannot do. On the one hand, it affirmed what we already learned in Desert Storm: U.S. forces will make short work of any conventionally organized and equipped adversary foolish enough to put up a fight.

On the other hand, developments since the fall of Baghdad have also affirmed what we learned in Mogadishu: against a determined insurgent armed with even primitive weapons, air power, stealth, and precision weapons – all the signature capabilities that distinguish the preferred American style of warfare – won't do the trick. Defeating guerrillas requires something more and something different. The United States military is no closer today to devising a technological solution to the riddle of unconventional war than it was when Vietnam ended in defeat.

Sixth, the margin of U.S. military supremacy is thinner than advertised. Ours is undoubtedly the mightiest military the world has ever seen, with a more than ample inventory of high-performance fighter jets, aircraft carriers, and top-of-the-line nuclear submarines. But our inventory of soldiers and Marines is grossly inadequate – inadequate at least to implement President Bush's grandiose plans for sprinkling the blessings of liberty throughout the Greater Middle East. Despite the administration's obdurate insistence to the contrary, the fact is that the United States today has too few soldiers doing too many things.

In just one year, the Iraq morass has brought U.S. ground forces within a hair's breadth of overstretch. Expedients such as relying on reserves and hiring thousands of mercenaries have not fixed the problem; they embody it. Announced plans to divert troops from Korea to Iraq and to deploy stateside training cadres show just how bare the cupboard has become.

If the United States is intent on playing the role of global hegemon, we need to put more young Americans in uniform – lots more. If as citizens we're not willing to pay that price, then the Iraq experience should oblige policymakers to scale back their ambitions.

Seventh, the myth of American casualty aversion is just that. The conventional wisdom of the 1990's was that a risk-averse military and a casualty-phobic public constituted major obstacles impeding the effective use of force. For the Clinton administration and its defenders, this became a convenient device for off-loading onto others responsibility for American military fecklessness. The onus for the pseudo-campaigns of the decade leading up to 9/11 – the zenith coming in 1998 when U.S. Navy cruise missiles demolished an empty pharmaceutical factory in Khartoum – lay not with the commander-in-chief but with foot-dragging generals and fainthearted citizens who lacked the stomach for serious military action.

Historians can debate whether or not the sensitivity to casualties was ever as great as it once appeared. But there is little room for debate that the events of Sept. 11, 2001 swept aside any such constraints. Traditional American ferocity and bloody-mindedness reasserted themselves with a vengeance. All that was needed was competence at the top to harness and direct it. But as the Iraq debacle has made plain, competence remains, as it was in the 1990's, in precariously short supply.

Eighth, so too with the myth of an American genius for spreading democracy. From the very day that U.S. forces entered Baghdad, the officials charged with raising a new Iraq out of the ashes of the old have displayed remarkable ineptitude. However admirable the hard work of those who have risked life and limb to give the Iraqi people a fresh start, the overall effort has misfired.

Far from replicating the success achieved in postwar Germany and Japan after 1945, L. Paul Bremer has managed to reprise the sorry record achieved in places like South Vietnam. If the United States insists that it needs to be in the nation-building business, then it's time to go back to square one, drawing on the disappointments of Iraq to devise the techniques, create the institutions, and develop the leaders to do better next time out. Or, perhaps more wisely, we might conclude that bringing democracy to the Arab world is akin to making bricks without straw – a trick best left to others.

Ninth, it's hard to win when you don't know whom you're fighting. Much has been made about the blunders in strategic intelligence such as the failure to anticipate 9/11 and the bogus assertions regarding Saddam's weapons of massive destruction. But the inadequacies of tactical intelligence have been at least as great, if not greater.

In a situation truly without precedent in all of American military history, American forces in Iraq have for more than a year been engaged in a full-fledged shooting war and still do not know whom they are fighting. The reliance on generic terms to describe the "terrorists," "insurgents," or "foreign fighters" tells the story. Exactly who is the enemy? How is he organized? Who gives the orders? What are his aims? We don't know. And as long as we don't, the enemy will retain the initiative.

In short, the Iraq War shows that the imperative of intelligence reform goes far beyond any problems attributed to the CIA.

Tenth, civil-military relations at the top are broken. The Iraq War has confirmed what had already become evident during the 1990's: the relationship between senior military leaders and the top echelon of civilian officials is dysfunctional. That dysfunction contributes to flawed decisions on crucial issues related to peace and war.

During the Clinton era, the problem was one of a weak commander-in-chief unable or unwilling to assert effective control over the generals. Donald Rumsfeld came into office intent on clearing up any confusion about who is in charge. But the Rumsfeld approach is to treat his principal military advisers with McNamara-like disdain. Those who speak up - like the Army chief of staff who had the temerity to suggest that occupying Iraq might require a considerable number of troops - are rebuked and marginalized.

The point is not to suggest turning war over to the soldiers. Unambiguous civilian control is essential. But effective civil-military interaction demands something more than simply throttling generals. It means incorporating professional military expertise into the debate over basic national security policy. That in turn requires a combination of trust, honesty, mutual respect, and mutual self-restraint that has been absent for many years. This is an intolerable situation that in all likelihood the Department of Defense itself cannot fix. It cries out for serious and sustained congressional attention.

As was the case with Vietnam, the debate over the lessons of Iraq promises to be a protracted one. Again as was the case with Vietnam, the temptation to exploit that debate for partisan purposes will be great. But the issue is too important to use as an excuse for bashing neoconservatives, scoring points against President Bush, or luxuriating in the peculiar satisfactions of *Schadenfreude*. To avoid repeating the errors that got us into this mess, we need to get those lessons right.

NORMAN PODHORETZ

14 World War IV: How It Started, What It Means, and Why We Have To Win

A Note to the Reader

THIS PAST SPRING, WHEN IT SEEMED THAT EVERYTHING THAT could go wrong in Iraq was going wrong, a plague of amnesia began sweeping through the country. Caught up in the particulars with which we were being assaulted 24 hours a day, we seemed to have lost sight of the context in which such details could be measured and understood and related to one another. Small things became large, large things became invisible, and hysteria filled the air.

Since then, of course, and especially after the handover of authority on June 30 to an interim Iraqi government, matters have become more complicated. But the relentless pressure of events, and the continuing onslaught both of details and of their often tendentious or partisan interpretation, have hardly let up at all. It is for this reason that, in what follows, I have tried to step back from the daily barrage and to piece together the story of what this nation has been fighting to accomplish since September 11, 2001.

In doing this, I have drawn freely from my own past writings on the subject, and especially from three articles that appeared in these pages two or more years ago.[1] In some instances, I have woven sections of these articles into a new setting; other passages I have adapted and updated.

Telling the story properly has required more than a straight narrative leading from 9/11 to the time of writing. For one thing, I have had to interrupt the narrative repeatedly in order to confront and clear away the many

[1] "How to Win World War IV" (February 2002), "The Return of the Jackal Bins" (April 2002), and "In Praise of the Bush Doctrine" (September 2002). A fourth piece I used was "Israel Isn't the Issue" (*Wall Street Journal*, September 20, 2001).

misconceptions, distortions, and outright falsifications that have been perpetrated. In addition, I have had to broaden the perspective so as to make it possible to see why the great struggle into which the United States was plunged by 9/11 can only be understood if we think of it as World War IV.

My hope is that telling the story from this perspective and in these ways will demonstrate that the road we have taken since 9/11 is the only safe course for us to follow. As we proceed along this course, questions will inevitably arise as to whether this or that move was necessary or right; and such questions will breed hesitations and even demands that we withdraw from the field. Some of this happened even in World War II, perhaps the most popular war the United States has ever fought, and much more of it in World War III (that is, the cold war); and now it is happening again, notably with respect to Iraq.

But as I will attempt to show, we are only in the very early stages of what promises to be a very long war, and Iraq is only the second front to have been opened in that war: the second scene, so to speak, of the first act of a five-act play. In World War II and then in World War III, we persisted in spite of impatience, discouragement, and opposition for as long as it took to win, and this is exactly what we have been called upon to do today in World War IV.

For today, no less than in those titanic conflicts, we are up against a truly malignant force in radical Islamism and in the states breeding, sheltering, or financing its terrorist armory. This new enemy has already attacked us on our own soil - a feat neither Nazi Germany nor Soviet Russia ever managed to pull off - and openly announces his intention to hit us again, only this time with weapons of infinitely greater and deadlier power than those used on 9/11. His objective is not merely to murder as many of us as possible and to conquer our land. Like the Nazis and Communists before him, he is dedicated to the destruction of everything good for which America stands. It is this, then, that (to paraphrase George W. Bush and a long string of his predecessors, Republican and Democratic alike) we in our turn, no less than the "greatest generation" of the 1940's and its spiritual progeny of the 1950's and after, have a responsibility to uphold and are privileged to defend.

Out of the Blue

The attack came, both literally and metaphorically, like a bolt out of the blue. Literally, in that the hijacked planes that crashed into the twin towers of the World Trade Center on the morning of September 11, 2001 had been flying in a cloudless sky so blue that it seemed unreal. I happened to be on jury duty that day, in a courthouse only a half-mile from what would soon be known as Ground Zero. Some time after the planes reached their targets, we all poured into the street – just as the second tower collapsed. And this sight, as if it were not impossible to believe in itself, was made all the more incredible by the perfection of the sky stretching so beautifully over it. I felt as though I had been deposited into a scene in one of those disaster movies being filmed (as they used to say) in glorious technicolor.

But the attack came out of the blue in a metaphorical sense as well. About a year later, in November 2002, a commission would be set up to investigate how and why such a huge event could have taken us by surprise and whether it might have been prevented. Because the commission's public hearings were not held until the middle of this year's exceptionally poisonous presidential election campaign, they quickly degenerated into an attempt by the Democrats on the panel to demonstrate that the administration of George W. Bush had been given adequate warnings but had failed to act on them.

Reinforcing this attempt was the testimony of Richard A. Clarke, who had been in charge of the counterterrorist operation in the National Security Council under Bill Clinton and then under Bush before resigning in the aftermath of 9/11. What Clarke for all practical purposes did – both at the hearings and in his hot-off-the-press book, *Against All Enemies* – was to blame Bush, who had been in office for a mere eight months when the attack occurred, while exonerating Clinton, who had spent eight long years doing little of any significance in response to the series of terrorist assaults on American targets in various parts of the world that were launched on his watch.

The point I wish to stress is not that Clarke was exaggerating or lying.[2] It is that the attack on 9/11 did indeed come out of the blue in the sense that

[2] He did, however, seem to have committed a sin of omission. Richard Lowry, the editor of *National Review*, reports that according to John Lehman, one of the Republican commissioners, "Clarke's original testimony included 'a searing indictment of some Clinton officials and Clinton policies.' That was the Clarke, evenhanded in his criticisms of both the Bush and Clinton administrations, whom Lehman and other Republican commissioners expected to show up at the public hearings. It was a surprise 'that he would come out against Bush that way.' Republicans were taken aback: 'It caught us flat-footed, but not the Democrats.'" In a different though related context, the commission quotes material written by Clarke while he was still in office that is inconsistent with his more recent, much-publicized denial of any relationship whatsoever between Iraq and al Qaeda.

no one ever took such a possibility seriously enough to figure out what to do about it. Even Clarke, who did stake a dubious claim to prescience, had to admit under questioning by one of the 9/11 commissioners that if all his recommendations had been acted upon, the attack still could not have been prevented. And in its final report, released on July 22 of this year, the commission, while digging up no fewer than ten episodes that with hindsight could be seen as missed "operational opportunities," thought that these opportunities could not have been acted on effectively enough to frustrate the attack. Indeed not - not, that is, in the real America as it existed at the time: an America in which hobbling constraints had been placed on both the CIA and the FBI; in which a "wall of separation" had been erected to obstruct communication or cooperation between law-enforcement and national-security agents; and in which politicians and the general public alike were still unable and/or unwilling to believe that terrorism might actually represent a genuine threat.

Slightly contradicting itself, the commission said that "the 9/11 attacks were a shock, but they should not have come as a surprise." Maybe so; and yet there was no one, either in government or out, to whom they did not come as a surprise, either in general or in the particular form they took. The commission also spoke of a "failure of imagination." Maybe so again; and yet the word "failure" seems inappropriate, implying as it does that success was possible. Surely a failure so widespread deserves to be considered inevitable.

* * *

To the *New York Times*, however, the failure was not at all inevitable. In a front-page editorial disguised as a "report," the *Times* credited the commission's final report with finding that "an attack described as unimaginable had in fact been imagined, repeatedly." But not a shred of the documentary evidence cited by the *Times* for this categorical statement actually predicted that al Qaeda would hijack commercial airliners and crash them into buildings in New York and Washington. Moreover, all of the evidence, such as it was, came from the 1990's. Nevertheless, the *Times* "report" contrived to convey the impression that in the fall of 2000 the Bush administration - then not yet in office - had received fair warning of an imminent attack. To bolster this impression, the *Times* went on to quote from a briefing given to Bush a month before 9/11. But the document in question was vague about details, and in any case was only one of many intelligence briefings with no special claim to credibility over conflicting assessments.

Thus the Bush administration, which had just been excoriated in hearings held by the Senate Intelligence Committee for having invaded Iraq on the basis of faulty intelligence, was now excoriated by some of the 9/11 commissioners for not having acted on the basis of even sketchier intelligence to head off 9/11 itself. This contradiction elicited a mordant comment from Charles Hill, a former government official who had been a regular "consumer" of intelligence:

> Intelligence collection and analysis is a very imperfect business. Refusal to face this reality has produced the almost laughable contradiction of the Senate Intelligence Committee criticizing the Bush administration for acting on third-rate intelligence, even as the 9/11 commission criticizes it for not acting on third-rate intelligence.[3]

However, the point I most wish to stress is that there was something unwholesome, not to say unholy, about the recriminations on this issue that befouled the commission's public hearings and some of the interim reports by the staff. It therefore came, so to speak, both as a shock and as a surprise that this same unholy spirit was almost entirely exorcised from the final report. In the end the commission agreed that no American President and no American policy could be held responsible in any degree for the aggression against the United States unleashed on 9/11.

Amen to that. For the plain truth is that the sole and entire responsibility rests with al Qaeda, along with the regimes that provided it with protection and support. Furthermore, to the extent that American passivity and inaction opened the door to 9/11, neither Democrats nor Republicans, and neither liberals nor conservatives, are in a position to derive any partisan or ideological advantage. The reason, quite simply, is that much the same methods for dealing with terrorism were employed by the administrations of both parties, stretching as far back as Richard Nixon in 1970 and proceeding through Gerald Ford, Jimmy Carter, Ronald Reagan (yes, Ronald Reagan), George H.W. Bush, Bill Clinton, and right up to the pre-9/11 George W. Bush.

A "Paper Tiger"

The record speaks dismally for itself. From 1970 to 1975, during the administrations of Nixon and Ford, several American diplomats were murdered

[3] Hill was referring here to the hearings of the 9/11 commission, not its final report, which did not single out the Bush administration for criticism on this score.

in Sudan and Lebanon while others were kidnapped. The perpetrators were all agents of one or another faction of the Palestine Liberation Organization (PLO). In Israel, too, many American citizens were killed by the PLO, though, except for the rockets fired at our embassy and other American facilities in Beirut by the Popular Front for the Liberation of Palestine (PFLP), these attacks were not directly aimed at the United States. In any case, there were no American military reprisals.

Our diplomats, then, were for some years already being murdered with impunity by Muslim terrorists when, in 1979, with Carter now in the White House, Iranian students - with either the advance or subsequent blessing of the country's clerical ruler, Ayatollah Khomeini - broke into the American embassy in Tehran and seized 52 Americans as hostages. For a full five months, Carter dithered. At last, steeling himself, he authorized a military rescue operation which had to be aborted after a series of mishaps that would have fit well into a Marx Brothers movie like *Duck Soup* if they had not been more humiliating than comic. After 444 days, and just hours after Reagan's inauguration in January 1981, the hostages were finally released by the Iranians, evidently because they feared that the hawkish new President might actually launch a military strike against them.

Yet if they could have foreseen what was coming under Reagan, they would not have been so fearful. In April 1983, Hizbullah - an Islamic terrorist organization nourished by Iran and Syria - sent a suicide bomber to explode his truck in front of the American embassy in Beirut, Lebanon. Sixty-three employees, among them the Middle East CIA director, were killed and another 120 wounded. But Reagan sat still.

Six months later, in October 1983, another Hizbullah suicide bomber blew up an American barracks in the Beirut airport, killing 241 U.S. Marines in their sleep and wounding another 81. This time Reagan signed off on plans for a retaliatory blow, but he then allowed his Secretary of Defense, Caspar Weinberger, to cancel it (because it might damage our relations with the Arab world, of which Weinberger was always tenderly solicitous). Shortly thereafter, the President pulled the Marines out of Lebanon.

Having cut and run in Lebanon in October, Reagan again remained passive in December, when the American embassy in Kuwait was bombed. Nor did he hit back when, hard upon the withdrawal of the American Marines from Beirut, the CIA station chief there, William Buckley, was kidnapped by Hizbullah and then murdered. Buckley was the fourth American to be kidnapped in Beirut, and many more suffered the same fate between 1982 and 1992 (though not all died or were killed in captivity).

* * *

These kidnappings were apparently what led Reagan, who had sworn that he would never negotiate with terrorists, to make an unacknowledged deal with Iran, involving the trading of arms for hostages. But whereas the Iranians were paid off handsomely in the coin of nearly 1,500 antitank missiles (some of them sent at our request through Israel), all we got in exchange were three American hostages - not to mention the disruptive and damaging Iran-*contra* scandal.

In September 1984, six months after the murder of Buckley, the U.S. embassy annex near Beirut was hit by yet another truck bomb (also traced to Hizbullah). Again Reagan sat still. Or rather, after giving the green light to covert proxy retaliations by Lebanese intelligence agents, he put a stop to them when one such operation, directed against the cleric thought to be the head of Hizbullah, failed to get its main target while unintentionally killing 80 other people.

It took only another two months for Hizbullah to strike once more. In December 1984, a Kuwaiti airliner was hijacked and two American passengers employed by the U.S. Agency for International Development were murdered. The Iranians, who had stormed the plane after it landed in Tehran, promised to try the hijackers themselves, but instead allowed them to leave the country. At this point, all the Reagan administration could come up with was the offer of a $250,000 reward for information that might lead to the arrest of the hijackers. There were no takers.

The following June, Hizbullah operatives hijacked still another airliner, an American one (TWA flight 847), and then forced it to fly to Beirut, where it was held for more than two weeks. During those weeks, an American naval officer aboard the plane was shot, and his body was ignominiously hurled onto the tarmac. For this the hijackers were rewarded with the freeing of hundreds of terrorists held by Israel in exchange for the release of the other passengers. Both the United States and Israel denied that they were violating their own policy of never bargaining with terrorists, but as with the arms-for-hostages deal, and with equally good reason, no one believed them, and it was almost universally assumed that Israel had acted under pressure from Washington. Later, four of the hijackers were caught but only one wound up being tried and jailed (by Germany, not the United States).

The sickening beat went on. In October 1985, the *Achille Lauro*, an Italian cruise ship, was hijacked by a group under the leadership of the PLO's

Abu Abbas, working with the support of Libya. One of the hijackers threw an elderly wheelchair-bound American passenger, Leon Klinghoffer, overboard. When the hijackers attempted to escape in a plane, the United States sent Navy fighters to intercept it and force it down. Klinghoffer's murderer was eventually apprehended and sent to prison in Italy, but the Italian authorities let Abu Abbas himself go. Washington - evidently having exhausted its repertoire of military reprisals - now confined itself to protesting the release of Abu Abbas. To no avail.

Libya's involvement in the *Achille Lauro* hijacking was, though, the last free pass that country's dictator, Muammar Qaddafi, was destined to get from the United States under Reagan. In December 1985, five Americans were among the 20 people killed when the Rome and Vienna airports were bombed, and then in April 1986 another bomb exploded in a discotheque in West Berlin that was a hangout for American servicemen. U.S. intelligence tied Libya to both of these bombings, and the eventual outcome was an American air attack in which one of the residences of Qaddafi was hit.

In retaliation, the Palestinian terrorist Abu Nidal executed three U.S. citizens who worked at the American University in Beirut. But Qaddafi himself - no doubt surprised and shaken by the American reprisal - went into a brief period of retirement as a sponsor of terrorism. So far as we know, it took nearly three years (until December 1988) before he could pull himself together to the point of undertaking another operation: the bombing of Pan Am flight 103 over Lockerbie, Scotland, in which a total of 270 people lost their lives. Of the two Libyan intelligence agents who were tried for planting the bomb, one was convicted (though not until the year 2001) and the other acquitted. Qaddafi himself suffered no further punishment from American warplanes.

In January 1989, Reagan was succeeded by the elder George Bush, who, in handling the fallout from the destruction of Pan Am 103, was content to adopt the approach to terrorism taken by all his predecessors. During the elder Bush's four-year period in the White House, there were several attacks on Americans in Turkey by Islamic terrorist organizations, and there were others in Egypt, Saudi Arabia, and Lebanon. None of these was as bloody as previous incidents, and none provoked any military response from the United States.

* * *

In January 1993, Bill Clinton became President. Over the span of his two terms in office, American citizens continued to be injured or killed in Israel and other countries by terrorists who were not aiming specifically at the

United States. But several spectacular terrorist operations occurred on Clinton's watch of which the U.S. was most emphatically the target.

The first, on February 26, 1993, only 38 days after his inauguration, was the explosion of a truck bomb in the parking garage of the World Trade Center in New York. As compared with what would happen on September 11, 2001, this was a minor incident in which "only" six people were killed and over 1,000 injured. The six Muslim terrorists responsible were caught, tried, convicted, and sent to prison for long terms.

But in following the by-now traditional pattern of treating such attacks as common crimes, or the work of rogue groups acting on their own, the Clinton administration willfully turned a deaf ear to outside experts like Steven Emerson and even the director of the CIA, R. James Woolsey, who strongly suspected that behind the individual culprits was a terrorist Islamic network with (at that time) its headquarters in Sudan. This network, then scarcely known to the general public, was called al Qaeda, and its leader was a former Saudi national who had fought on our side against the Soviets in Afghanistan but had since turned against us as fiercely as he had been against the Russians. His name was Osama bin Laden.

The next major episode was not long in trailing the bombing of the World Trade Center. In April 1993, less than two months after that attack, former President Bush visited Kuwait, where an attempt was made to assassinate him by - as our own investigators were able to determine - Iraqi intelligence agents. The Clinton administration spent two more months seeking approval from the UN and the "international community" to retaliate for this egregious assault on the United States. In the end, a few cruise missiles were fired into the Iraqi capital of Baghdad, where they fell harmlessly onto empty buildings in the middle of the night.

In the years immediately ahead, there were many Islamic terrorist operations (in Turkey, Pakistan, Saudi Arabia, Lebanon, Yemen, and Israel) that were not specifically aimed at the United States but in which Americans were nevertheless murdered or kidnapped. In March 1995, however, a van belonging to the U.S. consulate in Karachi, Pakistan, was hit by gunfire, killing two American diplomats and injuring a third. In November of the same year, five Americans died when a car bomb exploded in Riyadh, Saudi Arabia, near a building in which a U.S. military advisory group lived.

All this was trumped in June 1996 when another building in which American military personnel lived - the Khobar Towers in Dhahran, Saudi Arabia - was blasted by a truck bomb. Nineteen of our airmen were killed, and 240 other Americans on the premises were wounded.

In 1993, Clinton had been so intent on treating the World Trade Center bombing as a common crime that for some time afterward he refused even to meet with his own CIA director. Perhaps he anticipated that he would be told things by Woolsey – about terrorist networks and the states sponsoring them – that he did not wish to hear, because he had no intention of embarking on the military action that such knowledge might force upon him. Now, in the wake of the bombing of the Khobar Towers, Clinton again handed the matter over to the police; but the man in charge, his FBI director, Louis Freeh, who had intimations of an Iranian connection, could no more get through to him than Woolsey before. There were a few arrests, and the action then moved into the courts.

In June 1998, grenades were unsuccessfully hurled at the U.S. embassy in Beirut. A little later, our embassies in the capitals of Kenya (Nairobi) and Tanzania (Dar es Salaam) were not so lucky. On a single day – August 7, 1998 – car bombs went off in both places, leaving more than 200 people dead, of whom twelve were Americans. Credit for this coordinated operation was claimed by al Qaeda. In what, whether fairly or not, was widely interpreted, especially abroad, as a move to distract attention from his legal troubles over the Monica Lewinsky affair, Clinton fired cruise missiles at an al Qaeda training camp in Afghanistan, where bin Laden was supposed to be at that moment, and at a building in Sudan, where al Qaeda also had a base. But bin Laden escaped harm, while it remained uncertain whether the targeted factory in Sudan was actually manufacturing chemical weapons or was just a normal pharmaceutical plant.

This fiasco – so we have learned from former members of his administration – discouraged any further such action by Clinton against bin Laden, though we have also learned from various sources that he did authorize a number of covert counterterrorist operations and diplomatic initiatives leading to arrests in foreign countries. But according to Dick Morris, who was then Clinton's political adviser:

> The weekly strategy meetings at the White House throughout 1995 and 1996 featured an escalating drumbeat of advice to President Clinton to take decisive steps to crack down on terrorism. The polls gave these ideas a green light. But Clinton hesitated and failed to act, always finding a reason why some other concern was more important.

In the period after Morris left, more began going on behind the scenes, but most of it remained in the realm of talk or planning that went nowhere. In contrast to the flattering picture of Clinton that Richard Clarke would subsequently draw, Woolsey (who after a brief tenure resigned from the CIA out of sheer frustration) would offer a devastating retrospective summary of the President's overall approach:

> Do something to show you're concerned. Launch a few missiles in the desert, bop them on the head, arrest a few people. But just keep kicking the ball down field.

Bin Laden, picking up that ball on October 12, 2000, when the destroyer *USS Cole* had docked for refueling in Yemen, dispatched a team of suicide bombers. The bombers did not succeed in sinking the ship, but they inflicted severe damage upon it, while managing to kill seventeen American sailors and wounding another 39.

Clarke, along with a few intelligence analysts, had no doubt that the culprit was al Qaeda. But the heads neither of the CIA nor of the FBI thought the case was conclusive. Hence the United States did not so much as lift a military finger against bin Laden or the Taliban regime in Afghanistan, where he was now ensconced and being protected. As for Clinton, so obsessively was he then wrapped up in a futile attempt to broker a deal between the Israelis and the Palestinians that all he could see in this attack on an American warship was an effort "to deter us from our mission of promoting peace and security in the Middle East." The terrorists, he resoundingly vowed, would "fail utterly" in this objective.

Never mind that not the slightest indication existed that bin Laden was in the least concerned over Clinton's negotiations with the Israelis and the Palestinians at Camp David, or even that the Palestinian issue was of primary importance to him as compared with other grievances. In any event, it was Clinton who failed, not bin Laden. The Palestinians under Yasir Arafat, spurning an unprecedentedly generous offer that had been made by the Israeli prime minister Ehud Barak with Clinton's enthusiastic endorsement, unleashed a new round of terrorism. And bin Laden would soon succeed all too well in his actual intention of striking another brazen blow at the United States.

* * *

The sheer audacity of what bin Laden went on to do on September 11 was unquestionably a product of his contempt for American power. Our persistent refusal for so long to use that power against him and his terrorist brethren – or to do so effectively whenever we tried – reinforced his conviction that we were a nation on the way down, destined to be defeated by the resurgence of the same Islamic militancy that had once conquered and converted large parts of the world by the sword.

As bin Laden saw it, thousands or even millions of his followers and sympathizers all over the Muslim world were willing, and even eager, to die a martyr's death in the jihad, the holy war, against the "Great Satan," as the Ayatollah Khomeini had called us. But, in bin Laden's view, we in the West, and especially in America, were all so afraid to die that we lacked the will even to stand up for ourselves and defend our degenerate way of life.

Bin Laden was never reticent or coy in laying out this assessment of the United States. In an interview on CNN in 1997, he declared that "the myth of the superpower was destroyed not only in my mind but also in the minds of all Muslims" when the Soviet Union was defeated in Afghanistan. That the Muslim fighters in Afghanistan would almost certainly have failed if not for the arms supplied to them by the United States did not seem to enter into the lesson he drew from the Soviet defeat. In fact, in an interview a year earlier he had belittled the United States as compared with the Soviet Union. "The Russian soldier is more courageous and patient than the U.S. soldier," he said then. Hence, "Our battle with the United States is easy compared with the battles in which we engaged in Afghanistan."

Becoming still more explicit, bin Laden wrote off the Americans as cowards. Had Reagan not taken to his heels in Lebanon after the bombing of the Marine barracks in 1983? And had not Clinton done the same a decade later when only a few American Rangers were killed in Somalia, where they had been sent to participate in a "peacekeeping" mission? Bin Laden did not boast of this as one of his victories, but a State Department dossier charged that al Qaeda had trained the terrorists who ambushed the American servicemen. (The ugly story of what happened to us in Somalia was told in the film version of Mark Bowden's *Black Hawk Down*, which reportedly became Saddam Hussein's favorite movie.)

Bin Laden summed it all up in a third interview he gave in 1998:

> After leaving Afghanistan the Muslim fighters headed for Somalia and prepared for a long battle thinking that the Americans were like the Russians. The youth were surprised at the low morale of the American soldiers and realized, more than before, that the American soldier was a paper tiger and after a few blows ran in defeat.

Miscalculation

Bin Laden was not the first enemy of a democratic regime to have been emboldened by such impressions. In the 1930's, Adolf Hitler was convinced by the failure of the British to arm themselves against the threat he posed, as well as by the policy of appeasement they adopted toward him, that they were decadent and would never fight no matter how many countries he invaded.

Similarly with Joseph Stalin in the immediate aftermath of World War II. Encouraged by the rapid demobilization of the United States, which to him meant that we were unprepared and unwilling to resist him with military force, Stalin broke the pledges he had made at Yalta to hold free elections in the countries of Eastern Europe he had occupied at the end of the war. Instead, he consolidated his hold over those countries, and made menacing gestures toward Greece and Turkey.

After Stalin's death, his successors repeatedly played the same game whenever they sensed a weakening of the American resolve to hold them back. Sometimes this took the form of maneuvers aimed at establishing a balance of military power in their favor. Sometimes it took the form of using local Communist parties or other proxies as their instrument. But thanks to the decline of American power following our withdrawal from Vietnam - a decline reflected in the spread during the late 1970's of isolationist and pacifist sentiment, which was in turn reflected in severely reduced military spending - Leonid Brezhnev felt safe in sending his own troops into Afghanistan in 1979.

It was the same decline of American power, so uncannily personified by Jimmy Carter, that, less than two months before the Soviet invasion of Afghanistan, had emboldened the Ayatollah Khomeini to seize and hold American hostages. To be sure, there were those who denied that this daring action had anything to do with Khomeini's belief that the United States under Carter had become impotent. But this denial was impossible to sustain in the face of the contrast between the attack on our embassy in Tehran and the protection the Khomeini regime extended to the Soviet embassy there when a group of protesters tried to storm it after the invasion of Afghanistan. The radical Muslim fundamentalists ruling Iran hated Communism and the Soviet Union at least as much as they hated us - especially now that the Soviets had invaded a Muslim country. Therefore the difference in Khomeini's treatment of the two embassies could not be explained by ideological or political factors. What could and did explain it was his fear of Soviet retaliation as against his expectation that the United States, having lost its nerve, would go to any lengths to avoid the use of force.

And so it was with Saddam Hussein. In 1990, with the first George Bush sitting in the White House, Saddam Hussein invaded Kuwait in what was widely, and accurately, seen as a first step in a bid to seize control of the oil fields of the Middle East. The elder Bush, fortified by the determination of

Margaret Thatcher, who was then prime minister of England, declared that the invasion would not stand, and he put together a coalition that sent a great military force into the region. This alone might well have frightened Saddam Hussein into pulling out of Kuwait if not for the wave of hysteria in the United States about the tens of thousands of "body bags" that it was predicted would be flown home if we actually went to war with Iraq. Not unreasonably, Saddam concluded that, if he held firm, it was we who would blink and back down.

The fact that Saddam miscalculated, and that in the end we made good on our threat, did not overly impress Osama bin Laden. After all – dreading the casualties we would suffer if we went into Baghdad after liberating Kuwait and defeating the Iraqi army on the battlefield – we had allowed Saddam to remain in power. To bin Laden, this could only have looked like further evidence of the weakness we had shown in the ineffectual policy toward terrorism adopted by a long string of American Presidents. No wonder he was persuaded that he could strike us massively on our own soil and get away with it.

Yet just as Saddam had miscalculated in 1990–91, and would again in 2002, bin Laden misread how the Americans would react to being hit where, literally, they lived. In all likelihood he expected a collapse into despair and demoralization; what he elicited instead was an outpouring of rage and an upsurge of patriotic sentiment such as younger Americans had never witnessed except in the movies, and had most assuredly never experienced in their own hearts and souls, or, for those who enlisted in the military, on their own flesh.

* * *

In that sense, bin Laden did for this country what the Ayatollah Khomeini had done before him. In seizing the American hostages in 1979, and escaping retaliation, Khomeini inflicted a great humiliation on the United States. But at the same time, he also exposed the foolishness of Jimmy Carter's view of the world. The foolishness did not lie in Carter's recognition that American power – military, economic, political, and moral – had been on a steep decline at least since Vietnam. This was all too true. What was foolish was the conclusion Carter drew from it. Rather than proposing policies aimed at halting and then reversing the decline, he took the position that the cause was the play of historical forces we could do nothing to stop or even slow down. As he saw it, instead of complaining or flailing about in a vain and dangerous effort to recapture our lost place in the sun, we needed first to acknowledge, accept, and adjust to this inexorable historical development, and then to act upon it with "mature restraint."

In one fell swoop, the Ayatollah Khomeini made nonsense of Carter's delusionary philosophy in the eyes of very large numbers of Americans, including many who had previously entertained it. Correlatively, new heart was given to those who, rejecting the idea that American decline was inevitable, had argued that the cause was bad policies and that the decline could be turned around by returning to the better policies that had made us so powerful in the first place.

The entire episode thereby became one of the forces behind an already burgeoning determination to rebuild American power that culminated in the election of Ronald Reagan, who had campaigned on the promise to do just that. For all the shortcomings of his own handling of terrorism, Reagan did in fact keep his promise to rebuild American power. And it was this that set the stage for victory in the multifaceted cold war we had been waging since 1947, when the United States under President Harry Truman (aroused by Stalin's miscalculation) decided to resist any further advance of the Soviet empire.

Few, if any, of Truman's contemporaries would have dreamed that this product of a Kansas City political machine, who as a reputedly run-of-the-mill U.S. Senator had spent most of his time on taxes and railroads, would rise so resolutely and so brilliantly to the threat represented by Soviet imperialism. Just so, 54 years later in 2001, another politician with a small reputation and little previous interest in foreign affairs would be confronted with a challenge perhaps even greater than the one faced by Truman; and he too astonished his own contemporaries by the way he rose to it.

Enter the Bush Doctrine

In "The Sources of Soviet Conduct" (1947), the theoretical defense he constructed of the strategy Truman adopted for fighting the war ahead, George F. Kennan (then the director of the State Department's policy planning staff, and writing under the pseudonym "X") described that strategy as

> a long-term, patient but firm and vigilant containment of Russian expansive tendencies . . . by the adroit and vigilant application of counterforce at a series of constantly shifting geographical and political points.

In other words (though Kennan himself did not use those words), we were faced with the prospect of nothing less than another world war; and (though in later years, against the plain sense of the words that he himself did use, he tried to claim that the "counterforce" he had in mind was not military) it would not be an entirely "cold" one, either. Before it was over, more than 100,000 Americans would die on the far-off battlefields of Korea and Vietnam, and the blood of many others allied with us in the political and ideological struggle against the Soviet Union would be spilled on those same battlefields, and in many other places as well.

For these reasons, I agree with one of our leading contemporary students of military strategy, Eliot A. Cohen, who thinks that what is generally called the "cold war" (a term, incidentally, coined by Soviet propagandists) should be given a new name. "The cold war," Cohen writes, was actually "World War III, which reminds us that not all global conflicts entail the movement of multimillion-man armies, or conventional front lines on a map." I also agree that the nature of the conflict in which we are now engaged can only be fully appreciated if we look upon it as World War IV. To justify giving it this name - rather than, say, the "war on terrorism" - Cohen lists "some key features" that it shares with World War III:

> that it is, in fact, global; that it will involve a mixture of violent and nonviolent efforts; that it will require mobilization of skill, expertise, and resources, if not of vast numbers of soldiers; that it may go on for a long time; and that it has ideological roots.

There is one more feature that World War IV shares with World War III and that Cohen does not mention: both were declared through the enunciation of a presidential doctrine.

The Truman Doctrine of 1947 was born with the announcement that "it must be the policy of the United States to support free peoples who are resisting attempted subjugation by armed minorities or by outside pressure." Beginning with a special program of aid to Greece and Turkey, which were then threatened by Communist takeovers, the strategy was broadened within a few months by the launching of a much larger and more significant program of economic aid that came to be called the Marshall Plan. The purpose of the Marshall Plan was to hasten the reconstruction of the war-torn economies of Western Europe: not only because this was a good thing in itself, and not only because it would serve American interests, but also because it could help eliminate the grievances on which Communism fed. But then came a Communist coup in Czechoslovakia. Following as it had upon the installation by the Soviet Union of puppet regimes in the occupied countries of Eastern Europe, the Czech coup demonstrated that economic measures would not be enough by themselves to ward off a comparable danger posed to Italy and France by huge local Communist parties entirely subservient to Moscow. Out of this realization – and out of a parallel worry about an actual Soviet invasion of Western Europe – there emerged the North Atlantic Treaty Organization (NATO).

Containment, then, was a three-sided strategy made up of economic, political, and military components. All three would be deployed in a shifting relative balance over the four decades it took to win World War III.[4]

If the Truman Doctrine unfolded gradually, revealing its entire meaning only in stages, the Bush Doctrine was pretty fully enunciated in a single speech, delivered to a joint session of Congress on September 20, 2001. It was then clarified and elaborated in three subsequent statements: Bush's first State of the Union address on January 29, 2002; his speech to the graduating class of the U.S. Military Academy at West Point on June 1, 2002; and the remarks on the Middle East he delivered three weeks later, on June 24. This difference aside, his contemporaries were at least as startled as Truman's had been, both by the substance of the new doctrine and by the transformation it bespoke in its author. For here was George W. Bush, who in foreign affairs had been a more or less passive disciple of his father, talking for all the world like a fiery follower of Ronald Reagan.

In sharp contrast to Reagan, generally considered a dangerous ideologue, the first President Bush – who had been Reagan's Vice President and had then succeeded him in the White House – was often accused of being deficient in what he himself inelegantly dismissed as "the vision thing." The charge was fair in that the elder Bush had no guiding sense of what role the United States might play in reshaping the post-cold-war world. A strong adherent of the "realist" perspective on world affairs, he believed that the maintenance of stability was the proper purpose of American foreign policy, and the only wise and prudential course to follow. Therefore, when Saddam Hussein upset the balance of power in the Middle East by invading Kuwait in 1991, the elder Bush went to war not to create a new configuration in the region but to restore the status quo ante. And it was precisely out of the same overriding concern for stability that, having achieved this objective by driving Saddam out of Kuwait, Bush then allowed him to remain in power.

* * *

[4] The analysis offered by Kennan in "The Sources of Soviet Conduct" – as against his own later revisionist interpretation of it – turned out to be right in almost every important detail, except for the timing. He thought it would take only fifteen years for the strategy to succeed in causing the "implosion" of the Soviet empire.

As for the second President Bush, before 9/11 he was, to all appearances, as deficient in the "vision thing" as his father before him. If he entertained any doubts about the soundness of the "realist" approach, he showed no sign of it. Nothing he said or did gave any indication that he might be dissatisfied with the idea that his main job in foreign affairs was to keep things on an even keel. Nor was there any visible indication that he might be drawn to Ronald Reagan's more "idealistic" ambition to change the world, especially with the "Wilsonian" aim of making it "safe for democracy" by encouraging the spread to as many other countries as possible of the liberties we Americans enjoyed.

Which is why Bush's address of September 20, 2001 came as so great a surprise. Delivered only nine days after the attacks on the World Trade Center and the Pentagon, and officially declaring that the United States was now at war, the September 20 speech put this nation, and all others, on notice that whether or not George W. Bush had been a strictly conventional realist in the mold of his father, he was now politically born again as a passionate democratic idealist of the Reaganite stamp.

It was also this speech that marked the emergence of the Bush Doctrine, and that pointed just as clearly to World War IV as the Truman Doctrine had to War World III. Bush did not explicitly give the name World War IV to the struggle ahead, but he did characterize it as a direct successor to the two world wars that had immediately preceded it. Thus, of the "global terrorist network" that had attacked us on our own soil, he said:

> We have seen their kind before. They're the heirs of all the murderous ideologies of the 20th century. By sacrificing human life to serve their radical visions, by abandoning every value except the will to power, they follow in the path of fascism, Nazism, and totalitarianism. And they will follow that path all the way to where it ends in history's unmarked grave of discarded lies.

As this passage, coming toward the beginning of the speech, linked the Bush Doctrine to the Truman Doctrine and to the great struggle led by Franklin D. Roosevelt before it, the wind-up section demonstrated that if the second President Bush had previously lacked "the vision thing," his eyes were blazing with it now. "Great harm has been done to us," he intoned toward the end. "We have suffered great loss. And in our grief and anger we have found our mission and our moment." Then he went on to spell out the substance of that mission and that moment:

> The advance of human freedom, the great achievement of our time and the great hope of every time, now depends on us. Our nation, this generation, will lift the dark threat of violence from our people and our future. We will

> rally the world to this cause by our efforts, by our courage. We will not tire, we will not falter, and we will not fail.

Finally, in his peroration, drawing on some of the same language he had been applying to the nation as a whole, Bush shifted into the first person, pledging his own commitment to the great mission we were all charged with accomplishing:

> I will not forget the wound to our country and those who inflicted it. I will not yield, I will not rest, I will not relent in waging this struggle for freedom and security for the American people. The course of this conflict is not known, yet its outcome is certain. Freedom and fear, justice and cruelty, have always been at war, and we know that God is not neutral between them.

Not even Ronald Reagan, the "Great Communicator" himself, had ever been so eloquent in expressing the "idealistic" impetus behind his conception of the American role in the world.[5]

This was not the last time Bush would sound these themes. Two-and-a-half years later, at a moment when things seemed to be going badly in the war, it was with the same ideas he had originally put forward on September 20, 2001 that he sought to reassure the nation. The occasion would be a commencement address at the Air Force Academy on June 2, 2004, where he would repeatedly place the "war against terrorism" in direct succession to World War II and World War III. He would also be unusually undiplomatic in making no bones about his rejection of realism:

> For decades, free nations tolerated oppression in the Middle East for the sake of stability. In practice, this approach brought little stability and much oppression, so I have changed this policy.

And again, even less diplomatically:

> Some who call themselves realists question whether the spread of democracy in the Middle East should be any concern of ours. But the realists in this case have lost contact with a fundamental reality: America has always been less secure when freedom is in retreat; America is always more secure when freedom is on the march.

To top it all off, he would go out of his way to assert that his own policy, which he properly justified in the first place as a better way to protect

[5] In expressing his determination to win the war, however, Bush was mainly reaching back to the language of Winston Churchill, who vowed as World War II was getting under way in 1940: "We shall not flag or fail. We shall go on to the end."

American interests than the alternative favored by the realists, also bore the stamp of the Reaganite version of Wilsonian idealism:

> This conflict will take many turns, with setbacks on the course to victory. Through it all, our confidence comes from one unshakable belief: We believe in Ronald Reagan's words that "the future belongs to the free."

* * *

The first pillar of the Bush Doctrine, then, was built on a repudiation of moral relativism and an entirely unapologetic assertion of the need for and the possibility of moral judgment in the realm of world affairs. And just to make sure that the point he had first made on September 20, 2001 had hit home, Bush returned to it even more outspokenly and in greater detail in the State of the Union address of January 29, 2002.

Bush had won enthusiastic plaudits from many for the "moral clarity" of his September 20 speech, but he had also provoked even greater dismay and disgust among "advanced" thinkers and "sophisticated" commentators and diplomats both at home and abroad. Now he intensified and exacerbated their outrage by becoming more specific. Having spoken in September only in general terms about the enemy in World War IV, Bush proceeded in his second major wartime pronouncement to single out three such nations - Iraq, Iran, and North Korea - which he described as forming an "axis of evil."

Here again he was following in the footsteps of Ronald Reagan, who had denounced the Soviet Union, our principal enemy in World War III, as an "evil empire," and who had been answered with a veritably hysterical outcry from chancelleries and campuses and editorial pages all over the world. Evil? What place did a word like that have in the lexicon of international affairs, assuming it would ever occur to an enlightened person to exhume it from the grave of obsolete concepts in any connection whatsoever? But in the eyes of the "experts," Reagan was not an enlightened person. Instead, he was a "cowboy," a B-movie actor, who had by some freak of democratic perversity landed in the White House. In denouncing the Soviet empire, he was accused either of signaling an intention to trigger a nuclear war or of being too stupid to understand that his wildly provocative rhetoric might do so inadvertently.

The reaction to Bush was perhaps less hysterical and more scornful than the outcry against Reagan, since this time there was no carrying-on about a nuclear war. But the air was just as thick with the old sneers and jeers. Who but an ignoramus and a simpleton - or a fanatical religious fundamentalist, of the very type on whom Bush was declaring war - would resort to archaic moral absolutes like "good" and "evil"? On the one hand, it was egregiously simple-minded to brand a whole nation as evil, and on the other, only a fool could bring himself to believe, as Bush (once more like Reagan) had evidently done in complete and ingenuous sincerity, that the United States, of all countries, represented the good. Surely only a know-nothing illiterate could be oblivious of the innumerable crimes committed by America both at home and abroad – crimes that the country's own leading intellectuals had so richly documented in the by-now standard academic view of its history.

Here is how Gore Vidal, one of those intellectuals, stated the case:

> I mean, to watch Bush doing his little war dance in Congress ... about "evil-doers" and this "*axis* of evil" ... I thought, he doesn't even know what the word axis means. Somebody just gave it to him.... This is about as mindless a statement as you could make. Then he comes up with about a dozen other countries that have "evil" people in them, who might commit "terrorist acts." What is a terrorist act? Whatever he thinks is a terrorist act. And we are going to go after them. Because we are good and they are evil. And we're "gonna git 'em."

This was rougher and cruder than the language issuing from editorial pages and think tanks and foreign ministries and even most other intellectuals, but it was no different from what nearly all of them thought and how many of them talked in private.[6]

As soon became clear, however, Bush was not deterred. In subsequent statements he continued to uphold the first pillar of his new doctrine and to affirm the universality of the moral purposes animating this new war:

> Some worry that it is somehow undiplomatic or impolite to speak the language of right and wrong. I disagree. Different circumstances require different methods, but not different moralities. Moral truth is the same in every culture, in every time, and in every place.... We are in a conflict between good and evil, and America will call evil by its name.

Then, in a fascinating leap into the great theoretical debate of the post-cold-war era (though without identifying the main participants), Bush came down squarely on the side of Francis Fukuyama's much-misunderstood

[6] It is worth noting that Churchill, who had been the target of many derogatory epithets in his long career but who was never regarded even by his worst enemies as "simple-minded," had no hesitation in attaching a phrase like "monster of wickedness" to Hitler. Nor did the political philosopher Hannah Arendt, whose mind was, if anything, overcomplicated rather than too simple, have any problem in her masterpiece, *The Origins of Totalitarianism*, with calling both Nazism and Communism "absolute evil."

view of "the end of history," according to which the demise of Communism had eliminated the only serious competitor to our own political system:[7]

> The 20th century ended with a single surviving model of human progress, based on non-negotiable demands of human dignity, the rule of law, limits on the power of the state, respect for women and private property and free speech and equal justice and religious tolerance.

Having endorsed Fukuyama, Bush now brushed off the political scientist Samuel Huntington, whose rival theory postulated a "clash of civilizations" arising from the supposedly incompatible values prevailing in different parts of the world:

> When it comes to the common rights and needs of men and women, there is no clash of civilizations. The requirements of freedom apply fully to Africa and Latin America and the entire Islamic world. The peoples of the Islamic nations want and deserve the same freedoms and opportunities as people in every nation. And their governments should listen to their hopes.

The Second Pillar

If the first of the four pillars on which the Bush Doctrine stood was a new moral attitude, the second was an equally dramatic shift in the conception of terrorism as it had come to be defined in standard academic and intellectual discourse.

Under this new understanding - confirmed over and over again by the fact that most of the terrorists about whom we were learning came from prosperous families - terrorism was no longer considered a product of economic factors. The "swamps" in which this murderous plague bred were swamps not of poverty and hunger but of political oppression. It was only by "draining" them, through a strategy of "regime change," that we would be making ourselves safe from the threat of terrorism and simultaneously giving the peoples of "the entire Islamic world" the freedoms "they want and deserve."

In the new understanding, furthermore, terrorists, with rare exceptions, were not individual psychotics acting on their own but agents of organizations that depended on the sponsorship of various governments. Our aim, therefore, could not be merely to capture or kill Osama bin Laden and

[7] Fukuyama did not return the compliment. While not exactly rejecting the Bush Doctrine, he would later criticize it and call for a "recalibration." He would do this more in sorrow than in anger, but still in terms that were otherwise not always easy to distinguish from those of what I characterize below as the respectable opposition.

wipe out the al Qaeda terrorists under his direct leadership. Bush vowed that we would also uproot and destroy the entire network of interconnected terrorist organizations and cells "with global reach" that existed in as many as 50 or 60 countries. No longer would we treat the members of these groups as criminals to be arrested by the police, read their Miranda rights, and brought to trial. From now on, they were to be regarded as the irregular troops of a military alliance at war with the United States, and indeed the civilized world as a whole.

Not that this analysis of terrorism had exactly been a secret. The State Department itself had a list of seven state sponsors of terrorism (all but two of which, Cuba and North Korea, were predominantly Muslim), and it regularly issued reports on terrorist incidents throughout the world. But aside from such things as the lobbing of a cruise missile or two, diplomatic and/or economic sanctions that were inconsistently and even perfunctorily enforced, and a number of covert operations, the law-enforcement approach still prevailed.

September 11 changed much - if not yet all - of that; still in use were atavistic phrases like "bringing the terrorists to justice." But no one could any longer dream that the American answer to what had been done to us in New York and Washington would begin with an FBI investigation and end with a series of ordinary criminal trials. War had been declared on the United States, and to war we were going to go.

But against whom? Since it was certain that Osama bin Laden had masterminded September 11, and since he and the top leadership of al Qaeda were holed up in Afghanistan, the first target, and thus the first testing ground of this second pillar of the Bush Doctrine, chose itself.

* * *

Before resorting to military force, however, Bush issued an ultimatum to the extreme Islamic radicals of the Taliban who were then ruling Afghanistan. The ultimatum demanded that they turn Osama bin Laden and his people over to us and that they shut down all terrorist training camps there. By rejecting this ultimatum, the Taliban not only asked for an invasion but, under the Bush Doctrine, also asked to be overthrown. And so, on October 7, 2001, the United States - joined by Great Britain and about a dozen other countries - launched a military campaign against both al Qaeda and the regime that was providing it with "aid and safe haven."

As compared with what would come later, there was relatively little opposition either at home or abroad to the opening of this first front of World War IV. The reason was that the Afghan campaign could easily be justified as a retaliatory strike against the terrorists who had attacked us. And while there was a good deal of murmuring about the dangers of pursuing a policy of "regime change," there was very little sympathy in practice (outside the Muslim world, that is) for the Taliban.

Whatever opposition was mounted to the battle of Afghanistan mainly took the form of skepticism over the chances of winning it. True, such skepticism was in some quarters a mask for outright opposition to American military power in general. But once the Afghan campaign got under way, the main focus shifted to everything that seemed to be going awry on the battlefield.

For example, only a couple of weeks into the campaign, when there were missteps involving the use of the Afghan fighters of the Northern Alliance, observers like R.W. Apple of the *New York Times* immediately rushed to conjure up the ghost of Vietnam. This restless spirit, having been called forth from the vasty deep, henceforth refused to be exorcised, and would go on to elbow its way into every detail of the debates over all the early battles of World War IV. On this occasion, its message was that we were falling victim to the illusion that we could rely on an incompetent local force to do the fighting on the ground while we supplied advice and air support. This strategy would inevitably fail, and would suck us into the same "quagmire" into which we had been dragged in Vietnam. After all, as Apple and others argued, the Soviet Union had suffered its own "Vietnam" in Afghanistan – and unlike us, it had not been hampered by the logistical problems of projecting power over a great distance. How could we expect to do better?

* * *

When, however, the B-52's and the 15,000-pound "Daisy Cutter" bombs were unleashed, they temporarily banished the ghost of Vietnam and undercut the fears of some and the hopes of others that we were heading into a quagmire. Far from being good for nothing but "pounding the rubble," as the critics had sarcastically charged, the Daisy Cutters exerted, as even a *New York Times* report was forced to concede, "a terrifying psychological impact as they exploded just above ground, wiping out everything for hundreds of yards."

But the Daisy Cutters were only the half of it. As we were all to discover, our "smart-bomb" technology had advanced far beyond the stage it had reached when first introduced in 1991. In Afghanistan in 2001, such bombs – guided by "spotters" on the ground equipped with radios, laptops, and lasers, and often riding on horseback, and also aided by unmanned satellite drones and other systems in the air – were both incredibly precise in avoiding civilian casualties and absolutely lethal in destroying the enemy. It was this "new kind of American power," added the *New York Times* report, that "enabled a ragtag opposition" (i.e., the same Northern Alliance supposedly dragging us into a quagmire) to rout the "battle-hardened troops" of the Taliban regime in less than three months, and with the loss of very few American troops.

In the event, Osama bin Laden was not captured and al Qaeda was not totally destroyed. But it was certainly damaged by the campaign in Afghanistan. As for the Taliban regime, it was overthrown and replaced by a government that would no longer give aid and comfort to terrorists. Moreover, while Afghanistan under the new government may not have been exactly democratic, it was infinitely less oppressive than its totalitarian predecessor. And thanks to the clearing of political ground that had been covered over by the radical Islamic extremism of the Taliban, the seeds of free institutions were being sown and given a fighting chance to sprout and grow.

The campaign in Afghanistan demonstrated in the most unmistakable terms what followed from the new understanding of terrorism that formed the second pillar of the Bush Doctrine: countries that gave safe haven to terrorists and refused to clean them out were asking the United States to do it for them, and the regimes ruling these countries were also asking to be overthrown in favor of new leaders with democratic aspirations. Of course, as circumstances permitted and prudence dictated, other instruments of power, whether economic or diplomatic, would be deployed. But Afghanistan showed that the military option was open, available for use, and lethally effective.

The Third Pillar

The third pillar on which the Bush Doctrine rested was the assertion of our right to preempt. Bush had already pretty clearly indicated on September 20, 2001 that he had no intention of waiting around to be attacked again ("We will pursue nations that provide aid or safe haven to terrorism"). But in the State of the Union speech in January 2002, he became much more explicit on this point too:

> We'll be deliberate, yet time is not on our side. I will not wait on events, while dangers gather. I will not stand by, as peril draws closer and closer. The

> United States of America will not permit the world's most dangerous regimes to threaten us with the world's most destructive weapons.

To those with ears to hear, the January speech should have made it abundantly clear that Bush was now proposing to go beyond the fundamentally retaliatory strike against Afghanistan and to take preemptive action. Yet at first it went largely unnoticed that this right to strike, not in retaliation for but in anticipation of an attack, was a logical extension of the general outline Bush had provided on September 20. Nor did the new position attract much attention even when it was reiterated in the plainest of words on January 29. It was not until the third in the series of major speeches elaborating the Bush Doctrine – the one delivered on June 1, 2002 at West Point to the graduating class of newly commissioned officers of the United States Army – that the message got through at last.

Perhaps the reason the preemption pillar finally became clearly visible at West Point was that, for the first time, Bush placed his new ideas in historical context:

> For much of the last century, America's defense relied on the cold-war doctrines of deterrence and containment. In some cases, those strategies still apply. But new threats also require new thinking. Deterrence – the promise of massive retaliation against nations – means nothing against shadowy terrorist networks with no nation or citizens to defend.

This covered al Qaeda and similar groups. But Bush then proceeded to explain, in addition, why the old doctrines could not work with a regime like Saddam Hussein's in Iraq:

> Containment is not possible when unbalanced dictators with weapons of mass destruction can deliver those weapons or missiles or secretly provide them to terrorist allies.

Refusing to flinch from the implications of this analysis, Bush repudiated the previously sacred dogmas of arms control and treaties against the proliferation of weapons of mass destruction as a means of dealing with the dangers now facing us from Iraq and other members of the axis of evil:

> We cannot defend America and our friends by hoping for the best. We cannot put our faith in the word of tyrants, who solemnly sign nonproliferation treaties, and then systematically break them.

Hence, Bush inexorably continued,

> If we wait for threats to fully materialize, we will have waited too long. . . . [T]he war on terror will not be won on the defensive. We must take the battle to the

> enemy, disrupt his plans, and confront the worst threats before they emerge. In the world we have entered, the only path to safety is the path of action. And this nation will act.

At this early stage, the Bush administration was still denying that it had reached any definite decision about Saddam Hussein; but everyone knew that, in promising to act, Bush was talking about him. The immediate purpose was to topple the Iraqi dictator before he had a chance to supply weapons of mass destruction to the terrorists. But this was by no means the only or – surprising though it would seem in retrospect – even the decisive consideration either for Bush or his supporters (or, for that matter, his opponents).[8] And in any case, the long-range strategic rationale went beyond the proximate causes of the invasion. Bush's idea was to extend the enterprise of "draining the swamps" begun in Afghanistan and then to set the entire region on a course toward democratization. For if Afghanistan under the Taliban represented the religious face of Middle Eastern terrorism, Iraq under Saddam Hussein was its most powerful secular partner. It was to deal with this two-headed beast that a two-pronged strategy was designed.

Unlike the plan to go after Afghanistan, however, the idea of invading Iraq and overthrowing Saddam Hussein provoked a firestorm hardly less intense than the one that was still raging over Bush's insistence on using the words "good" and "evil."

* * *

Even before the debate on Iraq in particular, there had been strong objection to the whole idea of preemptive action by the United States. Some maintained that such action would be a violation of international law, while others contended that it would set a dangerous precedent under which, say, Pakistan might attack India or vice-versa. But once the

[8] As John Podhoretz would later write: "Those who supported the war, in overwhelming numbers, believed there were multiple justifications for it. Those who opposed and oppose it, in equally overwhelming numbers, weren't swayed by the WMD arguments. Indeed, many of them had no difficulty opposing the war while believing that Saddam possessed vast quantities of such weapons. Take Sen. Edward Kennedy. 'We have known for many years,' he said in September 2002, 'that Saddam Hussein is seeking and developing weapons of mass destruction.' And yet only a few weeks later he was one of 23 senators who voted against authorizing the Iraq war. Take French President Jacques Chirac, who believed Saddam had WMD and still did everything in his power to block the war. So whether policymakers supported or opposed the war effort was not determined by their conviction about the presence of weapons of mass destruction."

discussion shifted from the Bush Doctrine in general to the question of Iraq, the objections became more specific.

Most of these were brought together in early August 2002 (only about two months after Bush's speech at West Point) in a piece entitled "Don't Attack Saddam." The author was Brent Scowcroft, who had been National Security Adviser to the elder President Bush. Scowcroft asserted, first, that there was

> scant evidence to tie Saddam to terrorist organizations, and even less to the September 11 attacks. Indeed, Saddam's goals have little in common with the terrorists who threaten us, and there is little incentive for him to make common cause with them.

That being the case, Scowcroft continued, "An attack on Iraq at this time would seriously jeopardize, if not destroy, the global counterterrorist campaign we have undertaken," the campaign that must remain "our preeminent security priority."

But this was not the only "priority" that to Scowcroft was "preeminent":

> Possibly the most dire consequences [of attacking Saddam] would be the effect in the region. The shared view in the region is that Iraq is principally an obsession of the U.S. The obsession of the region, however, is the Israeli-Palestinian conflict.

Showing little regard for the American "obsession," Scowcroft was very solicitous of the regional one:

> If we were seen to be turning our backs on that bitter [Israeli-Palestinian] conflict... in order to go after Iraq, there would be an explosion of outrage against us. We would be seen as ignoring a key interest of the Muslim world in order to satisfy what is seen to be a narrow American interest.

This, added Scowcroft, "could well destabilize Arab regimes in the region," than which, to a quintessential realist like him, nothing could be worse.

In coming out publicly, and in these terms, against the second President Bush's policy, Scowcroft underscored the extent to which the son had diverged from the father's perspective. In addition, by lending greater credence to the already credible rumor that the elder Bush opposed invading Iraq, Scowcroft's article belied what would soon become one of the favorite theories of the hard Left - namely, that the son had gone to war in order to avenge the attempted assassination of his father.

On the other hand, by implicitly assenting to the notion that toppling Saddam was merely "a narrow American interest," Scowcroft gave a certain measure of aid and comfort to the hard Left and its fellow travelers within the liberal community. For from these circles the cry had been going out that it was the corporations, especially Halliburton (which Vice President Dick Cheney had formerly headed) and the oil companies that were dragging us into an unnecessary war.

So, too, with Scowcroft's emphasis on resolving "the Israeli-Palestinian conflict" – a standard euphemism for putting pressure on Israel, whose "intransigence" was taken to be the major obstacle to peace. By strongly insinuating that the Israeli prime minister Ariel Sharon was a greater threat to us than Saddam Hussein, Scowcroft provided a respectable rationale for the hostility toward Israel that had come shamelessly out of the closet within hours of the attacks of 9/11 and that had been growing more and more overt, more and more virulent, and more and more widespread ever since. To the "paleoconservative" Right, where the charge first surfaced, it was less the oil companies than Israel that was mainly dragging us into invading Iraq. Before long, the Left would add the same accusation to its own indictment, and in due course it would be imprinted more and more openly on large swatches of mainstream opinion.

A cognate count in this indictment held that the invasion of Iraq had been secretly engineered by a cabal of Jewish officials acting not in the interest of their own country but in the service of Israel, and more particularly of Ariel Sharon. At first the framers and early spreaders of this defamatory charge considered it the better part of prudence to identify the conspirators not as Jews but as "neoconservatives." It was a clever tactic, in that Jews did in fact constitute a large proportion of the repentant liberals and leftists who, having some two or three decades earlier broken ranks with the Left and moved rightward, came to be identified as neoconservatives. Everyone in the know knew this, and for those to whom it was news, the point could easily be gotten across by singling out only those neoconservatives who had Jewish-sounding names and to ignore the many other leading members of the group whose clearly non-Jewish names might confuse the picture.

* * *

This tactic had been given a trial run by Patrick J. Buchanan in opposing the first Gulf war of 1991. Buchanan had then already denounced the Johnny-come-lately neoconservatives for having hijacked and corrupted the conservative movement, but now he descended deeper into the fever swamps by insisting that there were "only two groups beating the drums ... for war in the Middle East – the Israeli Defense Ministry and its amen corner in the United States." Among those standing in the "amen corner" he subsequently singled out four prominent hawks with Jewish-sounding names, counterposing them to "kids with names like McAllister, Murphy, Gonzales, and Leroy Brown" who would actually do the fighting if these Jews had their way.

Ten years later, in 2001, in the writings of Buchanan and other paleo-conservatives within the journalistic fraternity (notably Robert Novak, Arnaud de Borchgrave, and Paul Craig Roberts), one of the four hawks of 1991, Richard Perle, made a return appearance. But Perle was now joined in starring roles by Paul Wolfowitz and Douglas Feith, both occupying high positions in the Pentagon, and a large supporting cast of identifiably Jewish intellectuals and commentators outside the government (among them Charles Krauthammer, William Kristol, and Robert Kagan). Like their predecessors in 1991, the members of the new ensemble were portrayed as agents of their bellicose counterparts in the Israeli government. But there was also a difference: the new group had managed to infiltrate the upper reaches of the American government. Having pulled this off, they had conspired to manipulate their non-Jewish bosses - Vice President Cheney, Secretary of Defense Donald Rumsfeld, National Security Adviser Condoleezza Rice, and George W. Bush himself - into invading Iraq.

Before long, this theory was picked up and circulated by just about everyone in the whole world who was intent on discrediting the Bush Doctrine. And understandably so: for what could suit their purposes better than to "expose" the invasion of Iraq - and by extension the whole of World War IV - as a war started by Jews and being waged solely in the interest of Israel?

To protect themselves against the taint of anti-Semitism, purveyors of this theory sometimes disingenuously continued to pretend that when they said "neoconservative" they did not mean "Jew." Yet the theory inescapably rested on all-too-familiar anti-Semitic canards - principally that Jews were never reliably loyal to the country in which they lived, and that they were always conspiring behind the scenes, often successfully, to manipulate the world for their own nefarious purposes.[9]

Quite apart from its pernicious moral and political implications, the theory was ridiculous in its own right. To begin with, it asked one to believe

[9] The classic expression of this fantasy was, of course, *The Protocols of the Elders of Zion*, a document that had been forged by the Czarist secret police in the late 19th century but that had more recently been resurrected and distributed by the millions throughout the Arab-Muslim world, and beyond. It would also form the basis of a dramatic television series produced in Egypt.

the unbelievable: that strong-minded people like Bush, Rumsfeld, Cheney, and Rice could be fooled by a bunch of cunning subordinates, whether Jewish or not, into doing anything at all against their better judgment, let alone something so momentous as waging a war, let alone a war in which they could detect no clear relation to American interests.

In the second place, there was the evidence uncovered by the purveyors of this theory themselves. That evidence, to which they triumphantly pointed, consisted of published articles and statements in which the alleged conspirators openly and unambiguously advocated the very policies they now stood accused of having secretly foisted upon an unwary Bush administration. Nor had these allegedly secret conspirators ever concealed their belief that toppling Saddam Hussein and adopting a policy aimed at the democratization of the entire Middle East would be good not only for the United States and for the people of the region but also for Israel. (And what, an uncharacteristically puzzled Richard Perle asked a hostile interviewer, was wrong with that?)

Which brings us to the fourth pillar on which the Bush Doctrine was erected.

The Fourth Pillar

Listening to the laments of Scowcroft and many others, one would think that George W. Bush had been ignoring "the Israeli-Palestinian conflict" altogether in his misplaced "obsession" with Iraq. In fact, however, even before 9/11 it had been widely and authoritatively reported that Bush was planning to come out publicly in favor of establishing a Palestinian state as the only path to a peaceful resolution of the conflict; and in October, after a short delay caused by 9/11, he became the first American President actually to do so. Yet at some point in the evolution of his thinking over the months that followed, Bush seems to have realized that there was something bizarre about supporting the establishment of a Palestinian state that would be run by a terrorist like Yasir Arafat and his henchmen. Why should the United States acquiesce, let alone help, in adding yet another state to those harboring and sponsoring terrorism precisely at a time when we were at war to rid the world of just such regimes?

Presumably it was under the prodding of this question that Bush came up with an idea even more novel in its way than the new conception of terrorism he had developed after 9/11. This idea was broached only three weeks after his speech at West Point, on June 24, 2002, when he issued a statement adding conditions to his endorsement of a Palestinian state:

> Today, Palestinian authorities are encouraging, not opposing terrorism. This is unacceptable. And the United States will not support the establishment of a Palestinian state until its leaders engage in a sustained fight against the terrorists and dismantle their infrastructure.

But engaging in such a fight, he added, required the election of "new leaders, leaders not compromised by terror," who would embark on building "entirely new political and economic institutions based on democracy, market economics, and action against terrorism."

It was with these words that Bush brought his "vision" (as he kept calling it) of a Palestinian state living peacefully alongside Israel into line with his overall perspective on the evil of terrorism. And having traveled that far, he went the distance by repositioning the Palestinian issue into the larger context from which Arab propaganda had ripped it. Since this move passed almost unnoticed, it is worth dwelling on why it was so important.

Even before Israel was born in 1948, the Muslim countries of the Middle East had been fighting against the establishment of a sovereign Jewish state – *any* Jewish state – on land they believed Allah had reserved for those faithful to his prophet Muhammad. Hence the Arab-Israeli conflict had pitted hundreds of millions of Arabs and other Muslims, in control of more than two dozen countries and vast stretches of territory, against a handful of Jews who then numbered well under three-quarters of a million and who lived on a tiny sliver of land the size of New Jersey. But then came the Six-Day war of 1967. Launched in an effort to wipe Israel off the map, it ended instead with Israel in control of the West Bank (formerly occupied by Jordan) and Gaza (which had been controlled by Egypt). This humiliating defeat, however, was eventually turned into a rhetorical and political victory by Arab propagandists, who redefined the ongoing war of the whole Muslim world against the Jewish state as, instead, a struggle merely between the Palestinians and the Israelis. Thus was Israel's image transformed from a David to a Goliath, a move that succeeded in alienating much of the old sympathy previously enjoyed by the outnumbered and besieged Jewish state.

Bush now reversed this reversal. Not only did he reconstruct a truthful framework by telling the Palestinian people that they had been treated for decades "as pawns in the Middle East conflict." He also insisted on being open and forthright about the nations that belonged in this larger picture and about what they had been up to:

> I've said in the past that nations are either with us or against us in the war on terror. To be counted on the side of peace, nations must act. Every leader actually committed to peace will end incitement to violence in official media and publicly denounce homicide bombs. Every nation actually committed to peace will stop the flow of money, equipment, and recruits to terrorist groups seeking the destruction of Israel, including Hamas, Islamic Jihad, and Hizbullah. Every nation committed to peace must block the shipment of Iranian supplies to these groups and oppose regimes that promote terror, like Iraq. And Syria must choose the right side in the war on terror by closing terrorist camps and expelling terrorist organizations.

Here, then, Bush rebuilt the context in which to understand the Middle East conflict. In the months ahead, pressured by his main European ally, the British prime minister Tony Blair, and by his own Secretary of State, Colin Powell, Bush would sometimes seem to backslide into the old way of thinking. But he would invariably recover. Nor would he ever lose sight of the "vision" by which he was guided on this issue, and through which he had simultaneously made a strong start in fitting not the Palestinian Authority alone but the entire Muslim world, "friends" no less than enemies, into his conception of the war against terrorism.

With the inconsistency thus removed and the resultant shakiness repaired by the addition of this fourth pillar to undergird it, the Bush Doctrine was now firm, coherent, and complete.

Saluting the Flag Again

Both as a theoretical construct and as a guide to policy, the new Bush Doctrine could not have been further from the "Vietnam syndrome" – that loss of self-confidence and concomitant spread of neoisolationist and pacifist sentiment throughout the American body politic, and most prominently in the elite institutions of American culture, which began during the last years of the Vietnam war. I have already pointed to a likeness between the Truman Doctrine's declaration that World War III had started and the Bush Doctrine's equally portentous declaration that 9/11 had plunged us into World War IV. But fully to measure the distance traveled by the Bush Doctrine, I want to look now at yet another presidential doctrine – the one developed by Richard Nixon in the late 1960's precisely in response to the Vietnam syndrome.

Contrary to legend, our military intervention into Vietnam under John F. Kennedy in the early 1960's had been backed by every sector of mainstream opinion, with the elite media and the professoriate leading the cheers. At the beginning, indeed, the only criticism from the mainstream concerned tactical issues. Toward the middle, however, and with Lyndon B. Johnson having succeeded Kennedy in the White House, doubts began to arise concerning the political wisdom of the intervention, and by the time Nixon had replaced Johnson, the moral character of the United States was being indicted and besmirched. Large numbers of Americans, including even many of the people who had led the intervention in the Kennedy years, were now joining the tiny minority on the Left who at the time had denounced them for stupidity and immorality, and were now saying that going into Vietnam had progressed from a folly into a crime.

To this new political reality the Nixon Doctrine was a reluctant accommodation. As getting into Vietnam under Kennedy and Johnson had worked to undermine support for the old strategy of containment, Nixon – along with his chief adviser in foreign affairs, Henry Kissinger – thought that our way of getting out of Vietnam could conversely work to create the new strategy that had become necessary.

First, American forces would be withdrawn from Vietnam gradually, while the South Vietnamese built up enough power to assume responsibility for the defense of their own country. The American role would then be limited to providing arms and equipment. The same policy, suitably modified according to local circumstances, would be applied to the rest of the world as well. In every major region, the United States would now depend on local surrogates rather than on its own military to deter or contain any Soviet-sponsored aggression, or any other potentially destabilizing occurrence. We would supply arms and other forms of assistance, but henceforth the deterring and the fighting would be left to others.

On every point, the new Bush Doctrine contrasted sharply with the old Nixon Doctrine. Instead of withdrawal and fallback, Bush proposed a highly ambitious forward strategy of intervention. Instead of relying on local surrogates, Bush proposed an active deployment of our own military power. Instead of deterrence and containment, Bush proposed preemption and "taking the fight to the enemy." And instead of worrying about the stability of the region in question, Bush proposed to destabilize it through "regime change."

The Nixon Doctrine had obviously harmonized with the Vietnam syndrome. What about the Bush Doctrine? Was the political and military strategy it put forward comparably in tune with the post-9/11 public mood?

Certainly this is how it seemed in the immediate aftermath of the attacks: so much so that a group of younger commentators were quick to proclaim the birth of an entirely new era in American history. What December 7, 1941 had done to the old isolationism, they announced, September 11, 2001 had done to the Vietnam syndrome. It was politically dead, and the cultural fallout of that war – all the damaging changes wrought by the 1960's and the 1970's – would now follow it into the grave.

The most obvious sign of the new era was that once again we were saluting our now ubiquitously displayed flag. This was the very flag that, not so long ago, leftist radicals had thought fit only for burning. Yet now, even on the old flag-burning Left, a few prominent personalities were painfully wrenching their unaccustomed arms into something vaguely resembling a salute.

It was a scene reminiscent of the response of some Communists to the suppression by the new Soviet regime of the sailors' revolt that erupted in Kronstadt in the early 1920's. Far more murderous horrors would pour out of the malignant recesses of Stalinist rule, but as the first in that long series of atrocities leading to disillusionment with the Soviet Union, Kronstadt became the portent of them all. In its way, 9/11 served as an inverse Kronstadt for a number of radical leftists of today. What it did was raise questions about what one of them was now honest enough to describe as their inveterately "negative faith in America the ugly."

September 11 also brought to mind a poem by W.H. Auden written upon the outbreak of World War II and entitled "September 1, 1939." Although it contained hostile sentiments about America, remnants of Auden's own Communist period, the opening lines seemed so evocative of September 11, 2001 that they were often quoted in the early days of this new war:

> I sit in one of the dives
> On Fifty-second Street
> Uncertain and afraid
> As the clever hopes expire
> Of a low dishonest decade.

Auden's low dishonest decade was the 1930's, and its clever hopes centered on the construction of a workers' paradise in the Soviet Union. Our counterpart was the 1960's, and its less clever hopes centered not on construction, however illusory, but on destruction – the destruction of the institutions that made up the American way of life. For America was conceived in that period as the great obstacle to any improvement in the lot of the wretched of the earth, not least those within its own borders.

* * *

As a "founding father" of neoconservatism who had broken ranks with the Left precisely because I was repelled by its "negative faith in America the ugly," I naturally welcomed this new patriotic mood with open arms. In the years since making that break, I had been growing more and more impressed with the virtues of American society. I now saw that America was a country in which more liberty and more prosperity abounded than human beings had ever enjoyed in any other country or any other time. I now recognized that these blessings were also more widely shared than even the most visionary utopians had ever imagined possible. And I now understood that this was an immense achievement, entitling the United States of America to an honored place on the roster of the greatest civilizations the world had ever known.

The new patriotic mood therefore seemed to me a sign of greater intellectual sanity and moral health, and I fervently hoped that it would last. But I could not fully share the confidence of some of my younger political friends that the change was permanent - that, as they exulted, nothing in American politics and American culture would ever be the same again. As a veteran of the political and cultural wars of the 1960's, I knew from my own scars how ephemeral such a mood might well turn out to be, and how vulnerable it was to seemingly insignificant forces.

In this connection, I was haunted by one memory in particular. It was of an evening in the year 1960, when I went to address a meeting of left-wing radicals on a subject that had then barely begun to show the whites of its eyes: the possibility of American military involvement in a faraway place called Vietnam. Accompanying me that evening was the late Marion Magid, a member of my staff at *Commentary*, of which I had recently become the editor. As we entered the drafty old hall on Union Square in Manhattan, Marion surveyed the 50 or so people in the audience, and whispered to me: "Do you realize that every young person in this room is a tragedy to some family or other?"

The memory of this quip brought back to life some sense of how unpromising the future had then appeared to be for that bedraggled-looking assemblage. No one would have dreamed that these young people, and the generation about to descend from them politically and culturally, would within the blink of a historical eye come to be hailed as "the best informed, the most intelligent, and the most idealistic this country has ever known." Those words, even more incredibly, would emanate from what the new movement regarded as the very belly of the beast: from, to be specific, Archibald Cox, a professor at the Harvard Law School and later Solicitor General of the United States. Similar encomia would flow unctuously from the mouths of parents, teachers, clergymen, artists, and journalists.

More incredible yet, the ideas and attitudes of the new movement, cleaned up but essentially unchanged, would within a mere ten years turn one of our two major parties upside down and inside out. In 1961, President John F. Kennedy had famously declared that we would "pay any price, bear any burden,... to assure the survival and the success of liberty." By 1972, George McGovern, nominated for President by Kennedy's own party, was campaigning on the slogan, "Come Home, America." It was a slogan that to an uncanny degree reflected the ethos of the embryonic movement I had addressed in Union Square only about a decade before.

The New "Jackal Bins"

In going over this familiar ground, I am trying to make two points. One is that the nascent radical movement of the late 1950's and early 1960's was up against an adversary, namely, the "Establishment," that looked unassailable. Even so – and this is my second point – to the bewilderment of almost everyone, not least the radicals themselves, they blew and they blew and they blew the house down.

Here we had a major development that slipped in under the radar of virtually all the pundits and the trend-spotters. How well I remember John Roche, a political scientist then working in the Johnson White House, being quoted by the columnist Jimmy Breslin as having derisively labeled the radicals a bunch of "Upper West Side jackal bins." As further investigation disclosed, Roche had actually said "Jacobins," a word so unfamiliar to his interviewer that "jackal bins" was the best Breslin could do in transcribing his notes.

Much ink has been spilled, gallons of it by me, in the struggle to explain how and why a great "Establishment" representing so wide a national consensus could have been toppled so easily and so quickly by so small and marginal a group as these "jackal bins." In the domain of foreign affairs, of course, the usual answer is Vietnam. In this view, it was by deciding to fight an unpopular war that the Establishment rendered itself vulnerable.

The ostensible problem with this explanation, to say it again, is that at least until 1965 Vietnam was a popular war. All the major media – from the *New York Times* to the *Washington Post*, from *Time* to *Newsweek*, from CBS to

ABC – supported our intervention. So did most of the professoriate. And so did the public. Even when all but one or two of the people who had either directly led us into Vietnam, or had applauded our intervention, commenced falling all over themselves to join the antiwar parade, public opinion continued supporting the war.

But it did not matter. Public opinion had ceased to count. Indeed, as the Tet offensive of 1968 revealed, reality itself had ceased to count. As all would later come to agree and some vainly struggled to insist at the time, Tet was a crushing defeat not for us but for the North Vietnamese. But Walter Cronkite had only to declare it a defeat for us from the anchor desk of the CBS *Evening News*, and a defeat it became.

Admittedly, in electoral politics, where numbers are decisive, public opinion remained potent. Consequently, none of the doves contending for the presidency in 1968 or 1972 could beat Richard Nixon. Yet even Nixon felt it necessary to campaign on the claim that he had a "plan" not for winning but for getting us out of Vietnam.

All of which is to say that, on Vietnam, elite opinion trumped popular opinion. Nor were the effects restricted to foreign policy. They extended into the newly antagonistic attitude toward everything America was and represented.

It hardly needs stressing that this attitude found a home in the world of the arts, the universities, and the major media of news and entertainment, where intellectuals shaped by the 1960's, and their acolytes in the publishing houses of New York and in the studios of Hollywood, held sway. But it would be a serious mistake to suppose that the trickle-down effect of the professoriate's attitude was confined to literature, journalism, and show business.

John Maynard Keynes once said that "Practical men who believe themselves to be quite exempt from any intellectual influences, are usually the slaves of some defunct economist." Keynes was referring specifically to businessmen. But practical functionaries like bureaucrats and administrators are subject to the same rule, though they tend to be the slaves not of economists but of historians and sociologists and philosophers and novelists who are very much alive even when their ideas have, or should have, become defunct. Nor is it necessary for the "practical men" to have studied the works in question, or even ever to have heard of their authors. All they need do is read the *New York Times*, or switch on their television sets, or go to the movies – and, drip by drip, a more easily assimilable form of the original material is absorbed into their heads and their nervous systems.

These, in sum, were some of the factors that made me wonder whether the terrorist attacks of September 11, 2001 would turn out to mark a genuine turning point comparable to the bombing of Pearl Harbor on December 7, 1941. I was well aware that, before Pearl Harbor, several groups ranging across the political spectrum had fought against our joining the British, who had been at war with Nazi Germany since 1939. There were the isolationists, both liberal and conservative, who detected no American interest in this distant conflict; there were the right-wing radicals who thought that if we were going to go to war, it ought to be on the side of Nazi Germany against Communist Russia, not the other way around; and there were the left-wing radicals who saw the war as a struggle between two equally malign imperialistic systems in which they had no stake. Under the influence of these groups, a large majority of Americans had opposed our entry into the war right up to the moment of the Japanese attack on Pearl Harbor. But from that moment on, the opposition faded away. The antiwar groups either lost most of their members or lapsed into a morose silence, and public opinion did a 180-degree turn.

At first, September 11 did seem to resemble Pearl Harbor in its galvanizing effect, while by all indications the first battle of World War IV – the battle of Afghanistan – was supported by a perhaps even larger percentage of the public than Vietnam had been at the beginning. Nevertheless, even though the opposition in 2001 was still numerically insignificant, it was much stronger than it had been in the early days of Vietnam. The reason was that it now maintained a tight grip over the institutions that, in the later stages of that war, had been surrendered bit by bit to the anti-American Left.

* * *

There was, for openers, the literary community, which could stand in for the world of the arts in general. No sooner had the Twin Towers been toppled and the Pentagon smashed than a fierce competition began for the gold in the anti-American Olympics. Susan Sontag, one of my old ex-friends on the Left, seized an early lead in this contest with a piece in which she asserted that 9/11 was an attack "undertaken as a consequence of specific American alliances and actions." Not content with suggesting that we had brought this aggression on ourselves, she went on to compare the backing in Congress for our "robotic President" to "the unanimously applauded, self-congratulatory bromides of a Soviet Party Congress."

Another of my old ex-friends, Norman Mailer, surprisingly slow out of the starting gate, soon came up strong on the inside by comparing the Twin Towers to "two huge buck teeth," and pronouncing the ruins at Ground

Zero "more beautiful than the buildings were." Still playing the enfant terrible even as he was closing in on his eightieth year, Mailer denounced us as "cultural oppressors and aesthetic oppressors" of the Third World. In what did this oppression consist? It consisted, he expatiated, in our establishing "enclaves of our food out there, like McDonald's" and in putting "our high-rise buildings" around the airports of even "the meanest, scummiest, capital[s] in the world." For these horrendous crimes we had, on 9/11, received a measure – and only a small measure at that – of our just deserts.

Then there were the universities. A report issued shortly after 9/11 by the American Council of Trustees and Alumni (ACTA) cited about a hundred malodorous statements wafting out of campuses all over the country that resembled Sontag and Mailer in blaming the attacks not on the terrorists but on America. Among these were three especially choice specimens. From a professor at the University of New Mexico: "Anyone who can blow up the Pentagon gets my vote." From a professor at Rutgers: "[We] should be aware that the ultimate cause [of 9/11] is the fascism of U.S. foreign policy over the past many decades." And from a professor at the University of Massachusetts: "[The American flag] is a symbol of terrorism and death and fear and destruction and oppression."

When the ACTA report was issued, protesting wails of "McCarthyism" were heard throughout the land, especially from the professors cited. Like them, Susan Sontag, too, claimed that her freedom of speech was being placed in jeopardy. In this peculiar reading of the First Amendment, much favored by leftists in general, they were free to say anything they liked, but the right to free speech ended where criticism of what they had said began.

Actually, however, with rare exceptions, attempts to stifle dissent on the campus were largely directed at the many students and the few faculty members who *supported* the 9/11 war. All these attempts could be encapsulated into a single phenomenon: on a number of campuses, students or professors who displayed American flags or patriotic posters were forced to take them down. As for Susan Sontag's freedom of speech, hardly had the ink dried on her post-9/11 piece before she became the subject of countless fawning reports and interviews in periodicals and on television programs around the world.

* * *

Speaking of television, it was soon drowning us with material presenting Islam in glowing terms. Mainly, these programs took their cue from the President and other political leaders. Out of the best of motives, and for prudential reasons as well, elected officials were striving mightily to deny that the war against terrorism was a war against Islam. Hence they never ceased heaping praises on the beauties of that religion, about which few of them knew anything.

But it was from the universities, not from the politicians, that the substantive content of these broadcasts derived, in interviews with academics, many of them Muslims themselves, whose accounts of Islam were selectively roseate. Sometimes they were even downright untruthful, especially in sanitizing the doctrine of jihad or holy war, or in misrepresenting the extent to which leading Muslim clerics all over the world had been celebrating suicide bombers – not excluding those who had crashed into the World Trade Center and the Pentagon – as heroes and martyrs.

I do not bring this up in order to enter into a theological dispute. My purpose, rather, is to offer another case study in the continued workings of the trickle-down effect I have already described. Thus, hard on the heels of 9/11, the universities began adding innumerable courses on Islam to their curricula. On the campus, "understanding Islam" inevitably translated into apologetics for it, and most of the media dutifully followed suit. The media also adopted the stance of neutrality between the terrorists and ourselves that prevailed among the relatively moderate professoriate, as when the major television networks ordered their anchors to avoid exhibiting partisanship.

Here the great exception was the Fox News Channel. The *New York Times*, in an article deploring the fact that Fox was covering the war from a frankly pro-American perspective, expressed relief that no other network had so cavalierly discarded the sacred conventions dictating that journalists, in the words of the president of ABC News, must "maintain their neutrality in times of war."

Although the vast majority of those who blamed America for having been attacked were on the Left, a few voices on the Right joined this perverted chorus. Speaking on Pat Robertson's TV program, the Reverend Jerry Falwell delivered himself of the view that God was punishing the United States for the moral decay exemplified by a variety of liberal groups among us. Both later apologized for singling out these groups, but each continued to insist that God was withdrawing His protection from America because all of us had become great sinners. And in the amen corner that quickly formed on the secular Right, commentators like Robert Novak and Pat Buchanan added that we had called the attack down on our heads not so much by our willful disobedience to divine law as by our manipulated obedience to Israel.

* * *

Oddly enough, however, within the Arab world itself, there was much less emphasis on Israel as the root cause of the attacks than was placed on it by most, if not all, of Buchanan's fellow paleoconservatives on the Right. Even to Osama bin Laden himself, support of Israel ranked only third on a list of our "crimes" against Islam.

Not, to be sure, that Arabs everywhere - together with most non-Arab Middle Eastern Muslims like the Iranians - had given up their dream of wiping Israel off the map. To anyone who thought otherwise, Fouad Ajami of Johns Hopkins, an American who grew up as a Muslim in Lebanon, had this to say about the Arab world's "great refusal" to accept Israel under any conditions whatsoever:

> The great refusal persists in that "Arab street" of ordinary men and women, among the intellectuals and the writers, and in the professional syndicates.... The force of this refusal can be seen in the press of the governments and of the oppositionists, among the secularists and the Islamists alike, in countries that have concluded diplomatic agreements with Israel and those that haven't.

Ajami emphasized that the great refusal remained "fiercest in Egypt," notwithstanding the peace treaty it had signed with Israel in 1978. It might have been expected, then, that the Egyptians would be eager to blame the widespread animus against the U.S. in their own country on American policy toward Israel, especially since Egypt, being second only to the Jewish state as a recipient of American aid, had a powerful incentive to explain away so ungrateful a response to the benevolent treatment it was receiving at our hands. But no. Only about two weeks before 9/11, Ab'd Al-Mun'im Murad, a columnist in *Al-Akhbar*, a daily newspaper sponsored by the Egyptian government, wrote:

> The conflict that we call the Arab-Israeli conflict is, in truth, an Arab conflict with Western, and particularly American, colonialism. The U.S. treats [the Arabs] as it treated the slaves inside the American continent. To this end, [the U.S.] is helped by the smaller enemy, and I mean Israel.

In another piece, the same writer expanded on this unusually candid acknowledgment:

> The issue no longer concerns the Israeli-Arab conflict. The real issue is the Arab-American conflict - Arabs must understand that the U.S. is not "the American friend" - and its task, past, present, and future, is [to impose] hegemony on the world, primarily on the Middle East and the Arab world.

Then, in a third piece, also published in late August, Murad gave us an inkling of the reciprocal "task" he had in mind to be performed on America:

> The Statue of Liberty, in New York Harbor, must be destroyed because of... the idiotic American policy that goes from disgrace to disgrace in the swamp of bias and blind fanaticism.... The age of the American collapse has begun.

If this was the kind of thing we were getting from an Arab country that everyone regarded as "moderate," in radical states like Iraq and Iran nothing less would suffice than identifying America as the "Great Satan." As for the Palestinians, their contempt for America was hardly exceeded by their loathing of Israel. For example, the mufti – or chief cleric – appointed by the Palestinian Authority under Yasir Arafat had prayed that God would "destroy America," while the editor of a leading Palestinian journal proclaimed:

> History does not remember the United States, but it remembers Iraq, the cradle of civilization.... History remembers every piece of Arab land, because it is the bosom of human civilization. On the other hand, the [American] murderers of humanity, the creators of the barbaric culture and the bloodsuckers of nations, are doomed to death and destined to shrink to a microscopic size, like Micronesia.

The absence of even a word here about Israel showed that if the Jewish state had never come into existence, the United States would still have stood as an embodiment of everything that most of these Arabs considered evil. Indeed, the hatred of Israel was in large part a surrogate for anti-Americanism, rather than the reverse. Israel was seen as the spearhead of the American drive for domination over the Middle East. As such, the Jewish state was a translation of America into, as it were, Hebrew – the "little enemy," the "little Satan." To rid the region of it would thus be tantamount to cleansing an area belonging to Islam (*dar al-Islam*) of the blasphemous political, social, and cultural influences emanating from a barbaric and murderous force. But the force, so to speak, was with America, of which Israel was merely an instrument.

Although Buchanan and Novak were earlier and more outspoken in blaming 9/11 on American friendliness toward Israel, this idea was not confined to the Right or to the marginal precincts of paleoconservatism. On the contrary: while it popped up on the Right, it thoroughly pervaded the radical Left and much of the soft Left, and was even espoused by a number of liberal centrists like Mickey Kaus. For the moment, indeed, the blame-Israel-firsters were concentrated most heavily on the Left.

It was also on the Left, and above all in the universities, that their fraternal twins, the blame-America-firsters, were located. Yet Eric Foner, a professor of history at my own alma mater, Columbia, risibly claimed that the ACTA report was misleading since the polls proved that there was "firm support" for the war among college students. "If our aim is to indoctrinate students with unpatriotic beliefs," Foner smirked, "we're obviously doing a very poor job of it."

True enough. But what Foner, as a historian, must have known but neglected to mention was that even at the height of the radical fevers on the campus in the 1960's, only a minority of students sided with the antiwar radicals. Still, even though they were in the majority, the non-radical students were unable to make themselves heard above the antiwar din, and whenever they tried, they were shouted down. This is how it was, too, on the campus after 9/11. There were, here and there, brave defiers of the academic orthodoxies. But mostly, the silent majority remained silent, for fear of incurring the disapproval of their teachers, or even of being punished for the crime of "insensitivity."

* * *

Such, then, was the assault that began to be mounted within hours of 9/11 by the guerrillas-with-tenure in the universities, along with their spiritual and political disciples scattered throughout other quarters of our culture. Could this "tiny handful of aging Rip van Winkles," as they were breezily brushed off by one commentator, grow into a force as powerful as the "jackal bins" of yesteryear? Was the upsurge of confidence in America, and American virtue, that spontaneously materialized on 9/11 strong enough to withstand them this time around?

Some who shared my apprehensions believed that if things went well on the military front, all would be well on the home front, too. And that is how it appeared from the effect wrought by the spectacular success of the Afghanistan campaign, which disposed of the "quagmire" theory and also dampened antiwar activity on at least a number of campuses. Nevertheless, the mopping-up operation in Afghanistan created an opportunity for more subtle forms of opposition to gain traction. There were complaints that the terrorists captured in Afghanistan and then sent to a special facility in Guantanamo were not being treated as regular prisoners of war. And there were also allegations of the threat to civil liberties posed in America itself by measures like the Patriot Act, which had been designed to ward off any further terrorist attacks at home. Although these concerns were mostly based on misreadings of the Geneva Convention and of the Patriot Act itself, some people no doubt raised them in good faith. But there is also no doubt that such issues could – and did – serve as a respectable cover for wholesale opposition to the entire war.

Another respectable cover was the charge that Bush was following a policy of "unilateralism." The alarm over this supposedly unheard-of outrage was first sounded by the chancelleries and chattering classes of Western Europe when Bush stated that, in taking the fight to the terrorists and their sponsors, we would prefer to do so with allies and with the blessing of the UN, but if necessary we would go it alone and without an imprimatur from the Security Council.

This was too much for the Europeans. Having duly offered us their condolences over 9/11, they could barely let a decent interval pass before going back into the ancient family business of showing how vastly superior in wisdom and finesse they were to the Americans, whose primitive character was once again on display in the "simplistic" ideas and crude moralizing of George W. Bush. Now they urged that our military operations end with Afghanistan, and that we leave the rest to diplomacy in deferential consultation with the great masters of that recondite art in Paris and Brussels.

Taking their cue from these masters, the *New York Times*, along with many other publications ranging from the Center to the hard Left – and soon to be seconded by all the Democratic candidates in the presidential primaries, except for Senator Joseph Lieberman – began hitting Bush for recklessness and overreaching. What we saw developing here was a broader coalition than the antiwar movement spawned by Vietnam had managed to put together, especially in its first few years. The antiwar movement then had been made up almost entirely of leftists and liberals, whereas this new movement was bringing together the whole of the hard Left, elements of the soft Left, and sectors of the American Right.

Treading the path previously marked out by his colleague Mickey Kaus on the issue of Israel, Michael Kinsley of the soft Left allied himself with Pat Buchanan in bringing forth yet another respectable cover. This was to indict the President for evading the Constitution by proposing to fight undeclared wars. Meanwhile, the same charge was moving into the political mainstream through Democratic Senators like Robert Byrd, Edward M. Kennedy, and Tom Daschle, though they also continued carrying on about quagmires and slippery slopes and "unilateralism."

I for one was certain that, as the military facet of World War IV widened – with Iraq clearly being the next most likely front – opposition would not only grow but would acquire enough assurance to dispense with any respectable covers. Which was to say that it would be taken over by extremists and radicalized. About this I turned out to be correct, while those who scoffed at the "jackal bins" and the "aging Rip Van Winkles" as a politically insignificant bunch turned out to be wrong. But I never imagined that the new antiwar movement would so rapidly arrive at the stage of virulence it had taken years for its ancestors of the Vietnam era to reach.

Varieties of Anti-Americanism

A possible explanation of the great velocity achieved by the new antiwar movement was that, like the respectable critique immediately preceding it, the radical opposition was following the lead of European opinion. In this instance, encouragement and reinforcement came from the almost incredible degree of hostility to America that erupted in the wake of 9/11 all over the European continent, and most blatantly in France and Germany, and that gathered even more steam in the run-up to the battle of Iraq. If demonstrations and public-opinion polls could be believed, huge numbers of Europeans loathed the United States so deeply that they were unwilling to side with it even against one of the most tyrannical and murderous despots on earth.

That this was the feeling in the Muslim world did not come as a surprise. Unlike in Europe, where the attacks of 9/11 did elicit a passing moment of sympathy for the United States ("We Are All Americans Now," proclaimed a headline the next day in the leading leftist daily in Paris), in the realm of Islam the news of 9/11 brought dancing in the streets and screams of jubilation. Almost to a man, Muslim clerics in their sermons assured the faithful that in striking a blow against the "Great Satan," Osama bin Laden had acted as a jihadist, or holy warrior, in strict accordance with the will of God.

This could have been predicted from a debate on the topic "Bin Laden – The Arab Despair and American Fear" that was televised on the Arabic-language network Al-Jazeera about two months before 9/11. Using "American Fear" in the title was a bit premature, since this was a time when very few Americans were frightened by Islamic terrorism, for the simple reason that scarcely any had ever heard of bin Laden or al Qaeda. Be that as it may, at the conclusion of the program, the host said to the lone guest who had been denouncing bin Laden as a terrorist: "I am looking at the viewers' reactions for one that would support your positions – but . . . I can't find any." He then cited "an opinion poll in a Kuwaiti paper which showed that 69 percent of Kuwaitis, Egyptians, Syrians, Lebanese, and Palestinians think bin Laden is an Arab hero and an Islamic jihad warrior." And on the basis of the station's own poll, he also estimated that among all Arabs "from the Gulf to the Ocean," the proportion sharing this view of bin Laden was "maybe even 99 percent."

Surely, then, the chairman of the Syrian Arab Writers Association was speaking for hordes of his "brothers" in declaring shortly after 9/11 that

> When the twin towers collapsed... I felt deep within me like someone delivered from the grave; I [felt] that I was being carried in the air above the corpse of the mythological symbol of arrogant American imperialist power.... My lungs filled with air, and I breathed in relief, as I had never breathed before.

If this was how the Arab/Muslim world largely felt about 9/11, what could have been expected from that world when the United States picked itself up off the ground - Ground Zero, to be exact - and began fighting back? What could have been expected is precisely what happened: another furious outburst of anti-Americanism. Only this time the outbursts were infused not by jubilation but by the desperate hope that the United States would somehow be humiliated. This hope was soon extinguished by the quick defeat of the Taliban regime in Afghanistan, but it was immediately rekindled by the way Saddam Hussein was standing up against America. Saddam had killed hundreds of thousands of Muslims in Iran, and countless Arabs in his own country and Kuwait. Obviously, however, to his Arab and Muslim "brothers" this was completely canceled out by his defiance of the United States.

Was there, perhaps, an element of the same twisted sentiment in the willingness of millions upon millions of Europeans to lend de-facto aid and comfort to this monster? Of course, the claim was that most such people were neither pro-Saddam nor anti-American: all they wanted was to "give peace a chance." But this claim was belied by the slogans, the body language, the speeches, and the manifestos of the "peace" party. Though hatred of America may not have been universal among opponents of American military action, it was obviously very widespread and very deep. And though other considerations (pacifist sentiment, concern about civilian casualties, contempt for George Bush, faith in the UN, etc.) were at work, these factors had no trouble coexisting harmoniously with extreme hostility to the United States.

Thus, within two months of 9/11, a survey of influential people in 23 countries was undertaken by the Pew Research Center, the Princeton

Survey Research Associates, and the *International Herald Tribune*. Here is how a British newspaper summarized the findings:

> Did America somehow ask for the terrorist outrages in New York and Washington?... [M]ost people of influence in the rest of the world... believe that, to a certain extent, the U.S. was asking for it.... From its closest allies, in Europe, to the Middle East, Russia, and Asia, a uniform 70 percent said people considered it good that after September 11 Americans had realized what it was to be vulnerable.

It would therefore seem that the Italian playwright Dario Fo, winner of the Nobel Prize for Literature in 1997, was more representative of European opinion than he may at first have appeared when spewing out the following sentiment:

> The great speculators wallow in an economy that every year kills tens of millions of people with poverty – so what is 20,000 [*sic*] dead in New York? Regardless of who carried out the massacre, this violence is the legitimate daughter of the culture of violence, hunger, and inhumane exploitation.

In France, a leading philosopher and social theorist, Jean Baudrillard, produced a somewhat different type of apologia for the terrorists of 9/11 and their ilk. This was so laden with postmodern jargon and so convoluted that it bordered on parody ("The collapse of the towers of the World Trade Center is unimaginable, but this does not suffice to make it a real event"). But Baudrillard's piece did at least contain a revealing confession:

> That we have dreamed of this event, that everyone without exception has dreamed of it,... is unacceptable for the Western moral conscience, but it is still a fact.... Ultimately, they [al Qaeda] did it, but we willed it.

* * *

Much the same idea, in even more straightforward terms, was espoused across the Channel by Mary Beard, a teacher of classics at my other alma mater, Cambridge University, who wrote: "[H]owever tactfully you dress it up, the United States had it coming.... World bullies... will in the end pay the price." With this the highly regarded novelist Martin Amis agreed. But Beard's old-fashioned English plainness evidently being a little too plain for him, Amis resorted to a bit of fancy continental footwork in formulating his own endorsement of the idea that America had been asking for it:

> Terrorism is political communication by other means. The message of September 11 ran as follows: America, it is time you learned how implacably you are hated.... Various national characteristics – self-reliance, a fiercer

> patriotism than any in Western Europe, an assiduous geographical incuriosity – have created a deficit of empathy for the sufferings of people far away.

What on earth was going on here? After 9/11, most Americans had gradually come to recognize that we were hated by the terrorists who had attacked us and their Muslim cheerleaders not for our failings and sins but precisely for our virtues as a free and prosperous country. But why should we be hated by hordes of people living in other free and prosperous countries? In their case, presumably, it must be for our sins. And yet most of us knew for certain that, whatever sins we might have committed, they were not the ones of which the Europeans kept accusing us.

To wit: far from being a nation of overbearing bullies, we were humbly begging for the support of tiny countries we could easily have pushed around. Far from being "unilateralists," we were busy soliciting the gratuitous permission and the dubious blessing of the Security Council before taking military action against Saddam Hussein. Far from "rushing into war," we were spending months dancing a diplomatic gavotte in the vain hope of enlisting the help of France, Germany, and Russia. And so on, and so on, down to the last detail in the catalogue.

What, then, was going on? An answer to this puzzling question that would eventually gain perhaps the widest circulation came from Robert Kagan of the Carnegie Endowment. In a catchy formulation that soon became famous, Kagan proposed that Americans were from Mars and Europeans were from Venus. Expanding on this formulation, he wrote:

> On the all-important question of power – the efficacy of power, the morality of power, the desirability of power – American and European perspectives are diverging. Europe is turning away from power, or to put it a little differently, it is moving beyond power into a self-contained world of laws and rules and transnational negotiation and cooperation. It is entering a post-historical paradise of peace and relative prosperity, the realization of Kant's "Perpetual Peace." The United States, meanwhile, remains mired in history, exercising power in the anarchic Hobbesian world where international laws and rules are unreliable and where true security and the defense and promotion of a liberal order still depend on the possession and use of military might.

In developing his theory, Kagan got many things right and cast a salubrious light into many dark corners. But it also seemed to me that he was putting the shoes of his theory on the wrong feet. Although I fully accepted Kagan's description of the divergent attitudes toward military power, I did not agree that the Europeans were already living in the future while the United States remained "mired" in the past. In my judgment, the opposite was closer to the truth.

The "post-historical paradise" into which the Europeans were supposedly moving struck me as nothing more than the web of international institutions that had been created at the end of World War II under the leadership of the United States in the hope that they would foster peace and prosperity. These included the United Nations, the World Bank, the World Court, and others. Then after 1947, and again under the leadership of the United States, adaptations were made to the already existing institutions and new ones like NATO were added to fit the needs of World War III. With the victorious conclusion of World War III in 1989–90, the old international order became obsolete, and new arrangements tailored to a new era would have to be forged. But more than a decade elapsed before 9/11 finally made the contours of the "post-cold-war era" clear enough for these new arrangements to begin being developed.

Looked at from this angle, the Bush Doctrine revealed itself as an extremely bold effort to break out of the institutional framework and the strategy constructed to fight the last war. But it was more: it also drew up a blueprint for a new structure and a new strategy to fight a different breed of enemy in a war that was just starting and that showed signs of stretching out into the future as far as the eye could see. Facing the realities of what now confronted us, Bush had come to the conclusion that few if any of the old instrumentalities were capable of defeating this new breed of enemy, and that the strategies of the past were equally helpless before this enemy's way of waging war. To move into the future meant to substitute preemption for deterrence, and to rely on American military might rather than the "soft power" represented by the UN and the other relics of World War III. Indeed, not even the hard power of NATO – which had specifically been restricted by design to the European continent and whose deployment in other places could, and would be, obstructed by the French – was of much use in the world of the future.

Examined from this same angle, the European justifications for resisting the Bush Doctrine – the complaints about "unilateralism," trigger-happiness, and the rest – were unveiled as mere rationalizations. Here I went along with Kagan in tracing these rationalizations to a decline in the power of the Europeans. He put it very well:

> World War II all but destroyed European nations as global powers.... For a half-century after World War II, however, this weakness was masked by the unique geopolitical circumstances of the cold war. Dwarfed by the two superpowers on its flanks, a weakened Europe nevertheless served as the

> central strategic theater of the worldwide struggle between Communism and democratic capitalism.... Although shorn of most traditional measures of great-power status, Europe remained the geopolitical pivot, and this, along with lingering habits of world leadership, allowed Europeans to retain international influence well beyond what their sheer military capabilities might have afforded. Europe lost this strategic centrality after the cold war ended, but it took a few more years for the lingering mirage of European global power to fade.

* * *

So far, so good. Where I parted company with Kagan's analysis was over his acquiescence in the claim that the Europeans had in fact made the leap into the post-national, or postmodern, "Kantian paradise" of the future. To me it seemed clear that it was they, and not we Americans, who were "mired" in the past. They were fighting tooth and nail against the American effort to move into the future precisely because holding onto the ideas, the strategic habits, and the international institutions of the cold war would allow them to go on exerting "international influence well beyond what their sheer military capabilities might have afforded." It was George W. Bush – that "simplistic" moralizer and trigger-happy "cowboy," that flouter of international law and reckless unilateralist – who had possessed the wit to see the future and had summoned up the courage to cross over into it.

But Bush was also a politician, and as such he felt it necessary to make some accommodation to the pressures coming at him both at home and from abroad. What this required was an occasional return visit to the past. On such visits, as when he would seek endorsements from the UN Security Council, he showed a polite measure of deference to those, again both at home and abroad, who insisted on reading the Bush Doctrine not as a blueprint for the future but as a reckless repudiation of the approach favored by the allegedly more sophisticated Europeans and their American counterparts. In Kagan's apt description of how the Europeans saw themselves:

> Europeans insist they approach problems with greater nuance and sophistication. They try to influence others through subtlety and indirection.... They generally favor peaceful responses to problems, preferring negotiation, diplomacy, and persuasion to coercion. They are quicker to appeal to international law, international conventions, and international opinion to adjudicate disputes. They try to use commercial and economic ties to bind nations together. They often emphasize process over result, believing that ultimately process can become substance.

None of this was new: the Europeans had made almost exactly the same claim of superior sophistication during the Reagan years. At that time – in 1983 – it had elicited a definitive comment from Owen Harries (the former head of policy planning in the Australian Department of Foreign Affairs and himself a member of the realist school):

> When one is exposed to this claim of superior realism and sophistication, one's first inclination is to ask where exactly is the evidence for it. If one considers some of the salient episodes in the history of Europe in this century – the events leading up to 1914, the Versailles peace conference, Munich, the extent of the effort Europe has been prepared to make to secure its own defense since 1948, and the current attitude toward the defense of its vital interests in the Persian gulf – one is not irresistibly led to concede European superiority.

Two decades later, Harries as a realist would have his own grave reservations about the Bush Doctrine. But I had no hesitation in adding the "sophisticated" European opposition to it as the latest episode in the long string of disastrously mistaken judgments he had enumerated back in 1983.

Unrealistic Realists

The astonishing success of the campaigns in Afghanistan and Iraq made a hash of the skepticism of the many pundits who had been so sure that we had too few troops or were following the wrong battle plan. Instead of getting bogged down, as they had predicted, our forces raced through these two campaigns in record time; and instead of ten of thousands of body bags being flown home, the casualties were numbered in the hundreds. As the military historian Victor Davis Hanson summarized what had transpired in Iraq:

> In a span of about three weeks, the United States military overran a country the size of California. It utterly obliterated Saddam Hussein's military hardware . . . and tore apart his armies. Of the approximately 110 American deaths in the course of the hostilities, fully a fourth occurred as a result of accidents, friendly fire, or peacekeeping mishaps rather than at the hands of enemy soldiers. The extraordinarily low ratio of total American casualties per number of U.S. soldiers deployed . . . is almost unmatched in modern military history.

True, the aftermath of major military operations, especially in Iraq, turned out to be rougher than the Pentagon seems to have expected. Thanks to the guerrilla insurgency mounted by a coalition of intransigent Saddam loyalists, radical Shiite militias, and terrorists imported from Iran and Syria, American soldiers continued to be killed. Nevertheless, by any historical standard – the more than 6,500 who died on D-Day alone in World War II, to cite only one example – our total losses remained amazingly low.

But it was not military matters that aroused the equally sour skepticism of the realists. Their doubts centered, rather, on the issue of whether the Bush Doctrine was politically viable. Most of all, they questioned the idea that democratization represented the best and perhaps even the only way to defeat militant Islam and the terrorism it was using as its main weapon against us. Bush had placed his bet on a belief in the universality of the desire for freedom and the prosperity that freedom brought with it. But what if he was wrong? What if the Middle East was incapable of democratization? What if the peoples of that region did not wish to be as free and as prosperous as we were? And what if Islam as a religion was by its very nature incompatible with democracy?

These were hard questions about which reasonable men could and did differ. But those of us who backed Bush's bet had our own set of doubts about the doubts of the realists. They seemed to forget that the Middle East of today had not been created by Allah in the 7th century, and that the miserable despotisms there had not evolved through some inexorable historical process powered entirely by internal cultural forces. Instead, the states in question had all been conjured into existence less than a hundred years ago out of the ruins of the defeated Ottoman empire in World War I. Their boundaries were drawn by the victorious British and French with the stroke of an often arbitrary pen, and their hapless peoples were handed over in due course to one tyrant after another.

Mindful of this history, we backers of the Bush Doctrine wondered why it should have been taken as axiomatic that these states would and/or should last forever in their present forms, and why the political configuration of the Middle East should be eternally immune from the democratizing forces that had been sweeping the rest of the world.

And we wondered, too, whether it could really be true that Muslims were so different from most of their fellow human beings that they liked being pushed around and repressed and beaten and killed by thugs – even if the thugs wore clerical garb or went around quoting from the Quran. We wondered whether Muslims really preferred being poor and hungry and ill-housed to enjoying the comforts and conveniences that we in the West took so totally for granted that we no longer remembered to be grateful for them. And we wondered why, if all this were the case, there had been so great an outburst of relief and happiness among the people of Kabul after we drove out their Taliban oppressors.

* * *

Yes, came the response, but what about the people of Iraq? Most supporters of the invasion - myself included - had predicted that we would be greeted there with flowers and cheers; yet our troops encountered car bombs and hatred. Nevertheless, and contrary to the impression created by the media, survey after survey demonstrated that the vast majority of Iraqis *did* welcome us, and *were* happy to be liberated from the murderous tyranny under which they had lived for so long under Saddam Hussein. The hatred and the car bombs came from the same breed of jihadists who had attacked us on 9/11, and who, unlike the skeptics in our own country, were afraid that we were actually succeeding in democratizing Iraq. Indeed, this was the very warning sent by the terrorist leader Abu Musab al Zarqawi to the remnants of al Qaeda still hunkered down in the caves of Afghanistan: "Democracy is coming, and there will be no excuse thereafter [for terrorism in Iraq]."

Speaking for many of his fellow realists, Fareed Zakaria of *Newsweek* disagreed with al Zarqawi that democracy was coming to Iraq and contended that it was premature to try establishing it there or anywhere else in the Middle East:

> We do not seek democracy in the Middle East - at least not yet. We seek first what might be called the preconditions for democracy... the rule of law, individual rights, private property, independent courts, the separation of church and state.... We should not assume that what took hundreds of years in the West can happen overnight in the Middle East.

Now, those of us who believed in the Bush Doctrine saw nothing wrong with pursuing Zakaria's agenda. But we rejected the charge - often made not only by realists like Zakaria but also by paleoconservatives like Buchanan - that our position was too "ideological" or naively "idealistic" or even "utopian." We agreed entirely with what the President had long since contended: that the realist alternative of settling for autocratic and despotic regimes in the Middle East had neither brought the regional stability it promised nor - as 9/11 horribly demonstrated - made us safe at home. Bush had also long since given his answer to the question posed by "some who call themselves realists" as to whether "the spread of democracy in the Middle East should be any concern of ours." It was, he affirmed in the strongest terms, a concern of ours precisely because democratization would make us more secure, and he accused the realists of having "lost contact with a fundamental reality" on this point. In this respect, I would argue, Bush was adopting a course akin to the one taken by the Marshall Plan, which had simultaneously served American interests and benefited others. Like the Marshall Plan, his new policy was a synthesis of realism and idealism: a case of doing well by doing good.

Those of us who supported the new policy also took issue with the view that democracy and capitalism could grow only in a soil that had been cultivated for centuries. We reminded the realists that in the aftermath of World War II, the United States managed within a single decade to transform both Nazi Germany and imperial Japan into capitalist democracies. And in the aftermath of the defeat of Communism in World War III, a similar process got under way on its own steam in Central and Eastern Europe, and even in the old heartland of the evil empire itself. Why not the Islamic world? The realist answer was that things were different there. To which our answer was that things were different everywhere, and a thousand reasons to expect the failure of any enterprise could always be conjured up to discourage making an ambitious effort.

To this, in turn, the counter frequently was that the Bush administration had wildly underestimated the special difficulties of democratizing Iraq and had correlatively misjudged the time so great a transformation would take, even assuming it to be possible at all. Yet talk about a "cakewalk" and the like mainly came from outside the administration; and in any event it had been applied to the future military campaign (which definitely did turn out to be a cakewalk), not to the ensuing reconstruction of Iraq. As to the latter, the administration kept repeating that we would stay in Iraq "for as long as it takes and not a day longer." How long would that be? For those who opposed the Bush Doctrine, a year (or even a month?) after the end of major combat operations was already much too much; for those of us who supported it, "as long as it takes and not a day longer" still seemed, given the stakes, the only satisfactory formula.

As with democratization, so with the reform and modernization of Islam. In considering this even more difficult question, we found ourselves asking whether Islam could really go on for all eternity resisting the kind of reformation and modernization that had begun within Christianity and Judaism in the early modern period. Not that we were so naive as to imagine that Islam could be reformed overnight, or from the outside. In its heyday, Islam was able to impose itself on large parts of the world by the sword; there was no chance today of an inverse instant transformation of Islam by the force of American arms.

There was, however, a very good chance that a clearing of the ground, and a sowing of the seeds out of which new political, economic, and social conditions could grow, would gradually give rise to correlative religious pressures from within. Such pressures would take the form of an ultimately irresistible demand on theologians and clerics to find warrants in the Quran and the *sharia* under which it would be possible to remain a good Muslim while enjoying the blessings of decent government, and even of political and economic liberty. In this way a course might finally be set toward the reform and modernization of the Islamic religion itself.

The Democrats of 2004

What I have been trying to say is that the obstacles to a benevolent transformation of the Middle East – whether military, political, or religious – are not insuperable. In the long run they can be overcome, and there can be no question that we possess the power and the means and the resources to work toward their overcoming. But do we have the skills and the stomach to do what will be required? Can we in our present condition play even so limited and so benign an imperial role as we did in occupying Germany and Japan after World War II?

Some of our critics on the European Right sneer at us not, as the Left does, for being imperialists but for being such clumsy ones – for lacking the political dexterity to oversee the emergence of successor governments more amenable to reform and modernization than the despotisms now in place. I confess that I am prey to anxieties about our capabilities, and to others stemming from our character as a nation. And in thinking about our long record of inattention and passivity toward terrorism before 9/11, I fear a relapse into appeasement, diplomatic evasion, and ineffectual damage control.

Anxieties and fears like these were given a great boost by the attacks on the Bush Doctrine that became so poisonous in the 2004 presidential primary campaigns of the Democratic party. I have already told of my early apprehensions about the potential spread of the antiwar movement from the margins to the center, and my subsequent amazement in watching it go so far so fast. Whereas it took twelve years for the radicals I addressed in that drafty union hall in 1960 to capture the Democratic party behind George McGovern, their political and spiritual heirs of 2001 seemed to be pulling off the same trick in less than two. This time their leader of choice was the raucously antiwar Howard Dean. Though he eventually failed to win the nomination, his early successes frightened most of the relatively moderate candidates into a sharp leftward turn on Iraq, and drove out the few who supported the campaign there. As for John Kerry, in order to win the nomination, he had to disavow the vote he had cast authorizing the President to use force against Saddam Hussein.

To make matters worse, the campaign to discredit the action in Iraq moved from the hustings into the halls of Congress, where it wore the camouflage of a series of allegedly nonpartisan hearings. In these hearings, the most prominent of which was held by the Senate Intelligence Committee, high officials of the Bush administration were hectored by Democratic legislators (and even a few Republicans) in terms that often came close to sounding like the many articles and books in circulation that were accusing the President of having lied to us in going after Saddam Hussein. This was no slow process of trickle-down; this was an instantaneous inundation of the whole political landscape.

Among the lies through which Bush supposedly misled John Kerry and everyone else was that there might have been some connection between Saddam and al Qaeda. Now, even those of us who believed in such a connection were willing to admit that the evidence was not (yet) definitive; but this was a far cry from denying that there was any basis for it at all.[10] So far a cry, that according to the reports that would be issued both by the Senate Intelligence Committee and the 9/11 Commission in the summer of 2004 (and contrary to how their conclusions would be interpreted in the media), al Qaeda did in fact have a cooperative, if informal, relationship with Iraqi agents working under Saddam.[11]

It was the same with another of the lies Bush allegedly told to justify the invasion of Iraq. In his State of the Union address of 2003, he said that "The British government has learned that Saddam Hussein recently sought significant quantities of uranium from Africa." Then an obscure retired diplomat named Joseph C. Wilson IV, who had earlier been sent to Niger by the CIA to check out this claim, earned his 15 minutes of fame – not to mention a best-selling book – by loudly denouncing this assertion as a lie. But it would in due course be established that every one of the notorious "sixteen words" Bush had uttered was true. This was the consensus of the Senate Intelligence Committee report, two separate British

[10] Stephen F. Hayes has done especially good work on this issue, both in a series of articles in the *Weekly Standard* and in his book *The Connection: How al Qaeda's Collaboration with Saddam Hussein Has Endangered America.*

[11] Additional corroboration of "meetings . . . between senior Iraqi representatives and senior al Qaeda operatives" would come from a comparable British investigation conducted by Lord Butler, whose report would be released around the same time as the Senate Intelligence Committee.

investigations, and a variety of European intelligence agencies, including even the French.[12] Not only that, but it turned out that Wilson's own report to the CIA had tended to *confirm* the suspicion that Saddam had been shopping for uranium in Africa, and not, as he went around declaring, to debunk it.[13] The liar here, then, was not Bush but Wilson.

* * *

But of course the biggest lie Bush was charged with telling was that Saddam possessed weapons of mass destruction. On this issue, too, those of us who still suspected that the WMD remained hidden, or that they had been shipped to Syria, or both, were willing to admit that we might well be wrong. But how could Bush have been *lying* when every intelligence agency in every country in the world was convinced that Saddam maintained an arsenal of such weapons? And how could Bush have "hyped" or exaggerated the reports he was given by our own intelligence agencies when the director of the CIA himself described the case as a "slam dunk"?

To be sure, again according to the Senate Intelligence Committee report, the case, far from being a "slam dunk," actually rested on weak or faulty evidence. Yet the committee itself "did not find any evidence that administration officials attempted to coerce, influence, or pressure analysts to change their judgments related to Iraq's weapons of mass destruction capabilities." The CIA, that is, did not tell the President what it thought he wanted to hear. It told him what it thought it knew; and what it told him, he had every reason to believe.[14]

In the wake of the WMD issue, several others emerged that did even more to shake the confidence of some who had been enthusiastic supporters of the operation in Iraq. On top of the mounting number of American soldiers being killed as they were trying to bring security to Iraq, and on the heels

[12] From the Butler Report: "We conclude also that the statement in President Bush's State of the Union Address of 28 January 2003 that 'The British Government has learned that Saddam Hussein recently sought significant quantities of uranium from Africa' was well-founded."

[13] From the Senate Intelligence Committee Report: "He [the CIA reports officer] said he judged that the most important fact in the report [by Wilson] was that Nigerian officials admitted that the Iraqi delegation had traveled there in 1999, and that the Nigerian prime minister believed the Iraqis were interested in purchasing uranium, because this provided some confirmation of foreign government service reporting."

[14] Going even further than the Senate Intelligence Committee, the Butler Report concluded: "We believe that it would be a rash person who asserted at this stage that evidence of Iraqi possession of stocks of biological or chemical agents, or even of banned missiles, does not exist or will never be found."

of the horrendous episodes of the murder and desecration of the bodies of four American contractors in Falluja, came the revelation that Iraqi prisoners in Abu Ghraib had been subjected to ugly mistreatment by their American captors.

Among supporters of the Bush Doctrine, these setbacks set off a great wave of defeatist gloom that was deepened by the nervous tactical shifts they produced in our military planners (such as the decision to hold back from cleaning out the terrorist militias hiding in and behind holy places in Falluja and Najaf). Even the formerly unshakable Fouad Ajami was shaken. In a piece entitled "Iraq May Survive, but the Dream Is Dead," he wrote: "Let's face it: Iraq is not going to be America's showcase in the Arab-Muslim world."

That the antiwar party would batten on all this - and would continue ignoring the enormous progress we had made in the reconstruction of Iraqi society - was only to be expected. It was also only natural for the Democrats to take as much political advantage of the setbacks as they could. But it was not necessarily to be expected that the Democrats would seize just as eagerly as the radicals upon every piece of bad news as another weapon in the war against the war. Nor was it necessarily to be expected that mainstream Democratic politicians would go so far off the intellectual and moral rails as to compare the harassment and humiliation of the prisoners in Abu Ghraib - none of whom, so far as anyone then knew, was even maimed, let alone killed - to the horrendous torturing and murdering that had gone on in that same prison under Saddam Hussein or, even more outlandishly, to the Soviet gulag in which many millions of prisoners died.

Yet this was what Edward M. Kennedy did on the floor of the Senate, where he declared that the torture chamber of Saddam Hussein had been reopened "under new management - U.S. management," and this was what Al Gore did when he accused Bush of "establishing an American gulag." Joining with the politicians was the main financial backer of the Democratic party's presidential campaign, George Soros, who actually said that Abu Ghraib was even worse than the attack of 9/11. On the platform with Soros when he made this morally disgusting statement was Senator Hillary Rodham Clinton, who let it go by without a peep of protest.

* * *

Equally ignominious was the response of mainstream Democrats to the most effective demagogic exfoliation of the antiwar radicals, Michael Moore's film *Fahrenheit 9/11*. Shortly after 9/11 - that is, long before the appearance of this movie but with many of its charges against Bush already on vivid display in Moore's public statements about Afghanistan – one liberal commentator had described him as a "well-known crank, regarded with considerable distaste even on the Left." The same commentator (shades of how the "jackal bins" of yore were regarded) had also dismissed as "preposterous" the idea that Moore's views "represent a significant body of antiwar opinion." Lending a measure of plausibility to this assessment was the fact that Moore elicited a few boos when, in accepting an Academy Award for *Bowling for Columbine* in 2003, he declared:

> We live in the time where we have fictitious election results that elect a fictitious president. We live in a time where we have a man sending us to war for fictitious reasons.... [W]e are against this war, Mr. Bush. Shame on you, Mr. Bush, shame on you.

By 2004, however, when *Fahrenheit 9/11* came out, things had changed. True, this movie – a compendium of every scurrility ever hurled at George W. Bush, and a few new ones besides, all gleefully stitched together in the best conspiratorial traditions of the "paranoid style in American politics" – did manage to embarrass even several liberal commentators. One of them described the film as a product of the "loony Left," and feared that its extremism might discredit the "legitimate" case against Bush and the war. Yet in an amazing reversal of the normal pattern in the distribution of prudence, such fears of extremism were more pronounced among liberal pundits than among mainstream Democratic politicians.

Thus, so many leading Democrats flocked to a screening of *Fahrenheit 9/11* in Washington that (as the columnist Mark Steyn quipped) the business of Congress had to be put on hold; and when the screening was over, nary a dissonant boo disturbed the harmony of the ensuing ovation. The chairman of the Democratic National Committee, Terry McAuliffe, pronounced the film "very powerful, much more powerful than I thought it would be." Then, when asked by CNN whether he thought "the movie was essentially fair and factually based," McAuliffe answered, "I do.... Clearly the movie makes it clear that George Bush is not fit to be President of this country." Senator Tom Harkin of Iowa seconded McAuliffe and urged all Americans to see the film: "It's important for the American people to understand what has gone on before, what led us to this point, and to see it sort of in this unvarnished presentation by Michael Moore."

Possibly some of the other important Democrats who attended the screening – including Senators Tom Daschle, Max Baucus, Barbara Boxer, and Bill Nelson; Congressmen Charles Rangel, Henry Waxman, and Jim McDermott; and elders of the party like Arthur Schlesinger, Jr. and

Theodore Sorensen – disagreed with Harkin and McAuliffe. But if so, they remained remarkably quiet about it.

As for John Kerry himself, he did not take time out to see *Fahrenheit 9/11*, explaining that there was no need since he had "lived it."

2004 and 1952

Returning now to the gloom that afflicted supporters of the Bush Doctrine in the spring of 2004: one of the reasons Fouad Ajami gave for it was that "our enemies have taken our measure; they have taken stock of our national discord over the war." Emboldened by our restraint in Falluja and elsewhere within Iraq, as well as by our concomitant willingness to bring the UN back into the political picture, our enemies had begun to breathe easier – and not only in Iraq:

> Once the administration talked of a "Greater Middle East" where the "deficits" of freedom, knowledge, and women's empowerment would be tackled, where our power would be used to erode the entrenched despotisms in the Arab-Muslim world.

But now, Ajami lamented, it had become clear that "we shall not chase the Syrian dictator to a spider hole, nor will we sack the Iranian theocracy." There were even indications that, abandoning the dream of democracy altogether, we might settle for the rule of a "strong man" in Iraq.

But how accurate was the measure our enemies had taken of us? Was it possible that their gauge was being thrown off by the overheated atmosphere of a more than usually bitter presidential campaign, and by the caution George Bush felt it necessary to adopt in seeking reelection?

This seemed to me then, and it still seems to me now, the most decisive question of all. I therefore want to conclude by examining it, and I want to do so by returning to the analogy I drew earlier between the start of World War III in 1947 and the start of World War IV in 2001.

When the Truman Doctrine was enunciated in 1947, it was attacked from several different directions. On the Right, there were the isolationists who – after being sidelined by World War II – had made something of a comeback in the Republican party under the leadership of Senator Robert Taft. Their complaint was that Truman had committed the United States to endless interventions that had no clear bearing on our national interest. But there was also another faction on the Right that denounced containment not as recklessly ambitious but as too timid. This group was still small, but within the next few years it would find spokesmen in Republican political figures like Richard Nixon and John Foster Dulles and conservative intellectuals like William F. Buckley, Jr. and James Burnham.

At the other end of the political spectrum, there were the Communists and their "liberal" fellow travelers who – strengthened by our alliance with the Soviet Union in World War II – had emerged as a relatively sizable group and would soon form a new political party behind Henry Wallace. In their view, the Soviets had more cause to defend themselves against us than we had to defend ourselves against them, and it was Truman, not Stalin, who posed the greater danger to "free peoples everywhere." But criticism also came from the political center, as represented by Walter Lippmann, the most influential and most prestigious commentator of the period. Lippmann argued that Truman had sounded "the tocsin of an ideological crusade" that was nothing less than messianic in its scope.

In the election of 1948, Truman had the seemingly impossible task of confronting all three of these challenges (and a few others as well). When, against what every poll had predicted, he succeeded in warding them off, he could reasonably claim a mandate for his foreign policy. And so it came about that, under the aegis of the Truman Doctrine, American troops were sent off in 1950 to fight in Korea. "What a nation can do or must do," Truman would later write, "begins with the willingness and the ability of its people to shoulder the burden," and Truman was rightly confident that the American people were willing to shoulder the burden of Korea.

Even so, enough bitter opposition remained within and around the Republican party to leave it uncertain as to whether containment was an *American* policy or only the policy of the Democrats. This uncertainty was exacerbated by the presidential election of 1952, when the Republicans behind Dwight D. Eisenhower ran against Truman's hand-picked successor Adlai Stevenson in a campaign featuring strident attacks on the Truman Doctrine by Eisenhower's running mate Richard Nixon and his future Secretary of State John Foster Dulles. Nixon, for example, mocked Stevenson as a graduate of the "Cowardly College of Communist Containment" run by Truman's Secretary of State Dean Acheson, while Dulles repeatedly called for ditching containment in favor of a policy of "rollback" and "liberation." And both Nixon and Dulles strongly signaled their endorsement of General Douglas MacArthur's insistence that Truman was wrong to settle for holding the line in Korea instead of going all the way – or, as MacArthur had famously put it, "There is no substitute for victory."

Yet when Eisenhower came into office, he hardly touched a hair on the head of the Truman Doctrine. Far from adopting a bolder and more aggressive strategy, the new President ended the Korean war on the basis of the status quo ante – in other words, precisely on the terms of containment. Even more telling was Eisenhower's refusal three years later to intervene when the Hungarians, apparently encouraged by the rhetoric of liberation still being employed in the broadcasts of Radio Free Europe, rose up in revolt against their Soviet masters. For better or worse, this finally dispelled any lingering doubt as to whether containment was the policy just of the Democratic party. With full bipartisan support behind it, the Truman Doctrine had become the official policy of the United States of America.

* * *

The analogy is obviously not perfect, but the resemblances between the political battles of 1952 and those of 2004 are striking enough to help us in thinking about what a few moments ago I called the most decisive of all the questions now facing the United States. To frame the question in slightly different terms from the ones I originally used: what will happen if the Democrats behind John Kerry defeat George W. Bush in November? Will they follow through on their violent denunciations of Bush's policy, or will they, like the Republicans of 1952 with respect to Korea, quietly forget their campaign promises of reliance on the UN and the Europeans, and continue on much the same course as Bush has followed in Iraq? And looking beyond Iraq itself, will they do unto the Bush Doctrine as the Republicans of 1952 did unto the Truman Doctrine? Will they treat Iraq as only one battle in the larger war – World War IV – into which 9/11 plunged us? Will they resolve to go on fighting that war with the strategy adumbrated by the Bush Doctrine, and for as long as it may take to win it?

From the way the Democrats have been acting and speaking, I fear that the answer is no. Nor was I reassured by the flamboyant display of hawkishness they put on at their national convention in July. Yet as a passionate supporter of the Bush Doctrine I pray that I am wrong about this. If John Kerry should become our next President, and he may, it would be a great calamity if he were to abandon the Bush Doctrine in favor of the law-enforcement approach through which we dealt so ineffectually with terrorism before 9/11, while leaving the rest to those weakest of reeds, the UN and the Europeans. No matter how he might dress up such a shift, it would – rightly – be interpreted by our enemies as a craven retreat, and dire consequences would ensue. Once again the despotisms of the Middle East would feel free to offer sanctuary and launching pads to Islamic terrorists; once again these terrorists would have the confidence to attack us – and this time on an infinitely greater scale than before.

If, however, the victorious Democrats were quietly to recognize that our salvation will come neither from the Europeans nor from the UN, and if they were to accept that the Bush Doctrine represents the only adequate response to the great threat that was literally brought home to us on 9/11, then our enemies would no longer be emboldened - certainly not to the extent they have recently been - by "our national discord over the war."

In World War III, despite the bipartisan consensus that became apparent after 1952 (and contrary to the roseate reminiscences of how it was then), plenty of "discord" remained, and there were plenty of missteps - most notably involving Vietnam - along the way to victory. There were also moments when it looked as though we were losing, and when our enemies seemed so strong that the best we could do was in effect to sue for a negotiated peace.

Now, with World War IV barely begun, a similar dynamic is already at work. In World War III, we as a nation persisted in spite of the inevitable setbacks and mistakes and the defeatism they generated, until, in the end, we won. To us the reward of victory was the elimination of a military, political, and ideological threat. To the people living both within the Soviet Union itself and in its East European empire, it brought liberation from a totalitarian tyranny. Admittedly, liberation did not mean that everything immediately came up roses, but it would be foolish to contend that nothing changed for the better when Communism landed on the very ash heap of history that Marx had predicted would be the final resting place of capitalism.

Suppose that we hang in long enough to carry World War IV to a comparably successful conclusion. What will victory mean this time around? Well, to us it will mean the elimination of another, and in some respects greater, threat to our safety and security. But because that threat cannot be eliminated without "draining the swamps" in which it breeds, victory will also entail the liberation of another group of countries from another species of totalitarian tyranny. As we can already see from Afghanistan and Iraq, liberation will no more result in the overnight establishment of ideal conditions in the Middle East than it has done in Eastern Europe. But as we can also see from Afghanistan and Iraq, better things will immediately happen, and a genuine opportunity will be opened up for even better things to come.

* * *

The memory of how it was toward the end of World War III suggests another intriguing parallel with how it is now in the early days of World

War IV. We have learned from the testimony of former officials of the Soviet Union that, unlike the elites here, who heaped scorn on Ronald Reagan's idea that a viable system of missile defense could be built, the Russians (including their best scientists) had no doubt that the United States could and would succeed in creating such a system and that this would do them in. Today the same kind of scorn is heaped by the same kind of people on George W. Bush's idea that the Middle East can be democratized, while our enemies in the region – like the Russians with respect to "Star Wars" – believe that we are actually succeeding.

One indication is the warning to this effect issued by al Zarqawi to al Qaeda, from which I have already quoted. But his letter is not the only sign that the secular despots and the Islamofascists in the Middle East are deeply worried over what the Bush Doctrine holds in store for them. There is Libya's Qaddafi, who has admitted that it was his anxiety about "being next" that induced him to give up his nuclear program. And there are the Syrians and the Iranians. Of course they keep making defiant noises and they keep trying to create as much trouble for us as possible, but with all due respect to the disappointed expectations of Fouad Ajami, I have to ask: why would they be sending jihadists and weapons into Iraq if not in a desperate last-ditch campaign to derail a process whose prospects are in their judgment only too fair and whose repercussions they fear are only too likely to send them flying?

This fear may, as Ajami says, have been tempered by our response to the troubles they themselves have been causing us. But it cannot have been altogether assuaged, since it is solidly grounded in the new geostrategic realities in their region that have been created under the aegis of the Bush Doctrine. Professor Haim Harari, a former president of the Weizmann Institute, describes these realities succinctly:

> Now that Afghanistan, Iraq, and Libya are out, two-and-a-half terrorist states remain: Iran, Syria, and Lebanon, the latter being a Syrian colony.... As a result of the conquest of Afghanistan and Iraq, both Iran and Syria are now totally surrounded by territories unfriendly to them. Iran is encircled by Afghanistan, by the Gulf States, Iraq, and the Muslim republics of the former Soviet Union. Syria is surrounded by Turkey, Iraq, Jordan, and Israel. This is a significant strategic change and it applies strong pressure on the terrorist countries. It is not surprising that Iran is so active in trying to incite a Shiite uprising in Iraq. I do not know if the American plan was actually to encircle both Iran and Syria, but that is the resulting situation.

Finally, there is the effect the Bush Doctrine has had on the forces pushing for liberalization throughout the Middle East. When Ronald Reagan used the word "evil" in speaking of the Soviet Union, and even confidently predicted its demise, he gave new hope to democratic dissidents in and out of the gulag. Back then, very much like Ajami on Bush, some of us fell into near despair when Reagan failed to act in full accordance with his own convictions. When, for example, he responded tepidly to the great Polish crisis of 1982 that culminated in the imposition of martial law, the columnist George F. Will, one of his staunchest supporters, angrily declared that the administration headed by Reagan "loved commerce more than it loathed Communism," and I wrote an article expressing "anguish" over his foreign policy. Yet even though (once more like Ajami today) our criticisms were mostly right in detail, we were proved wondrously wrong about the eventual outcome. It was different with the dissidents behind the Iron Curtain. They knew better than to get stuck on tactical details, and they never once lost heart.

* * *

So it has been with the Bush Doctrine. Bush has made reform and democratization the talk of the entire Middle East. Where before there was only silence, now there are countless articles and speeches and conferences, and even sermons, dedicated to the cause of political and religious liberalization and exploring ways to bring it about. Like the dissidents behind the Iron Curtain in the 1980's, the democratizers in the Middle East today evidently remain undiscouraged. Falluja and the rest notwithstanding, there has been, if anything, a steady increase in the volume and range of the reformist talk that was and continues to be inspired by the Bush Doctrine.[15]

I do not wish to exaggerate. Except in Iran, and perhaps also one or two other non-Arab Muslim states, the democratizers are still a relatively small group, and as yet their ranks seem to contain no one comparable in intellectual stature or moral and political influence to Sakharov or Solzhenitsyn or Sharansky. But the editor of the *Middle East Review of International Affairs*, Barry Rubin, who has generally been very skeptical about the chances for democratization in the region, offers a cautious assessment that seems reasonable to me:

> Democracy and reform are on the Arab world's agenda. It will be a long, uphill fight to bring change to those countries, but at least a process has begun. Liberals remain few and weak; the dictatorships are strong and the

[15] A representative sample can be found on the website of the Middle East Media Research Institute (http://www.memri.org/reform.html).

> Islamist threat will discourage openness or innovation. Still, at least there are more people trying to move things in the right direction.

To which I (though not Rubin) would add, thanks to George W. Bush.

Then there is Gaza, where at least some elements of the fabled Palestinian street have for the very first time exploded with denunciations not of Israel or the United States, but of Yasir Arafat's tyrannical and corrupt rule. For the first time, too, we find articles in the Arab press calling for Arafat's removal – in favor not of the Islamist alternative represented by Hamas but of a different kind of leadership.

Here, for example, is the *Jordan Times*:

> The rapid deterioration of the domestic political order in Gaza mirrors similar dilemmas that plague most of the Arab world, revolving around the tendency of small power elites or single men to monopolize political and economic power in their hands via their direct, personal control of domestic security and police systems. Gaza is yet another warning about the failure of the modern Arab security state and the need for a better brand of statehood based on law-based citizen rights rather than gun-based regime protection and perpetual incumbency.

And here is the *Arab Times* of Kuwait:

> Arafat should quit his position because he is the head of a corrupt authority. Arafat has destroyed Palestine. He has led it to terrorism, death, and a hopeless situation.

And there is this, from the *Gulf News* in Dubai:

> Palestinians are saying their president for life – Arafat – is the problem along with his cronies who rule them, rob them, and impoverish them. Arabs have a responsibility here too. They can say "Israel" until they are all blue in the face, but it does not change the fact that a large part of the fault lies with the Palestinians and the Arabs.

According to a Palestinian legislator quoted by the *Washington Post*, "what is happening in the streets of Gaza has [nothing] to do with reform. It's a simple power struggle." By contrast, the Iranian-born commentator Amir Taheri sees it as a new kind of "intifada aimed at bringing down yet another Arab tyranny." Chances are that there is some truth in both of these opposing judgments, and in any event it is still too early to tell how the turmoil in Gaza will play itself out. But it is surely not too early to say that there would have been no uprising against Arafat, and much less talk about reform, if not for George W. Bush's policies combined with his courageous willingness to back those of Ariel Sharon.

History's Call

In his first State of the Union address, President Bush affirmed that *history* had called America to action, and that it was both "our responsibility and our privilege to fight freedom's fight" - a fight he also characterized as "a unique opportunity for us to seize." Only last May, he reminded us that "We did not seek this war on terror," but, having been sought out by it, we responded, and now we were trying to meet the "great demands" that "history has placed on our country."

In this language, and especially in the repeated references to history, we can hear an echo of the concluding paragraphs of George F. Kennan's "X" essay, written at the outbreak of World War III:

> The issue of Soviet-American relations is in essence a test of the overall worth of the United States as a nation among nations. To avoid destruction the United States need only measure up to its own best traditions and prove itself worthy of preservation as a great nation.

Kennan then went on to his peroration:

> In the light of these circumstances, the thoughtful observer of Russian-American relations will experience a certain gratitude for a Providence which, by providing the American people with this implacable challenge, has made their entire security as a nation dependent on their pulling themselves together and accepting the responsibilities of moral and political leadership that history plainly intended them to bear.

Substitute "Islamic terrorism" for "Russian-American relations," and every other word of this magnificent statement applies to us as a nation today. In 1947, we accepted the responsibilities of moral and political leadership that history "plainly intended" us to bear, and for the next 42 years we acted on them. We may not always have acted on them wisely or well, and we often did so only after much kicking and screaming. But act on them we did. We thereby ensured our own "preservation as a great nation," while also bringing a better life to millions upon millions of people in a major region of the world.

Now "our entire security as a nation" - including, to a greater extent than in 1947, our physical security - once more depends on whether we are ready and willing to accept and act upon the responsibilities of moral and political leadership that history has yet again so squarely placed upon our shoulders. Are we ready? Are we willing? I think we are, but the jury is still out, and will not return a final verdict until well after the election of 2004.

FRANCIS FUKUYAMA

15 The Neoconservative Moment

ONE OF WASHINGTON'S MOST EXCLUSIVE CLUBS DURING THE 1990's was the annual board dinner of the *National Interest*. Presided over by founding editor Owen Harries and often kicked off with a presentation by Henry Kissinger, the group included Jeane Kirkpatrick, Irving, Bea, and Bill Kristol, Samuel Huntington, Paul Wolfowitz, Norman Podhoretz, Daniel Pipes, Charles Krauthammer, Marty Feldstein, Eliot Cohen, Peter Rodman, and a host of other conservative thinkers, writers, and doers, including just about everyone now characterized as a "neoconservative."

What I always found fascinating about these dinners was their unpredictability. People's views were very much set in concrete during the Cold War; while this group was divided into pro- and anti-détente camps, virtually everyone (myself included) had staked out territory years before. The Berlin Wall's fall brought a great change, and there was no clear mapping between one's pre-1989 views and the ones held thereafter. Roughly, the major fault line was between people who were more realist and those who were more idealist or Wilsonian. But everyone was trying to wrestle with the same basic question: In the wake of the disappearance of the overarching strategic threat posed by the former USSR, how did one define the foreign policy of a country that had suddenly become the global hegemon? How narrowly or broadly did one define this magazine's eponymous "national interest"?

It was at one of these dinners that Charles Krauthammer first articulated the idea of American unipolarity. In the winter of 1990–91, he wrote in *Foreign Affairs* of the "unipolar moment"; in the Winter 2002/03 issue of the *National Interest*, he expanded the scope of his thesis by arguing that "the unipolar moment has become the unipolar era." And in February 2004, he gave a speech at the annual dinner of the American Enterprise Institute in which he took his earlier themes and developed the ideas further, in the aftermath of the Iraq War. He defined four different schools of thought on foreign policy: isolationism, liberal internationalism, realism, and his own position that he defines as "democratic globalism," a kind of muscular Wilsonianism - minus international institutions - that seeks to use U.S. military supremacy to support U.S. security interests and democracy simultaneously.

Krauthammer is a gifted thinker and his ideas are worth taking seriously for their own sake. But, perhaps more importantly, his strategic thinking has become emblematic of a school of thought that has acquired strong influence inside the Bush Administration foreign policy team and beyond. It is for that reason that Krauthammer's writings, particularly his AEI speech, require careful analysis. It is in the spirit of our earlier debates that I offer the following critique.

* * *

The 2004 speech is strangely disconnected from reality. Reading Krauthammer, one gets the impression that the Iraq War - the archetypical application of American unipolarity - had been an unqualified success, with all of the assumptions and expectations on which the war had been based fully vindicated. There is not the slightest nod towards the new empirical facts that have emerged in the last year or so: the failure to find weapons of mass destruction in Iraq, the virulent and steadily mounting anti-Americanism throughout the Middle East, the growing insurgency in Iraq, the fact that no strong democratic leadership had emerged there, the enormous financial and growing human cost of the war, the failure to leverage the war to make progress on the Israeli-Palestinian front, and the fact that America's fellow democratic allies had by and large failed to fall in line and legitimate American actions *ex post*.

The failure to step up to these facts is dangerous precisely to the neo-neoconservative position that Krauthammer has been seeking to define and justify. As the war in Iraq turns from triumphant liberation to grinding insurgency, other voices - either traditional realists like Brent Scowcroft, nationalist-isolationists like Patrick Buchanan, or liberal internationalists like John Kerry - will step forward as authoritative voices and will have far more influence in defining American post-Iraq War foreign policy. The poorly executed nation-building strategy in Iraq will poison the well for future such exercises, undercutting domestic political support for a generous and visionary internationalism, just as Vietnam did.

It did not have to be this way. One can start with premises identical to Krauthammer's, agree wholeheartedly with his critiques of the other three positions, and yet come up with a foreign policy that is very different from the one he lays out. I believe that his strategy simultaneously defines our interests in such a narrow way as to make the neoconservative position indistinguishable from realism, while at the same time managing to be utterly unrealistic in its overestimation of U.S. power and our ability to control events around the world. It is probably too late to reclaim the label "neoconservative" for any but the policies undertaken by the Bush Administration, but it is still worth trying to reformulate a fourth alternative that combines idealism and realism - but in a fashion that can be sustained over the long haul.

Excessive Realism

Krauthammer and other commentators are correct that what is seen as "Kissingerian" realism is not an adequate basis for American foreign policy. A certain degree of messianic universalism with regard to American values and institutions has always been an inescapable component of American national identity: Americans were never comfortable with the kinds of moral compromises that a strict realist position entails. The question, which was the constant subject of those board dinners, was: What kinds of bounds do you put around the idealistic part of the agenda? Krauthammer answers this key question in the following manner:

> Where to intervene? Where to bring democracy? Where to nation-build? I propose a single criterion: where it counts. Call it democratic realism. And this is its axiom: *We will support democracy everywhere, but we will commit blood and treasure only in places where there is strategic necessity – meaning, places central to the larger war against the existential enemy, the enemy that poses a global mortal threat to freedom.* [italics in the original]

While this axiom appears to be clear and straightforward, it masks a number of ambiguities that make it less than helpful as a guideline for U.S. intervention. The first has to do with the phrase "strategic necessity," which of course can be defined more and less broadly. Krauthammer initially appears to be taking a realist position by opting for the narrow definition when he refers to an "existential enemy" or an enemy posing a "mortal" threat. If these words have any real meaning, then they should include only threats to our existence as a nation or as a democratic regime. There have been such threats in the past: the Soviet Union could have annihilated us physically and conceivably could have subverted democracy in North America. But it is questionable whether any such *existential* threats exist now. Iraq before the U.S. invasion was certainly not one: It posed an existential threat to Kuwait, Iran, and Israel, but it had no means of threatening the continuity of our regime. Al Qaeda and other radical Islamist groups aspire to be existential threats to American civilization but do not currently have anything like the capacity to actualize their vision: They are extremely dangerous totalitarians, but pose threats primarily to regimes in the Middle East.

This is not to say that Iraq and al Qaeda did not pose serious threats to American *interests*: the former was a very serious regional threat, and the latter succeeded in killing thousands of Americans on American soil. Use of WMD against the United States by a terrorist group would have terrible consequences, not just for the immediate victims but also for American freedoms in ways that could be construed as undermining our regime. But it is still of a lesser order of magnitude than earlier, state-based threats. The global Nazi and communist threats were existential both because their banner was carried by a great power, and because ideologically there were many people in the United States and throughout the Western world seduced by their vision. The Islamist threat has no such appeal, except perhaps in countries like France that have permitted high levels of immigration from Muslim countries.

I suspect that Krauthammer's intended use of the term "strategic necessity" is actually broader than is implied by his own words about existential threats. At the end of his axiom he leaps to the need to fight an "*enemy that poses a global mortal threat to freedom*," and elsewhere speaks of the United States as "custodian of the international system," suggesting a broadminded understanding of self-interest. Does "global" here mean threats that transcend specific regions, like radical Islamism or communism? If the enemy's reach has to be global, then North Korea would be excluded from the definition of a "strategic" threat. Or does "global" instead mean any mortal threat to freedom around the globe? Does the fact that an "enemy" poses a mortal threat to another free country but not to us qualify it as our "enemy?" Is Hamas, an Islamist group which clearly poses an existential threat to Israel, our enemy as well? Is Syria? And if these are our enemies, why should we choose to fight them in preference to threats to free countries closer to home like the FARC or ELN, which threaten democracy in Colombia, or Hugo Chavez in Venezuela? What makes something "central" in *this* global war? Was Iraq central to the war against radical Islamism?

It is clear that Krauthammer's axiom provides very little practical guidance for answering these questions. He might respond that applying the general principle requires prudential judgment. He might further respond that his position is very distinct from that of the realists because he is using democracy as an instrument to advance U.S. strategic interests: By transforming Iraqi politics and turning a bloodthirsty dictatorship into a Western-style democracy, new possibilities will open up for the entire region that promises to get at some of the root causes of terrorism. This is indeed an ambitious and highly idealistic agenda, and it is precisely in the prudential judgments underlying the current project of transforming the Middle East that his argument is fatally flawed.

Excessive Idealism

Of all of the different views that have now come to be associated with neoconservatives, the strangest one to me was the confidence that the United States could transform Iraq into a Western-style democracy, and go on from there to democratize the broader Middle East. It struck me as strange precisely because these same neoconservatives had spent much of the past generation warning – in the *National Interest*'s former sister publication, the *Public Interest*, for example – about the dangers of ambitious social engineering, and how social planners could never control behavior or deal with unanticipated consequences. If the United States cannot eliminate poverty or raise test scores in Washington, DC, how does it expect to bring democracy to a part of the world that has stubbornly resisted it and is virulently anti-American to boot?

Krauthammer picks up this theme in his speech. Noting how wrong people were after World War II in asserting that Japan could not democratize, he asks, "Where is it written that Arabs are incapable of democracy?" He is echoing an argument made most forthrightly by the eminent Middle East scholar Bernard Lewis, who has at several junctures suggested that pessimism about the prospects for a democratic Iraq betrays lack of respect for Arabs.

It is, of course, nowhere written that Arabs are incapable of democracy, and it is certainly foolish for cynical Europeans to assert with great confidence that democracy is impossible in the Middle East. We have, indeed, been fooled before, not just in Japan but in Eastern Europe prior to the collapse of communism.

But possibility is not likelihood, and good policy is not made by staking everything on a throw of the dice. Culture is not destiny, but culture plays an important role in making possible certain kinds of institutions – something that is usually taken to be a conservative insight. Though I, more than most people, am associated with the idea that history's arrow points to democracy, I have never believed that democracies can be created anywhere and everywhere through sheer political will. Prior to the Iraq War, there were many reasons for thinking that building a democratic Iraq was a task of a complexity that would be nearly unmanageable. Some reasons had to do with the nature of Iraqi society: the fact that it would be decompressing rapidly from totalitarianism, its ethnic divisions, the role of politicized religion, the society's propensity for violence, its tribal structure and the dominance of extended kin and patronage networks, and its susceptibility to influence from other parts of the Middle East that were passionately anti-American.

But other reasons had to do with the United States. America has been involved in approximately 18 nation-building projects between its conquest of the Philippines in 1899 and the current occupations of Afghanistan and Iraq, and the overall record is not a pretty one. The cases of unambiguous success – Germany, Japan, and South Korea – were all ones in which U.S. forces came and then stayed indefinitely. In the first two cases, we were not nation-building at all, but only re-legitimizing societies that had very powerful states. In all of the other cases, the U.S. either left nothing behind in terms of self-sustaining institutions, or else made things worse by creating, as in the case of Nicaragua, a modern army and police but no lasting rule of law.

This gets to a much more fundamental point about unipolarity. Krauthammer has always stressed the vast disparity of power between the United States and the rest of the world, vaster even than Rome's dominance at the height of its empire. But that dominance is clear-cut only along two dimensions of national power: the cultural realm and the ability to fight and win intensive conventional wars.

Americans have no particular taste or facility for nation-building; we want exit strategies rather than empires – a point Krauthammer reiterated at the start of his lecture. Where then does he think the domestic basis of support will come from for this unbelievably ambitious effort to politically transform one of the world's most troubled and hostile regions? And if the nation is really a commercial republic uncomfortable with empire, why is he so eager to expand its domain? Lurking like an unbidden guest at a dinner party is the reality of what has happened in Iraq since the U.S. invasion:

We have been our usual inept and disorganized selves in planning for and carrying out the reconstruction, something that was predictable in advance and should not have surprised anyone familiar with American history.

Allies, Institutions, and Legitimacy

The final area of weakness in Krauthammer's argument lies in his treatment of legitimacy, and how the United States relates to the rest of the world. Failure to appreciate America's own current legitimacy deficit hurts both the realist part of our agenda, by diminishing our actual power, and the idealist portion of it, by undercutting our appeal as the embodiment of certain ideas and values.

Krauthammer avoids confronting this issue by creating a bit of a parody of foreign critiques of American policy, something easily dismissed because it comes from "the butchers of Tiananmen Square or the cynics of the Quai d'Orsay." He manages to lump both the Democratic Party and most of our European allies into a single category of liberal internationalists. He argues that their opposition to the Iraq War was founded on a self-proclaimed normative commitment to multilateralism and international law. For liberal internationalists, war is legitimate only if it is sanctioned by the United Nations. But this high-mindedness, he argues, masks motives that are much baser: the Europeans are Lilliputians who want to tie the American Gulliver down and reduce American freedom of action. So they are both naive and hypocritical in the same breath.

What Krauthammer here describes as the Democratic/European position is one that is readily recognizable and does in fact characterize the views of many opponents of the Iraq War. But if he had listened carefully to what many Europeans were actually saying (something that Americans are not very good at doing these days), he would have discovered that much of their objection to the war was not a normative one having to do with procedural issues and the UN, but rather a prudential one having to do with the overall wisdom of attacking Iraq. Europeans tended not to be persuaded that Iraq was as dangerous as the Bush Administration claimed. They argued that Ba'athi Iraq had little to do with al Qaeda, and that attacking Iraq would be a distraction from the War on Terror. Many Europeans, moreover, did not particularly trust the United States to handle the postwar situation well, much less the more ambitious agenda of democratizing the Middle East. They believed that the ongoing Palestinian-Israeli conflict was a more dangerous source of instability and terrorism than Iraq and that the Bush Administration was undercutting its own credibility by appearing to side so strongly with the policies of Ariel Sharon.

All of these were and are, of course, debatable propositions. On the question of the threat posed by Iraq, everyone - Europeans and Americans - were evidently fooled into thinking that it possessed significant stockpiles of chemical and biological weapons. But on this issue, the European bottom line proved to be closer to the truth than the administration's far more alarmist position. The question of pre-war Iraq-al-Qaeda links has become intensely politicized in America since the war. My reading of the evidence is that these linkages existed (indeed, it would be very surprising if they did not), but that their significance was limited. We have learned since September 11 that al Qaeda did not need the support of a state like Iraq to do a tremendous amount of damage to the United States and that attacking Iraq was not the most direct way to get at al Qaeda. On the question of the manageability of postwar Iraq, the more skeptical European position was almost certainly right; the Bush Administration went into Iraq with enormous illusions about how easy the postwar situation would be. On the question of Palestine, the Europeans are likely wrong, or at least wrong in their belief that we could move to a durable settlement of the conflict if only the United States decided to use its influence with Israel.

The point here is not who is right, but rather that the prudential case was not nearly as open-and-shut as Krauthammer and other neoconservatives believe. He talks as if the Bush Administration's judgment had been vindicated at every turn, and that any questioning of it can only be the result of base or dishonest motives. Would that this were so. The fact that our judgment was flawed has created an enormous legitimacy problem for us, one that will hurt our interests for a long time to come.

* * *

The problem of judgment gets to the heart of what is wrong with the vision of a unipolar world that Krauthammer lays out. In his words, the United States "has been designated custodian of the international system" by virtue of its enormous margin of military superiority. If we had in fact been designated global custodian, we would have no legitimacy problem, but we have unfortunately designated ourselves. We have in effect said to the rest of the world, "look, trust us, we will look out for your interests. You can do this safely because we are not just any run-of-the-mill hyperpower. We are, after all, the United States." While we would not trust Russia, China, India, France, or even Britain with a similar kind of power, we believe that the rest of the world should trust us. This is because the United States is different from other countries, a democracy espousing universal values and therefore not subject to the same calculations of self-interest as other would-be hegemons.

There is actually something to this argument. But it is also not very difficult to see why it does not gain much traction outside the United States, and not just among those endemically hostile to America. Krauthammer-the-realist, after all, argues for a narrow definition of national interest, which does not suggest we will be a very reliable partner to a struggling friend when we do not have important interests at stake. And even if we were willing to bear other people's burdens, what about our judgment?

Legitimacy is a tricky concept. It is related to substantive principles of justice, but it is not the same thing as justice. That is, people believe that a set of institutions is legitimate because they believe they are just, but legitimacy is always relative to the people conferring legitimacy.

Legitimacy is important to us not simply because we want to feel good about ourselves, but because it is useful. Other people will follow the American lead if they believe that it is legitimate; if they do not, they will resist, complain, obstruct, or actively oppose what we do. In this respect, it matters not what *we* believe to be legitimate, but rather what *other* people believe is legitimate. If the Indian government says that it will not participate in a peacekeeping force in Iraq unless it has a UN Security Council mandate to do so, it does not matter in the slightest that we believe the Security Council to be an illegitimate institution: the Indians simply will not help us out.

Krauthammer and others have dismissed the importance of legitimacy by associating it entirely with the United Nations – and then shooting at that very easy target. Of course, the UN has deep problems with legitimacy. Since membership is not based on a substantive principle of legitimacy, but rather formal sovereignty, it has been populated from the beginning by a range of dictatorial and human-rights-abusing regimes. Our European allies themselves do not believe in the necessity of legitimization through the Security Council. When they found they could not get its support for the intervention in Kosovo because of the Russian veto, they were perfectly willing to bypass the UN and switch the venue to NATO instead.

But our legitimacy problem in Iraq went much deeper. Even if we had switched the venue to NATO – an alliance of democracies committed to the same underlying set of values – we could not have mustered a majority in support of our position, not to speak of the consensus required for collective action in that organization. The Bush Administration likes to boast of the size of the "coalition of the willing" that the United States was eventually able to pull together. One can take comfort in this only by abstracting from the *quality* of the support we received. Besides Britain and Australia, no one was willing to put boots on the ground during the active phase of combat, and now that post-conflict peacekeeping looks more like real warfare once again, Spain, Honduras, and other members of the coalition are pulling out. Those countries that did support the United States did so on the basis of an elite calculation of national interest - in almost all cases against the wishes of large majorities of their own populations. This is true alike for Tony Blair, our staunchest ally, and for Poland, the most pro-American country in Eastern Europe. While the behavior of Germany's Gerhard Schröder in actively opposing the war was deeply disappointing, I would still much rather have Germany on my side than a feckless and corrupt Ukraine.

* * *

It is clear, in other words, that a very large part of the world, including many people who are normally inclined to be our friends, did not believe in the legitimacy of our behavior towards Iraq. This is not because the Security Council failed to endorse the war, but because many of our friends did not trust us, that is, the Bush Administration, to use our huge margin of power wisely and in the interests of the world as a whole. This should matter to us, not just for realist reasons of state (our ability to attract allies to share the burden), but for idealist ones as well (our ability to lead and inspire based on the attractiveness of who we are).

I do not believe that the Bush Administration was in fact contemptuous of the need for legitimacy. What they believed and hoped, rather, was that legitimacy would be awarded *ex post* rather than *ex ante* by the international community. There was a widespread belief among members of the administration that once it became clear that the United States was going to disarm Iraq forcefully, other NATO allies including France would eventually come on board. Everyone was taken aback by the vehemence with which France and Germany opposed the war, and by the U.S. failure to line up normally compliant countries like Chile and Mexico during the Security Council vote.

The hope that we would be awarded *ex post* legitimacy was not an unreasonable calculation. It might indeed have materialized had the United States found a large and active WMD program in Iraq after the invasion, or if the transition to a democratic regime had been as quick and low-cost as the Bush Administration expected. Many people have argued that American unilateralism towards Iraq breaks a long pattern of transatlantic cooperation, but they are forgetting history. The United States during the Cold War repeatedly pushed its European allies to do things they were reluctant to do, often by staking out positions first and seeking approval later. In the end, American judgment on these issues was better than that of the Europeans, and legitimacy was in fact awarded retrospectively. When this happened, the United States was not blamed for unilateralism, but praised for its leadership.

One could then interpret the Iraq War simply as a one-time mistake or unfortunate miscalculation coming on the heels of a long string of successes. Certainly, it would be utterly wrong to conclude that the war teaches us that the United States should never stick its neck out and lead the broader Western world to actions that our allies oppose or are reluctant to undertake. Nor should we conclude that pre-emption and unilateralism will never be necessary.

On the other hand, it is not simply bad luck that we failed to win legitimacy as badly as we did this time. The world is different now than it was during the Cold War in ways that will affect our future ability to exert leadership and claim to speak on behalf of the world as a whole. This is so for three reasons.

The first difference is, of course, the demise of the Soviet Union and the absence of an overarching superpower threat. During the Cold War, there was rampant anti-Americanism around the world and popular opposition to U.S. policies. But our influence was anchored by center-right parties throughout Europe that were both grateful for America's historical role in the liberation of Europe and fearful of Soviet influence. The global terrorist threat may some day come to be interpreted in a similar fashion, but it is not yet.

A second difference has to do with the very fact of our military dominance. During the Cold War, when our power was more or less evenly matched against that of the Soviets, we cared a great deal about credibility and slippery slopes. We were afraid that withdrawal in the face of a challenge would be taken as a sign of weakness and exploited by the other side. Today, the United States is utterly dominant in the military sphere. Credibility in our willingness and ability to use force remains important, but we simply do not have to prove our toughness to the rest of the world at every turn.

The final difference has to do with the fact that the current battlefield is not Europe but the Middle East. There were always sharp differences of opinion between the United States and its allies on how to proceed with respect to the Soviet Union, but they pale in comparison to the differences between the United States and virtually everyone else in the world with respect to the Arab world. So it is to this issue that we must turn.

Dealing with the Middle East

Krauthammer has thought long and hard about the Israeli-Palestinian conflict, and his views on how the Israelis need to deal with the Palestinians color his views on how the United States should deal with the Arabs more broadly. Krauthammer has not supported strongly engaging the Arab world through political strategies. In the past, he has put forward a particular view of Arab psychology, namely, that they respect power above all as a source of legitimacy. As he once said in a radio interview, if you want to win their hearts and minds, you have grab a lower part of their anatomy and squeeze hard.

Towards the end of his AEI speech, Krauthammer speaks of the United States as being in the midst of a bitter and remorseless war with an implacable enemy that is out to destroy Western civilization. This kind of language is appropriate as a description of Israel's strategic situation since the outbreak of the second *intifada*. The question is whether this accurately describes the position of the United States as well. Are we like Israel, locked in a remorseless struggle with a large part of the Arab and Muslim world, with few avenues open to us for dealing with them other than an iron fist? And in general, does a strategic doctrine developed by a small, vulnerable country surrounded by implacable enemies make sense when applied to the situation of the world's sole superpower, a country that spends as much on defense as the next 16 most powerful countries put together?

I believe that there are real problems in transposing one situation to the other. While Israel's most immediate Arab interlocutors are indeed implacable enemies, the United States faces a much more complex situation. In al Qaeda and other radical Islamist groups, we do in fact confront an enemy that hates us for what we are rather than for what we do. For the reasons given above, I do not believe they are an existential threat to us, but they certainly would like to be, and it is hard to see how we can deal with them other than by killing, capturing, or otherwise militarily neutralizing them.

But the radicals swim in a much larger sea of Muslims – 1.2 billion of them, more or less – who are not yet implacable enemies of the United States. If one has any doubts about this, one has only to look at the first of the United Nations Development Program's two *Arab Human Development* reports, which contained a poll asking whether respondents would like to emigrate to the United States if they had the opportunity. In virtually every Arab country, a majority of respondents said yes. On the other hand, recent Pew surveys of global public opinion show that positive feelings about the United States in Jordan, Egypt, Turkey, Pakistan, and other supposedly friendly Muslim countries has sunk to disastrously low levels. What these data taken as a whole suggest is that for the broad mass of public opinion in Muslim countries, we are disliked or hated not for what we are, but rather for what we do. What they do not like is a familiar list of complaints about our foreign policy that we somehow continue to fail to take seriously: our lack of concern for the plight of the Palestinians, our hypocritical support for dictators in Muslim countries, and now our occupation of Iraq.

The War on Terror is, in other words, a classic counter-insurgency war, except that it is one being played out on a global scale. There are genuine bad guys out there who are much more bitter ideological enemies than the Soviets ever were, but their success depends on the attitudes of the broader populations around them who can be alternatively supportive, hostile or indifferent - depending on how we play our cards. As we are seeing vividly in Iraqi cities like Fallujah and Najaf, counter-insurgency wars are incredibly difficult to fight, because we must somehow destroy the enemy without alienating the broader population and making things worse. Counter-insurgency requires a tricky mixture of precisely targeted force, political judgment, and extremely good intelligence: a combination of carrots and sticks.

Israel used carrots during the Oslo process and then shifted to sticks after its collapse and the beginning of the second *intifada*. I do not want to second-guess either of these approaches, neither of which seems to have worked very well. But an American policy toward the Muslim world that, like Sharon's, is largely stick will be a disaster: we do not have enough sticks in our closet to "make them respect us." The Islamists for sure hated us from the beginning, but Krauthammerian unipolarity has increased hatred for the United States in the broader fight for hearts and minds. This suggests that we need a much more complex strategy that recalibrates the proportion of sticks and carrots. This has begun to happen with the leaking of the Bush Administration's Greater Middle East Initiative, but that is only the beginning of a much longer political struggle.

Israel's policy of constantly being on the offensive, pre-empting, and taking the initiative (as in its policy of targeted assassinations) is also something that does not scale well. Unlike Israel, the United States has a substantial margin of strategic depth and does not constantly have to run risks in order to stay on top. A sole superpower that is seen being as inclined to intervene pre-emptively and often will frighten not just its enemies but its friends as well. The United States must never abjure its right to pre-empt, but it is a right that needs to be exercised cautiously. Even talking about such a strategy, as we did in the *National Security Strategy* document, will tend to promote opposing coalitions and resistance to U.S. policies. Israel can afford to antagonize potential allies and disregard international public opinion as long as it can count on support from the United States. The United States could, I suppose, survive if it were similarly isolated, but it is hard to see why we would want to put ourselves in this position. It is hardly an advantageous position from which to launch an idealistic Wilsonian crusade to reshape the Middle East in our image.

What Now?

Since I have volunteered only to write a critique of the views expressed by Charles Krauthammer and am not myself running for president, I am under no obligation to lay out in depth a positive agenda for American foreign policy that would serve as a substitute. On the other hand, there are elements of a different neoconservative foreign policy that are implicit in what I have said thus far. The United States should understand the need to exercise power in pursuit of both its interests and its values, but also to be more prudent and subtle in that exercise. The world's sole superpower needs to remember that its margin of power is viewed with great suspicion around the world and will set off countervailing reactions if that power is not exercised judiciously.

This means, in the first instance, doing the simple work of diplomacy and coalition-building that the Bush Administration seemed reluctant to undertake prior to the Iraq War and not gratuitously to insult the "common opinions of mankind." We do not need to embrace the UN or multilateralism for its own sake, because we somehow believe that such institutions are inherently more legitimate than nation-states. On the other hand, we need likeminded allies to accomplish both the realist and the idealist portions of our agenda and should spend much more time and energy cultivating them.

The promotion of democracy through all of the available tools at our disposal should remain high on the agenda, particularly with regard to the Middle East. But the United States needs to be more realistic about its nation-building abilities, and cautious in taking on large social-engineering projects in parts of the world it does not understand very well. On the other hand, it is inevitable that we will get sucked into similar projects in the future (for example, after a sudden collapse of the North Korean regime), and we need to be much better prepared. This means establishing a permanent office with authority and resources appropriate for the job the next time around as part of a broader restructuring of the U.S. government's soft-power agencies.

To this list I would add a final element that for reasons of space I cannot elaborate here. The visionary founders of the postwar order were institution-builders, who created not just the much-maligned UN system, but the Bretton Woods institutions, NATO, the U.S.-Japan and U.S.-Korea alliances, the GATT, the WTO, and a host of other international organizations. Institution-building is not something that has occupied the time of officials in the Bush Administration, but it should. If the United States does not like the fact that the UN is dominated by non-democratic regimes, then it should invest in an effort to build up other institutions, like NATO or the Community of Democracies founded during the Clinton Administration, that are based on norms and values we share. The Community of Democracies initiative, which the French foreign minister Hubert Védrine tried to strangle at its birth, was never taken seriously by the Republicans, for, I assume, "not invented here" reasons. But such a global alliance of democracies, led by newer ones in Eastern Europe and Latin America, could play a legitimizing function around the world in a way that NATO cannot.

If the United States cannot create new global institutions, then it could try to pursue a vision of overlapping multilateral organizations on a regional basis. The Bush Administration has stumbled into a six-power format for dealing with North Korea; why not seek to make permanent a five-power caucus once we (hopefully) get past the current impasse over nuclear weapons with Pyongyang? Such an organization could play a very valuable coordinating function in the event of, say, a sudden North Korean collapse. Mutual suspicions between Japan, Korea, and China are high, and a multilateral forum would be a much better vehicle for sharing information and plans than the current system of bilateral alliances running through Washington. The Chinese in recent years have been pushing a series of regional pacts – ASEAN Plus Three, the China-ASEAN Free Trade Area, a Northeast Asian Free Trade Area, and ultimately, an East Asian Free Trade Area – that they argue may some day serve as the basis for regional security arrangements as well. While the Japanese have seen these as bids for regional leadership and have replied in kind with trade pacts centered on themselves, the Bush Administration has not, as far as I am aware, formulated anything like a coherent response. Do we simply want to swat down proposals for regional multilateral organizations, as we did in the case of Mahatir's East Asian Community in the early 1990's or Japan's proposal after the Asian financial crisis for a regional IMF, or do we want to engage with the region and shape such proposals in ways that can suit our own interests? I believe that East Asia is under-institutionalized and ripe for some creative thinking by the United States.

I believe that this kind of recalibration of American foreign policy still qualifies as falling in Krauthammer's fourth "democratic globalism" basket, being neither isolationist, liberal-idealist, nor realist. Whether it will ever be seen as neoconservative I doubt, but there is no reason why it should not have this title.

CHARLES KRAUTHAMMER

16 In Defense of Democratic Realism

On February 10, 2004, I delivered the Irving Kristol Lecture to the American Enterprise Institute outlining a theory of foreign policy that I called democratic realism. It was premised on the notion that the 1990's were a holiday from history, an illusory period during which we imagined that the existential struggles of the past six decades against the various totalitarianisms had ended for good. September 11 reminded us rudely that history had not ended, and we found ourselves in a new existential struggle, this time with an enemy even more fanatical, fatalistic, and indeed undeterable than in the past. Nonetheless, we had one factor in our favor. With the passing of the Soviet Union, we had entered a unique period in human history, a unipolar era in which America enjoys a predominance of power greater than any that has existed in the half-millennium of the modern state system. The challenge of the new age is whether we can harness that unipolar power to confront the new challenge, or whether we rely, as we did for the first decade of the post-Cold War era, on the vague internationalism that characterizes the foreign policy thinking of European elites and American liberalism.

The speech and the subsequent AEI monograph have occasioned some comment. None, however, as loquacious as Frank Fukuyama's twelve-page rebuttal in the previous issue of the *National Interest*. His essay is doubly useful. It is a probing critique of democratic realism, yet demonstrates inadvertently how little the critics have to offer as an alternative.

Democratic Realism

In my speech I describe the four major schools of American foreign policy. *Isolationism* defines the American national interest extremely narrowly and essentially wishes to pull up the drawbridge to Fortress America. Unfortunately, in the age of the supersonic jet, the submarine, and the ballistic missile, to say nothing of the suitcase bomb, the fortress has no moat, and the drawbridge, as was demonstrated on 9/11, cannot be drawn up. Isolationism has a long pedigree, but today it is a theory of nostalgia and reaction. It is as defunct post-9/11 as it was on December 11, 1941, the day the America First Committee disbanded.

More important is *liberal internationalism*, the dominant school of American liberalism and of the foreign policy establishment. Its pillars are (a) legalism, the construction of a web of treaties and agreements that will bind the international community in a normative web; (b) multilateralism, acting in concert with other countries in pursuit of "international legitimacy"; and (c) humanitarianism, a deep suspicion of national interest as a justification for projecting power – hence the congressional Democrats' overwhelming 1991 vote against the Gulf War, followed by a Democratic administration that launched humanitarian military interventions in Haiti, Bosnia, and Kosovo. Liberal internationalists see national interest as a form of communal selfishness and thus as inimical to their true objective: the construction of a new international system that mimics domestic society, being based on law, treaties, covenants, understandings, and norms that will ultimately abolish power politics. To do so, liberal internationalism is prepared to yield America's unique unipolar power piece by piece by subsuming it into the new global architecture in which America becomes not the arbiter of international events but a good and tame international citizen.

The third school, *realism*, emphasizes the primacy of power in international relations. It recognizes that the international system is a Hobbesian state of nature, not to be confused with the settled order of domestic society that enjoys a community of values, a monopoly of power, and most important, an enforcer of norms – all of which are lacking in the international system. Realism has no use for a liberal internationalism that serves only to divert the United States from its real tasks. The United States spent the 1990's, for example, endlessly negotiating treaties on the spread of WMD, which would have had absolutely no effect on the very terrorists and rogue states that are trying to get their hands on these weapons.

Realism has the virtue of most clearly understanding the new unipolarity and its uses, including the unilateral and pre-emptive use of power if necessary. But in the end, pure realism in any American context fails because it offers no vision beyond power. It is all means and no ends. It will not play in a country that was built on a proposition and that sees itself as the carrier of the democratic idea.

Hence, the fourth school, *democratic globalism*, often incorrectly called neoconservatism. It sees the spread of democracy, "the success of liberty," as John F. Kennedy put it in his inaugural address, as both the ends and the means of foreign policy. Its most public spokesmen, George W. Bush and Tony Blair, have sought to rally America and the world to a struggle over values. Its response to 9/11 is to engage in a War on Terror whose essential element is the global spread of democracy.

Democratic globalism is an improvement on realism because it understands the utility of democracy as a means for achieving global safety and security. Realists undervalue internal democratic structures. They see the state system as an arena of colliding billiard balls. Realists have little interest in what is inside. Democratic globalists understand that as a rule, fellow democracies provide the most secure alliances and most stable relationships. Therefore the spread of democracy – understood not just as elections, but as limited government, protection of minorities, individual rights, the rule of law, and open economies – has ultimately not just moral but geopolitical value.

The problem with democratic globalism, as I argued in my address, is that it is too ambitious and too idealistic. The notion, expressed by Tony Blair, that "the spread of freedom is . . . our last line of defense and our first line of attack" is a bridge too far. "The danger of democratic globalism," I wrote, "is its universalism, its open-ended commitment to human freedom, its temptation to plant the flag of democracy everywhere." Such a worldwide crusade would overstretch our resources, exhaust our morale and distract us from our central challenge. I therefore suggested an alternative, *democratic realism*, that is "targeted, focused, and limited," that intervenes not everywhere that freedom is threatened but only where it counts – in those regions where the defense or advancement of freedom is critical to success in the larger war against the existential enemy. That is how we fought the Cold War. The existential enemy then was Soviet communism. Today, it is Arab/Islamic radicalism. Therefore "where it really counts today is in that Islamic crescent stretching from North Africa to Afghanistan."

An Existential Threat

At its most fundamental, Fukuyama's critique is that I am misreading the new world because there is no existential struggle. By calling our war with Arab/Islamic radicalism existential, I exaggerate the threat and thus distort the whole fabric of American foreign policy. "Krauthammer," he writes, "speaks of the United States as being in the midst of a bitter and remorseless war with an implacable enemy that is out to destroy Western civilization." "Speaks of" – as one might speak of flying saucers. In reality, asserts Fukuyama, "al Qaeda and other radical Islamist groups aspire to be existential threats to American civilization but do not currently have anything like the capacity to actualize their vision."

Fukuyama apparently believes that the phrase "not currently" saves him from existential peril. But the problem is that precisely as we speak, al Qaeda is energetically trying to make up for the deficiencies from which Fukuyama so complacently derives comfort. When Hitler marched into the Rhineland in 1936, he did not "currently" have the means to overrun Europe. Many Europeans believed, delusionally, that he did not present an existential threat. By Fukuyama's logic, they were right.

What defines an existential threat is intent, objective, and potential capability. Existential struggle is a struggle over existence and identity. Until it lost heart late in life, Soviet communism was utterly committed to the eradication of what it called capitalism, in other words, the entire way of life of the West. Its mission was to do to the world what it had done to, say, Lithuania and Czechoslovakia – remake it in its image. Existential struggle is a fight to the end – extermination or, even better, conversion. That is what distinguishes it from non-existential struggles, in which the contending parties in principle can find compromise (over territory or resources or power).

Fukuyama is unimpressed with radical Islam because, in his view, it lacks the global appeal of such true existential threats as communism and Nazism. But Nazism had little global appeal. A master-race theory hardly plays well among the other races. Did it really have more sympathizers and fifth columnists in the West than does Islamism today? Islamist cells are being discovered regularly in just about every European capital, and some even in the United States. And these, of course, are just the fifth columnists we know about. The thought is sobering, given how oblivious we were to the presence among us of the 9/11 plotters. Just because Islamism in the West may not, like its Nazi or communist counterparts, take the form of a political party or capture Western celebrity intellectuals, does not minimize the threat or the power of its appeal. Radical Islam does not have its Sartre or its Pound. It is the conceit of intellectuals to think that this counts for more than a Richard Reid, armed this time not with a shoe-bomb but a nuclear suitcase or consignment of anthrax.

Disdaining the appeal of radical Islam is the conceit also of secularists. Radical Islam is not just as fanatical and unappeasable in its anti-Americanism, anti-Westernism, and anti-modernism as anything we have ever known. It has the distinct advantage of being grounded in a venerable religion of over one billion adherents that not only provides a ready supply of recruits – trained and readied in mosques and *madrassas* far more effective, autonomous, and ubiquitous than any Hitler Youth or Komsomol camp – but is able to draw on a long and deep tradition of zeal, messianic expectation, and a cult of martyrdom. Hitler and Stalin had to invent these out of whole cloth. Mussolini's version was a parody. Islamic radicalism flies under a flag with far more historical depth and enduring appeal than the ersatz religions of the swastika and hammer-and-sickle that proved so historically thin and insubstantial.

* * *

Fukuyama does not just underestimate the power of religion. He underestimates the power of technology. He is trapped in the notion that only Great Powers can threaten other Great Powers. Because the enemy today does not resemble a Germany or a Japan, the threat is "of a lesser order of magnitude." For a realist, he is remarkably blind to the revolution that technology has brought. The discovery of nuclear power is the greatest "order of magnitude" leap in potential destructiveness since the discovery of fire. True, the atomic bomb was detonated half a century ago; but the democratization of the knowledge of how to make it is new. Chemical and biological weapons are perhaps a century old; but the diffusion of the capacity to develop them is new. Radical Islam's obvious intent is to decapitate the American polity, cripple its economy, and create general devastation. We have seen what a mere 19 Islamists can do in the absence of WMD. We have seen what but two envelopes of mail-delivered anthrax can do to the world's most powerful capital. Imagine what a dozen innocuous vans in a dozen American cities dispersing aerosolized anthrax could do. Imagine what just a handful of the world's loose nukes, detonated simultaneously in New York, Washington, Chicago, and just a few other cities, would do to the United States. America would still exist on the map. But what kind of country – and what kind of polity – would be left? If that is not an existential threat, nothing is.

Fukuyama, of course, has a stake in denying the obvious nature of the threat, having made his reputation proclaiming the "end of history," which, if it means anything, means an end to precisely this kind of ideological existential threat. One can understand how he would be loath to acknowledge that history has returned, that the 1990's were not the end of history but a holiday from history, and that we find ourselves once again, sadly but unmistakably, with everything at stake. But he goes further. He has so persuaded himself in denial of this new reality that he needs some psychological reason to account for why I and other neoconservatives are so inexplicably convinced that we are in an existential struggle. His answer: Neoconservatives apparently identify so strongly with Israel that they have come to confuse America's predicament with Israel's. Neoconservatives think the United States is in the same boat as Israel. Fukuyama points out that it is not.

This is bizarre. Of course the United States is not in the same predicament as Israel. So what? You do not have to be Israel to be existentially threatened. If Israel's predicament represents the standard for existential threat, then the West never experienced it during the six decades of anti-fascist, anti-communist struggle that Fukuyama himself insists was existential. Israel is threatened with Carthaginian extinction. France was conquered by Nazi Germany, and is still France today. Poland and Hungary were conquered by the Soviet Union, and have become Poland and Hungary again. If Israel had been conquered in any of its wars, it would not be Israel today, nor ever again. Simply not matching up to the Israeli standard says nothing about whether one is engaged in an existential struggle.

What is interesting about Fukuyama's psychological speculation is that it allows him a novel way of Judaizing neoconservatism. His is not the crude kind, advanced by Pat Buchanan and Malaysia's Mahathir Mohamad, among others, that American neoconservatives (read: Jews) are simply doing Israel's bidding, hijacking American foreign policy in the service of Israel and the greater Jewish conspiracy. Fukuyama's take is more subtle and implicit. One is to understand that those spreading the mistaken idea that the War on Terror is existential are neoconservatives so deeply and unconsciously identified with the Jewish state that they cannot help seeing the world through its eyes.

What makes this idea quite ridiculous is that the leading proponents of the notion of existential threat are George Bush and Tony Blair. How did they come to their delusional identification with Israel? The American war cabinet consists of Dick Cheney, Colin Powell, Don Rumsfeld, and Condoleezza Rice. They speak passionately of the existential nature of the threat to the United States. Are they Marranos, or have they been hypnotized by "neoconservatives" into sharing the tribal bond?

"Neoconservatism"

Fukuyama entitles his critique, "The Neoconservative Moment," a play on the first exposition of my theory, "The Unipolar Moment," published 14 years ago. His intent is to take down the entire neoconservative edifice. His method is to offer a "careful analysis" of "Krauthammer's writings, particularly his AEI speech," because "his strategic thinking has become emblematic of a school of thought," that is, neoconservatism.

What Fukuyama fails to understand is that there are two major strains of neoconservative thinking on foreign policy, not one. There is the democratic globalism advocated by Blair and Bush and long elaborated by such thinkers as Robert Kagan and Bill Kristol. And there is the democratic realism that I and others have long advanced. Both are "democratic" because they advocate the spread of democracy as both an end and a means of American foreign policy. But one is "realism" because it rejects the universalist scope and high idealism of democratic "globalism" and always requires geopolitical necessity as a condition for intervention. This is hardly just a theoretical debate. It has very practical consequences. They were on stark display just half a decade ago, when there was a fundamental split among conservatives on the question of intervention in the Balkans. At the time, Kagan and Kristol (among many others) were strong advocates of intervention in the Balkans and of the war over Kosovo. I was not. I argued then, as I argue now, that while humanitarian considerations are necessary for any American intervention, they are not sufficient. American intervention must always be strategically grounded. In the absence of a strategic imperative, it is better to keep one's powder dry, precisely because that powder might be necessary to meet some coming strategic threat. On 9/11, that strategic threat revealed itself.

At the time of Kosovo, many realists took the same position I did, while many democratic globalists (lazily just called "neoconservatives") took the opposite view and criticized my reservations about intervention as a betrayal of democratic principles. Fukuyama's essay does not just conflate these two distinct foreign policy schools. He repeatedly characterizes me as a champion of democratic globalism, the school with which I explicitly take issue. (Thus: "his [Krauthammer's] own position that he defines as 'democratic globalism'. . . . ") It is odd in the extreme to write a long critique of a speech and monograph entitled "Democratic Realism" and then precis that critique thus: "Krauthammer's democratic globalism fails as a guiding principle of foreign policy and creates more questions than answers." Perhaps Fukuyama believes that he alone has a proprietary right to the word "realism." Perhaps he believes that by misrepresenting me as a globalist he can then identify me with every twist and turn of the Blair and Bush foreign policies.

One of the reasons I gave this speech is that I thought the universalist, bear-any-burden language of both Blair and Bush to advance the global spread of democracy is too open-ended and ambitious. The alternative I proposed tries to restrain the idealistic universalism with the realist consideration of strategic necessity. Hence the central axiom of democratic realism:

> We will support democracy everywhere, but we will commit blood and treasure only in places where there is a strategic necessity – meaning, places central to the larger war against the existential enemy, the enemy that poses a global mortal threat to freedom.

* * *

Fukuyama finds this central axiom "less than helpful as a guideline for U.S. intervention" because "it masks a number of ambiguities." He asks the following questions.

Does "global" here mean threats that transcend specific regions, like radical Islamism or communism?

Yes.

If the enemy's reach has to be global, then North Korea would be excluded from the definition of a "strategic" threat.

Yes. North Korea is a discrete problem. Islamism is not our only problem, no more than Soviet communism was our only problem in the second half of the 20th century. There can be others, though they are of a lesser order. North Korea is not on a deliberate mission to spread *Juche* communism around the globe or to destroy the United States. Its mission is regime survival, with intimations of threat to South Korea. Its ambitions do not extend beyond that. Which is why it is a very different kind of threat from the existential Arab/Islamist one we face, and falls outside the central imperative. It needs to be contained. But there is no imperative for its invasion, overthrow, and reconstruction – unless we find that, for commercial and regime-sustaining reasons, it is selling WMD to our real existential enemy. Under these circumstances it would be joining the global war on the other side.

Or does "global" instead mean any mortal threat to freedom around the globe?

Any serious threat to what was once known as the "free world" as a whole is "global." In the 1930's and 1940's, that meant fascism. In the second half of the 20th century, that meant communism. Today it means Arab/Islamic radicalism.

Does the fact that an "enemy" poses a mortal threat to another free country, but not to us, qualify it as our "enemy"?

No.

Is Hamas, an Islamist group which clearly poses an existential threat to Israel, our enemy as well?

As it defines itself today, as an enemy of Israel, no. Were it to join the war on the United States, then the answer would be yes.

Is Syria?

Because of its hostility to Israel? No. To the extent, however, that it allies itself with and supports the jihadists in Iraq, it risks joining the enemy camp.

And if these are our enemies, why should we choose to fight them in preference to threats to free countries closer to home like the FARC or ELN, which threaten democracy in Colombia, or Hugo Chavez in Venezuela?

We should not. See above.

What makes something "central" in this global war?

Whether a change in the political direction of a state or territory will have an important, perhaps decisive, effect in defeating Arab/Islamic radicalism. Afghanistan meets that test. So does Iraq.

Legitimacy

This is not terribly complicated. What then is Fukuyama's quarrel with democratic realism? He seems to accept democratic realism as a theory but then condemns it in practice because . . . well, because of Iraq. He has enthusiastically joined the crowd seizing upon the difficulties in Iraq as a refutation of any forward-looking policy that might have gotten us there, most specifically, any unilateralist, nation-building policy that got us there. Iraq, he says, is a mess, and the experience proves two things: the importance of "international legitimacy" and the futility of U.S. nation-building among Arabs.

On legitimacy, Fukuyama endorses my view that international support does not confer superior morality upon any action – other nations are acting out of self-interest, not priestly wisdom. He admits that the United Nations has "deep problems with legitimacy," and that Kosovo demonstrated that our European allies themselves do not believe in the necessity of legitimization through the Security Council. Nonetheless, he charges me with being too dismissive of the practical utility of international support and approval.

But no one denies the utility of international support. Of course there are practical advantages to having Security Council approval, NATO assistance, or whatever political cover that might induce, say, India or Turkey to offer assistance. You seek whatever approval, assistance, cover you can get. You even make accommodations and concessions to get it. None of this is in dispute. The only serious question is how far you go. Is "legitimacy" a limiting factor? When you fail to get it, do you abandon the policy? Should we have abandoned our policy of regime change in Iraq – military force being the only way to achieve it – because we lacked sufficient cover?

Fukuyama seems to be saying yes, we should have – although he deploys a Kerry-like ambiguity about what he would actually have done. He seems to be saying that we should have deferred to the opposition of our allies and to the absence of an international consensus, and not invaded Iraq – and that our experience in the aftermath of the war supports that prudential judgment.

But this assumes two things:

First, that a lack of legitimacy is the cause of our postwar problems. Our central problem, of course, has been the Sunni insurgency and the Moqtada Sadr rebellion. I hardly think that either of these groups, or the foreign jihadists who have come to join them, are impressed by UN resolutions. Indeed, the Security Council passed a unanimous postwar resolution legitimizing the American occupation. The UN even established a major presence in Baghdad right after the war. The insurgents were unimpressed: They blew the UN headquarters to smithereens. It is possible that we will fail to defeat these insurgencies, but the "legitimacy deficit" will hardly be the reason.

Second, it assumes that the choice in March 2003 was between invasion and postwar difficulties on the one hand and pre-invasion stability on the other. It assumes there were no serious prudential considerations that impelled us towards war. Of course the lack of Franco-German support made things more difficult. Of course the lack of international consensus constituted a prudential reason not to invade. But Fukuyama assumes these were the only prudential considerations, that doing nothing about Iraq had no cost, that the Iraq problem before the war was in some kind of sustainable equilibrium. It was not. The tense post-Gulf War settlement was unstable and created huge and growing liabilities for all concerned, most especially for the United States. First, it caused enormous suffering for the Iraqi people under a cruel and corrupt sanctions regime - suffering and starvation that throughout the Middle East and in much of Europe were blamed squarely on the United States. Second, the standoff with Iraq made it necessary to maintain a large American garrison in Saudi Arabia, land of the Islamic holy places - for many Muslims, a provocative and deeply offensive presence. Indeed, in his 1998 fatwa against the United States, Bin Laden listed these two offenses as crimes numbers one and two justifying jihad against America.

Moreover, the sanctions regime was collapsing. That collapse was temporarily halted by the huge pre-war infusion of American troops into Kuwait that forced the Security Council to reaffirm the sanctions - but only as a way to avert an American invasion. The troop deployment was itself unsustainable. Upon its withdrawal, the collapse of the sanctions regime would have continued, resulting in a re-energized and relegitimized regime headed by Saddam (and ultimately, even worse, by his sons) that was increasingly Islamicizing its Ba'athi ideology, re-arming and renewing WMD programs, and extending its connections with terror groups. As the quintessential realist Henry Kissinger wrote recently - in the full light and awareness of our postwar troubles - of "the calculus for preemption":

> Could the United States wait until weapons were actually produced by a country with the largest army in the region, the second-largest potential oil income, a record of having used these weapons against its own population and neighbors, and - according to the Sept. 11 commission - intelligence contact with Al-Qaeda?

There is no dispute that a paucity of international support is a prudential consideration in any major decision. But in Iraq, the paucity of international support is not the source of our troubles today, and before the war it was far outweighed by the prudential considerations in favor of removing Saddam. And finally, in any decision, the legitimacy issue is never decisive. In the 1980's, our European allies were almost universally opposed to American support for the Nicaraguan Contras. The common opinion of mankind was that American imperialism was trying to bring back Somozism. The policy had zero "international legitimacy." If Fukuyama's belief in international legitimacy is real, that should have been grounds for abandoning the policy - a policy that was right at the time and that history has decisively vindicated.

Nation-Building

The last of Fukuyama's questions about my "central axiom" was this: Was Iraq central to the war against radical Islamism? I believe it was and is. I argued that before the war, and I believe it is all the more true today. September 11 led to the inexorable conclusion that a half-century of American policy towards the Arab world had failed. Ever since Franklin Roosevelt made alliance with King Ibn Saud, the United States has chosen to leave the Arab world to its own political and social devices, so long as it remained a reasonably friendly petrol station. The arrangement lasted a very long time. Had 9/11 never happened, it would have lasted longer. The policy of Arab exceptionalism was never enunciated, but it was universally understood: America was pursuing democratization in Europe, East Asia, South and Central America - everywhere except the Arab world. Democratization elsewhere was remarkably successful and was the key to stability and pacification. The Arab exception proved costly. On 9/11, we reaped the whirlwind from that policy and finally understood that it was untenable. We could continue to fight Arab/Islamic radicalism by catching a terrorist leader here, rolling up a cell there. Or we could go to the heart of the problem and take the risky but imperative course of trying to reorder the Arab world. Success in Iraq would be a singular victory in the war on radical Islam. Failure in Iraq would be a singular defeat.

I never underestimated the task. I have written before, during, and after the war that the task was enormous, the risk great, and failure possible - but that the undertaking was necessary.

Fukuyama never addresses the necessity question. Instead, he invokes our difficulties and setbacks to discredit the very idea of nation-building in the Middle East, not just because of local conditions but because Americans are no good at nation-building. Iraq is a fool's errand that was bound to fail:

> We have been our usual inept and disorganized selves in planning for and carrying out the reconstruction, something that was predictable in advance.

Curiously, however, Fukuyama never predicted it in advance. He waited a year to ascertain wind direction, then predicted what had already occurred. At the time of decision before the war, Fukuyama now tells the *New York Times*, he had private doubts which he kept to himself: He did not think the war was wise, but "for all I knew, it might have worked." At the time, then, failure was not "predictable in advance," after all.

And how does he come to predict now? He writes as if the history to come has already been written. It has not. Iraq is rid of Saddam, and its future is in play. We are in the midst of a generational struggle, both in the War on Terror in general and in the reconstruction of Iraq. Fukuyama's unmistakable conclusion that Iraq is lost is, to put it mildly, premature. It is reminiscent of John Dos Passos's famous 1946 essay, "Americans are Losing the Victory in Europe." We have made serious mistakes in Iraq. We may yet fail. But Fukuyama's conclusion that Americans are simply no good at nation-building is retrospective presumption. We have succeeded in the monumental task of reconstructing Germany, Japan, and South Korea. We failed in Haiti and Somalia. What was the principal difference? Great knowledge of the local culture? Democratic tradition? In Korea we did not have any great knowledge of the culture nor did Korea have a democratic tradition upon which to draw. Yet South Korea is a remarkable success.

What was the key? Strategic value. When the stakes were high, and correctly perceived at home as such, we stayed the course and devoted the requisite effort and time to succeed. Where the strategic stakes were minimal, as in Haiti or Somalia, we failed because we correctly understood that nation-building is a huge task and that these places were not remotely worth the cost. The single most important factor in the success of nation-building is seriousness.

To say that the country that rebuilt Germany and Japan and South Korea from rubble – perhaps the three greatest achievements in nation-building ever – is intrinsically no good at the job is silly. And if that is the case, by the way, should we not be cutting our losses in Afghanistan as well, since it is far more tribal, primitive, and underdeveloped than Iraq?

* * *

What is remarkable about Fukuyama's pessimism about the spread of democracy in an enormous swath of humanity and amid one of its most venerable civilizations is that not long ago he declared that all of humanity had already made the critical turn toward democracy and its triumph was inevitable. As he now admits, "I, more than most people, am associated with the idea that history's arrow points to democracy." Except among Arabs, it seems. One searches Fukuyama's essay for a single "hearts and minds" idea to give "history's arrow" a bit of nudge in this critical region. What does one find? A single passing reference to the Bush Administration's "Greater Middle East Initiative," a tepid State Department aid and exchange program of democratic engagement – already hopelessly watered-down and understood by all to be a facade.

This will not do. Before 9/11 we were content to wait passively for however many generations it took for the Arabs to achieve what had been achieved with the help of American (often military) intervention in Europe, East Asia, and the Americas: democratization, modernization, and pacification. After 9/11 we no longer have the luxury of time.

The rejection of nation-building, whether on grounds of American incompetence or Arab recalcitrance, reduces the War on Terror to cops-and-robbers, to fighting al Qaeda operatives here and there, arresting some, killing others in some cave. It simply does not get to the root of the problem, which is the cauldron of political oppression, religious intolerance, and social ruin in the Arab-Islamic world - oppression transmuted and deflected by regimes with no legitimacy into the virulent, murderous anti-Americanism that exploded upon us on 9/11. You cannot be serious about post-9/11 foreign policy unless you confront this reality.

What Is To Be Done?

How does Fukuyama confront this reality? What is his alternative to democratic realism? The most bizarre part of his essay is the conclusion. When he finally comes around to offering an alternative, his three-point "recalibration," as he calls it, is so insignificant that he himself admits to "falling in Krauthammer's fourth 'democratic globalism' basket" - that is, he endorses the very foreign policy to which he ostensibly had such fundamental objections.

Of what does this three point "recalibration" consist?

1. "In the first instance, doing the simple work of diplomacy and coalition-building that the Bush Administration seemed reluctant to undertake prior to the Iraq War." Now, one can hold in high or low regard this administration's display of diplomatic skill in the six-month run-up to the Iraq War. But to imply that the administration did not work to build support both in the Security Council and outside it is absurd. It worked hard but fell short. What extra work does Fukuyama imagine would have enlisted France or Russia? Fukuyama then recommends that the United States "not gratuitously . . . insult the 'common opinions of mankind.'" Who is for that? If it is a recommendation for anything other than good manners, it is for granting other nations veto power over actions the United States believes essential to its national interest and to the common defense. But Fukuyama himself rejects this idea categorically, saying that it is "utterly wrong" to maintain that "the United States should never

stick its neck out and lead the broader Western world to actions that our allies oppose."

2. The United States should establish a new bureaucracy for nation-building. No objection here. We could use a Colonial Office in the State Department.

3. Consider establishing, in Fukuyama's words, a "global alliance of democracies, led by newer ones in Eastern Europe and Latin America" that "could play a legitimizing function around the world in a way that NATO cannot." Another perfectly good idea. I proposed it over a year ago.

So, a well-mannered diplomacy, a colonial office, and perhaps a new alliance of democracies. That's it? This is Fukuyama's alternative to democratic realism? Well, he adds: "I believe that East Asia is under-institutionalized and ripe for some creative thinking by the United States." Al Qaeda brings down the World Trade Center, war with the jihadists rages all over the world, Iraq is in play, and Fukuyama calls for thinking creatively about new East Asian institutions.

* * *

Fukuyama begins his essay by promising to "come up with a foreign policy that is very different from the one he [Krauthammer] lays out." He ends with a tweak: a couple of new institutions and more diplomacy. One finishes the essay in puzzlement. What was this polemic about? He declares himself an adherent of "democratic globalism," the very school of thought he was ostensibly taking on. "He retains," he tells the *New York Times*, "his neoconservative principles – a belief in the universal aspiration for democracy and the use of American power to spread democracy in the world." What is left of his promise of a very different foreign policy?

The reason he offers none is that, as he concedes, no plausible alternative theory presents itself. Isolationism is obsolete. Liberal internationalism is too naive to be effective. And realism fails to see the power and promise of democratic transformation. Democratic realism offers a clear framework for responding to the challenge posed by history's unwelcome return in September 2001. Fukuyama's endorsement of democratic realism is welcome, and his recalibrations duly noted.

PATRICK J. BUCHANAN

17 'Stay the Course!' Is Not Enough

IN THE AFTERMATH OF THE SUICIDE BOMBING OF THE MOSUL MESS hall, we are being admonished anew we must stay the course in Iraq. But "Stay the course!" is no longer enough.

President Bush needs to go on national television and tell us the unvarnished truth. Why are we still there? For some of Bush's countrymen, there is a sense of having been had, of having been made victim to one of the great bait-and-switches in the history of warfare.

The president, his War Cabinet, and the neocon punditocracy sold us on this war by implying that Saddam was implicated in 9/11, that he had a vast arsenal of chemical and biological weapons, that he was working on an atom bomb, that he would transfer his terror weapons to al Qaeda. We had to invade, destroy, and disarm his axis-of-evil regime. Only thus could we be secure.

None of this was true. But the president won that debate and was given a free hand to invade Iraq. He did so, and overthrew Saddam's regime in three weeks. "Mission Accomplished!"

That was 20 months ago. What is our mission now? When did it change? With 1,300 dead and nearly 10,000 wounded, why are we still at war with these people?

The president says the enemy is "terrorism" and "evil," and we fight for "democracy" and that "freedom" which is "God's gift to humanity." All very noble.

But why should Americans have to die for democracy in a nation that has never known it? Democracy in the Middle East is not vital to our national security. For though the Middle East has never been democratic, no Middle East nation has ever attacked us. And should we catch a nation that is supporting terror against us, we have the weapons to make them pay a hellish price, without invading and occupying their country.

The only nation in the 20th century to attack us was Japan. And Japan lashed out, insanely, in desperation, because we had cut off her oil and convinced the British and Dutch to cut off the vital commodities she needed to avoid imperial defeat in China. We were choking the Japanese empire to death.

We might all prefer that Arab nations be democratic. But that is not vital to us. If they remain despotic, that is their problem, so long as they do not threaten or attack us. But to invade an Islamic country to force it to adopt democratic reforms is democratic imperialism. If we practice it, we must expect that some of those we are reforming will resort to the time-honored weapon of anti-imperialists – terrorism, the one effective weapon the weak have against the strong.

Yet, if our goals appear gauzy and vague, our enemy's war aims appear specific, concrete, and understandable. They seek our expulsion from Iraq and the eradication of all "collaborators." And the tactics they are using are the same as those the FLN used to drive the French out of Algeria.

To us, democracy may mean New England town meetings. To the Sunnis, democracy means a one-man, one-vote path to power for the Shias, 60 percent of Iraq's population, who will dispossess them of the power and place they have held since Ottoman times. Why should people to whom politics is about power – "Who, whom?" in Lenin's phrase – not fight that? And why should we fight and die for a Shia-dominated Iraq?

Before addressing his countrymen, the president needs to ask and answer for himself some hard questions. Who told him this would be a "cakewalk"? Who misled him to believe we would be welcomed as liberators with bouquets of flowers? Who led him into a situation where his choice appears to be between a seemingly endless guerrilla war that could destroy his presidency, and walking away from Iraq and watching it collapse in mayhem and massacre of those who cast their lot with us? Why have these fools not been fired, like the CIA geniuses who sold JFK on the Bay of Pigs?

It is not just President Bush who is in this hellish mess. We're all in it together. But the president needs to know that if he intends to use U.S. military power to democratize the Middle East, Americans – 56 percent of whom now believe Iraq was a mistake – will not follow him.

Finally, the president must answer in his heart this question: Exactly how much more blood and money is he willing to plunge into a war for democracy in Iraq, and at what point must he decide – as LBJ and Nixon did in Vietnam – that the cost to America is so great that we must get out and risk the awful consequences of a mistaken war that we should never have launched?

ROBERT F. ELLSWORTH AND DIMITRI K. SIMES

18 Realism's Shining Morality

WE ARE PLEASED THAT PRESIDENT GEORGE W. BUSH ACHIEVED AN impressive victory over Senator John Kerry - but we do not believe that the president received a clear mandate for conducting foreign policy. Indeed, it was unfortunate that there was no real foreign policy debate during the campaign - and this at a time when the United States must make fateful choices.

The president, understandably, was unwilling to acknowledge serious errors of judgment in the conduct of U.S. foreign policy. Yet Senator Kerry failed to offer a credible alternative. His attacks on administration policy, especially vis-à-vis Iraq, were more nitpicking than a serious evaluation of what went wrong and what lessons the United States should learn.

President Bush built a strong record on the defining issue of our time - fighting terrorism. He destroyed al Qaeda's base in Afghanistan, removing the Taliban from power. And regarding Iraq, there were only two feasible options. One was to offer Saddam a quid pro quo settlement - allowing him and his murderous regime to stay in power in return for verifiably giving up weapons of mass destruction and abandoning his regional pretensions. There was little constituency in the United States for such a course of action. The second was regime change. Senator Kerry himself had voted in 1998 for this option. The Clinton team (many of whom also served as advisors to the Kerry camp) opted for half-measures - conducting regular air strikes against Saddam, attempting (with declining success) to maintain strangulating sanctions, and plotting covert action. It was clear that these were not achieving their objective - while giving Saddam every incentive to strike back at the United States. So resolving the situation once and for all by ending the Saddam regime seemed to be a more prudent solution. One need not be a neoconservative to reach such a conclusion.

But how foreign policy is conducted also matters, and here it is vitally important that President Bush, in his second term, avoid wrong choices that may bring catastrophic consequences. The second Bush Administration will have to deal with two fundamental dilemmas: first, how to reconcile the war against terror with a commitment to make the world safe for democracy; and second, how to assure that unchallenged U.S. military supremacy is used to enhance America's ability to shape the world rather than provoke global opposition to the United States, making us more isolated and accordingly less secure. The neoconservative vision for conducting American foreign policy is fraught with risks. And continuing to follow the prescriptions of the neoconservative faction in the Republican party may damage President Bush's legacy, imperil the country's fiscal stability, and complicate America's ability to exercise global leadership.

It has become an article of faith for the increasingly influential alliance of liberal interventionists and neoconservatives that the United States, as the world's democratic hegemonic power, is both entitled and even morally bound to use whatever tools are necessary to save the world from brutality and oppression and to promote democratization around the globe. Up to a point, the War on Terror and encouraging democracy worldwide are mutually reinforcing. President Bush is quite right that democracy, particularly if we are talking about democracy in a stable society coupled with a rule of law and with adequate protection of minority rights, is not only morally preferable to authoritarian rule, but also is the best prescription against the emergence of deeply alienated radical groups prone to terrorism. The "democracy project" also appeals to the highest aspirations of the American people. After all, the Cold War was never driven solely by the need to contain Soviet power, but by the moral conviction that defending freedom in the United States and in the world in general was something worth fighting and dying for – even, in the Berlin Crisis, risking nuclear war itself.

High-minded realists do not disagree with the self-appointed champions of global democracy (the neoconservatives and the liberal interventionists) that a strong preference for liberty and justice should be an integral part of U.S. foreign policy. But they realize that there are tradeoffs between pushing for democracy and working with other sovereign states – some not always quite democratic – to combat global terror. Realists also, following the advice of General Charles Boyd, understand the need to "separate reality from image" and "to tell the truth, if only to ourselves" – not to play fast and loose with facts to create the appearance of acting morally. And they are aware that there are important differences in how the United States helps the world achieve freedom. Indeed, in his first press conference after his triumph at the polls, President Bush used three different terms in talking about America's global pro-democracy effort. He discussed the need "to encourage freedom and democracy," to "promote free societies," and to "spread freedom and democracy."

"Encouraging" democracy is not a controversial position. Nearly everyone in the world accepts that the sole superpower is entitled and indeed expected to be true to its core beliefs. "Promoting" democracy is vaguer and potentially more costly. Still, if the United States does so without resorting to military force and takes into account the circumstances and perspectives of other nations, then it is likely not to run into too much international opposition. "Spreading" democracy, however, particularly spreading it by force, coercion, and violent regime change, is a different thing altogether. Those who suspect they may be on the receiving end of such treatment are unlikely to accept American moral superiority, are bound to feel threatened, and cannot reasonably be expected to cooperate with the United States on other important American priorities, including the War on Terror and nuclear proliferation.

Worse still, they may decide that acquiring nuclear weapons is the last – perhaps their only – option to deter an American attempt to overthrow their governments. This already appears to be the dynamic in the case of Iran and North Korea. Also, in dealing with the likes of Tehran and Pyongyang, there can be no certainty with whom they may share nuclear technology. Accordingly, there is a clear and present danger that pro-democracy zeal may enhance the greatest possible threat to U.S. security and the American way of life – the threat of nuclear terrorism.

We have already seen how overzealousness in the cause of democracy (along with a corresponding underestimation of the costs and dangers) has led to a dangerous overstretch in Iraq. As Shlomo Avineri, a professor at Hebrew University in Jerusalem, has observed, what is currently going on in Iraq is not "the war the U.S.-led coalition had in mind when the decision was taken to topple Saddam Hussein." The United States could have rid Iraq of Saddam and his most notorious associates without turning the whole country upside down. America could have made it clear from the start that Washington had no ambitions in Iraq beyond removing the threat from Saddam's regime and co-opted the United Nations and the Arab League to create a provisional post-Saddam government. It would have been possible to communicate to less-discredited members of the old regime – first and foremost the military command – that in return for coming clean on Iraq's programs to develop weapons of mass destruction, cooperating with coalition forces, introducing the rule of law, and accepting a broad-based transitional government that would incorporate Iraqi exiles (and here one could have envisaged Prime Minister Iyad Allawi playing a key role), they could retain some degree of influence in the new Iraq. Additionally, Iraq's neighbors, none of them friends of Saddam, could have been assured that they had nothing to worry from the American military presence on their borders, as long as they did not attempt to obstruct a U.S. occupation which their benign attitude could help to make shorter.

Instead, we opted to dismantle the Ba'ath party government altogether without having anything with which to replace it, dissolved the Iraqi army, and proudly pronounced that the liberation of Iraq was just a beginning of a grand democratic transformation of the Greater Middle East. It required an inordinate degree of naivety and, frankly, ignorance about the real conditions in Iraq and in the Middle East in general to believe that this overly ambitious scheme could work - especially when pursued without any visible effort to promote the Arab-Israeli settlement and from the position of being the sole sponsor of the Sharon government. An effort to reshape the Middle East according to American specifications was bound to face opposition on the ground in Iraq, from Iraq's neighbors such as Iran and Syria, and to say the least, dampen enthusiasm for helping the United States in Iraq even on the part of the most friendly Arab regimes such as Egypt, Saudi Arabia, and Jordan, all of which had cause for concern that they could become targets of the American master plan for restructuring the region.

America has had to pay for these errors with blood, treasure, diminished international prestige, and a weakened ability to focus adequately on and get much needed international cooperation on other urgent priorities, such as the emerging nuclear capabilities of North Korea and now of Iran. Reactions from other major powers strongly suggest that the Iraqi experience, for example, has made it considerably harder for the United States to get European, Russian, and Chinese cooperation on tough measures against Iran. (In the case of Moscow and Beijing, the experience with the 1999 U.S.-led attack on Yugoslavia was also a factor.) There is a reluctance to pass UN Security Council resolutions that would include a threat of force - a threat that would be quite useful in pressuring the Iranian government, but which many nations, including some of America's long-standing partners, are afraid would be used by the United States to justify unilateral military action.

Neoconservatives both in and outside the administration argue that all that is needed to make American foreign policy more effective is to change the tone of American statements and to engage in better public relations. This is fantasy. What is required is not just a change in salesmanship, but rather how U.S. policy is conducted.

Nothing short of a midcourse adjustment can allow America to reassert true world leadership – enjoying the concrete support of other major powers, not (with the notable exception of Great Britain) token contributions made by insufficient "coalitions of the willing."

We suggest an adjustment, rather than a wholescale course correction. In its first term, the Bush Administration showed it was capable of pursuing a realist foreign policy grounded in vital interests. After an initially rough start with China and Russia, the Bush team came to accept the importance of building partnerships with these major powers.

And after the tragedies of 9/11, President Bush was absolutely right in his call for a relentless and ruthless pursuit of terrorists wherever they may be, and, unlike many neoconservatives and liberal interventionists, he rejected double standards in dealing with the terrorist threat. He did not reclassify certain terrorists as "freedom fighters," even in the face of sometimes considerable pressure from special interests. Thus, he refused to criticize Russian President Vladimir Putin for his tough (even if not always effective) measures against terrorists acting in the name of the Chechen cause. President Bush has made it clear that groups that perpetrate horrific violence specifically directed against civilian targets are terrorists. No matter how noble the cause they espouse, and even if there are legitimate grievances at play, sympathy must never become a means to aid and abet terrorism.

After an initial bout of euphoria following the fall of Baghdad, the Bush Administration has come to realize that, as a practical matter, with the United States being preoccupied with Iraq, it is unlikely that force should be used to remove other repressive regimes as long as they do not threaten the United States. And in Iraq itself, once National Security Advisor Condoleezza Rice became responsible for guiding that country's political reconstruction, the focus changed from starry-eyed democratic experimentation to establishing stability and ensuring a quick transfer of authority to the new Iraqi government. This is a policy not only less threatening to Iraq's neighbors, but also one which has a better chance of success among Iraqis who are tired of disorder.

Of course, in the post-September 11 world, the leading superpower has no choice but to remain assertive, and that includes rare instances when America has to act unilaterally and to use military force pre-emptively. The question is, under which circumstances and in the name of what? No responsible American president, as Senator Kerry acknowledged during the campaign, can surrender the right to do whatever is required to defend American security, even when the UN, NATO, and other international bodies refuse to give consent. Realistically, other nations would not expect that much from us – even those who cherish their ability to use international law as a straightjacket on U.S. freedom of action.

As far as pre-emption is concerned, there is a growing consensus in the world that traditional notions of deterrence, appropriate against nation-states (which were in control of their territory and were vulnerable to massive retaliation in response to irresponsible behavior), simply cannot work in the age of sub-national terrorist coalitions and with the apocalyptic consequences of weapons of mass destruction increasingly available to non-state actors. The issue is not with pre-emption itself, but rather with the notion, now widespread in the world, that the United States may use pre-emption arbitrarily – not against genuine enemies threatening America, but against those whom the American political consensus at the moment decides to label as brutal and undemocratic. With their historic reluctance to have authority without the consent of the governed, Americans should be the first to understand why the rest of the world would not be prepared to surrender such overwhelming power to any one nation. After all, there is no such thing as a benign tyranny. The ability of one power to act freely without constraints, short of those it is willing to impose upon itself, would look like a tyranny even to those countries that, as a result of their democratic credentials, have little reason to fear American punishment themselves.

The president of the United States proudly proclaims that he is a man of faith, and so were the American Founding Fathers. However, the genius of the American experiment was based on the fact that great ideals were combined with an equally great pragmatism and that strong belief in one's cause was also measured by a decent respect for the passions of others. That is what makes the neoconservative creed such a departure from the American political tradition. President Bush will enhance his legacy and do a lot of good for U.S. foreign policy effectiveness if he makes high-minded realism his foreign policy motto. Such high-minded realism should be based on five important principles.

First, the War on Terror should be made the true organizing principle of U.S. foreign policy. That does not mean neglecting other important preferences such as U.S. economic interests, environmental issues, and human rights. But none of them should be pursued at the expense of the struggle against terror. After all, success or failure in the War on Terror could very well determine the fate of America.

Second, the Bush Administration should work hard in its second term to re-establish American leadership. This is not about allowing anyone else to checkmate the exercise of U.S. power. Rather, it requires a serious evaluation of tradeoffs between compromises in the name of greater international support and the freedom of action associated with acting alone when no multilateral solution is available. For example, in the instances of the North Korean and Iranian nuclear programs, it is wise for America to work hard to move other relevant nations as close as possible to the U.S. position - as imperfect as such consensus may be - rather than to adopt a threatening pose in splendid isolation. In that context it should be made clear that pre-emption is a last resort, applicable only when there is credible evidence of a real threat to vital U.S. interests.

Third, as a pre-eminent military power, whose capabilities no one disputes, we should follow the guidance of President Theodore Roosevelt to speak softly while carrying a big stick. America should not be timid in protecting and promoting its interests, but a modicum of humility when talking about our exceptional goodness would help others reconcile themselves to American preponderance and make it easier for them to accommodate our preferences. That is something that does not come naturally to neoconservative polemicists who seem to derive satisfaction from loudly beating their drums - but it would again be in the best American tradition and most likely to produce results.

Fourth, we should abandon the demonstrably false pretense that all nations and cultures share essentially the same values. Every country, every region, every civilization has its own cycle, circumstances, and path of development. We have disagreements over values and policies even with our democratic European allies and with Canada and Mexico just across the border - so we should not expect that the peoples of the Middle East would share our attitudes. One key passion in the Middle East is the rights of the Palestinians. This passion may seem exaggerated to us and manipulated by undemocratic Arab leaders. But the fact remains that it is strongly felt among the Muslim elites and masses alike. If we want our good intentions to be trusted in the Islamic world, and if we want to be able to encourage moderation and positive attitudes towards Western civilization among Muslims, a sympathetic attention to the Palestinian problem, obviously without abandoning the security of Israel, is a must. Yasir Arafat's departure may provide an important opening in that regard.

Finally, our focus on democracy should not be presented to others as an imperial command. Over the centuries we have been advised by leaders from John Adams to George Kennan to Ronald Reagan to be unto the world as a shining city on a hill, appealing to the better instincts of mankind – not to become a military empire demanding subservience. We certainly would not object to other countries emulating us, but it is more important that we have shared interests and work to address and promote them.

For President Bush to use his second term to enhance his legacy and to build – as he clearly wants – a lasting Republican majority, the United States needs to pursue a foreign policy based on thoughtful evaluation, dealing with the world as it is, rather than embracing polemical clichés passed off as ideas. And such a policy needs as its moral lodestone the traditional American value of prudence, not a neo-Trotskyite belief in a permanent revolution (even if it is a democratic rather than proletarian one). The neoconservative insistence that the United States can be made safe only by making other nations accept American values is a recipe for provoking a clash of civilizations rather than a way to enhance and promote America's global leadership.

In 1999, then-candidate Bush said, "Let us have an American foreign policy that reflects American character. The modesty of true strength, the humility of real greatness." September 11 has made this realistic and honorable approach even more essential for U.S. international conduct.

VICTOR DAVIS HANSON

19 Has Iraq Weakened Us?

WHATEVER THE RESULTS OF THE ELECTIONS SCHEDULED FOR LATE January in Iraq, a new pessimism about that country, as well as about the larger war on terror, has taken hold in many circles in the United States. Serious observers, not to mention shriller commentators like Paul Krugman and Maureen Dowd of the *New York Times*, have concluded not only that the United States is stuck in a hopeless quagmire in Iraq, but that our unwise unilateral intervention there is having painful repercussions both for our position as an honest promoter of reform and for our diplomatic and military maneuverability elsewhere in the world.

Joining the pessimism, Alistair Horne, the eminent British military historian, recently likened the American situation in Iraq to the French debacle in the "brutal Algerian eight-year war"; his obvious inference was that the ultimate denouement will be a similarly abrupt and humiliating Western withdrawal. Horne could adduce much apparent evidence to support this depressing proposition: the instability in the Sunni triangle over the last two years, mounting American combat fatalities, a seemingly endless insurgency, the increasing reluctance of allies to support in any serious material way the world's lone superpower, and a failure of moderate Iraqis to step forward and deny sanctuary to the terrorists in their midst. The more jihadists, Baathists, and *mujahideen* that Americans kill, the more of them have seemed to pour into Iraq from Syria and other places in the neighboring Islamic world, either for pay or out of religious zeal. As for the Iraqi "street," it appears to be both repulsed and paralyzed by this terrorist barbarity, and above all uncertain whether the Americans will stay long enough to ensure either safety or the promised democracy.

Meanwhile, American efforts at democratization are the object of much criticism at home, both on pragmatic and ideological grounds. Even some supporters of the war have come to see these postbellum efforts as naive, misconceived, or simply too taxing in the tribal and factional circumstances of Iraq. A November 2004 article in *Reason*, subtitled "Twilight of the Liberal Hawks," surveyed the second thoughts of a number of pundits and columnists, among them Paul Berman, Thomas Friedman, Kenneth Pollack, Fareed Zakaria, Andrew Sullivan, and Michael Ignatieff. Each of them, unhappy in his own particular way with the failure to deal with the post-April 2003 insurrection in Iraq, has criticized the Bush administration not only for its conduct of the Iraq operation but, at least by implication, for the much more ambitious project of an American-led democratizing of the greater Middle East.

The newly perceived area of strategic crisis emanates worldwide from its current center in Baghdad. With over 130,000 troops and $100 billion tied up on the ground in Iraq, where, critics ask, are we to find ready reserves for other hot spots on the horizon? Aside from the boiling Middle East, the Balkans are not yet pacified; our relationship with the South Koreans is in a state of dangerous flux; and Japan, lacking its own strategic arsenal, is sandwiched between a rising China and a nuclear North Korea. Add in the worry over protecting Taiwan, instability in the former Soviet republics, leftist rumblings in South America, and the United States may stand in need of additional and sizable rapid-reaction forces that it shows no signs of being able to recruit, train, or pay for in time to deal with most emergencies.

Nor is it only a matter of a current shortage of manpower. Looming domestic problems - a declining dollar, huge budget deficits, and dependence on overseas capital - are exacerbated by the fact that we have committed over a third of our available combat strength to Iraq and do not have the ready funds to recreate the divisions lost to budget cuts in the 1990's. It is at least partly with this perceived gap between responsibilities and resources in mind that even some conservatives have begun to weigh in with regret. In June 2004, William F. Buckley, Jr. concluded: "If I knew then what I know now about what kind of situation we would be in, I would have opposed the war." Although Buckley has since offered different thoughts, George F. Will still appears as pessimistic as he was when he announced in the headline of a May 2004 column: "Time for Bush to See the Realities of Iraq."

Finally, a number of retired generals and admirals - Wesley Clark, William J. Crowe, Barry McCaffrey, Tony McPeak, William Odom,

Stansfield Turner, and Anthony Zinni – have worried publicly over the demands placed on the United States in Iraq and the specter of another open-ended, Vietnam-like commitment sapping American assets, troop morale, and public support for the military. Moved by the hard facts of finite resources and the soft reality of censure at home and abroad, these former-officers-turned-political-commentators emphasize our increasing vulnerabilities and voice a reluctance to exercise any further American power abroad except under the aegis of the United Nations and with de-facto NATO blessing.

* * *

Political prognoses in wartime are notoriously mercurial, hinging on the weekly eddies of the battlefield. But these are sometimes poor indicators of larger strategic currents. If one thing can be said with confidence about Iraq, it is that the story is not over, since so far the daily bombings have neither prompted American withdrawal nor derailed scheduled elections and reforms. In World War II, the bloodiest moment of the Pacific theater was at Okinawa, finally declared secure a mere nine weeks before the Japanese surrender, while in Europe the Battle of the Bulge, a slog that cost more American lives than the drive to the Rhine, was not finished until only about 100 days before Germany collapsed. What can be seen in hindsight, and only in hindsight, is that while Americans were being butchered in Belgium and on Sugar Loaf Hill, larger forces were insidiously working to doom Germany and Japan in short order. The last gasps of resistance are sometimes the bloodiest and most unexpected.

Just so, Afghanistan a year ago was supposedly a hopeless case, torn apart by warlords and Taliban resurgence, and unfit for elections; today the country is mostly on the back pages, as if democracy were *de rigueur* for a nation recently dismissed as a relic of the Dark Ages. Similarly, with all the news of bombings and beheadings coming from Iraq, the larger picture, not so easily deciphered, shows signs of real progress in most of the country. The long overdue retaking of Falluja and ancillary military operations have sent their own signal: that a reelected George Bush intends to ensure the installation and the survival of a legitimately elected Iraqi government. The specter of that constitutional authority sending troops to quash mercenaries, Baathists, and Wahhabi jihadists is precisely what frightens al Qaeda and other avatars of Islamic fascism, who have rightly grasped that their failure in the Sunni triangle will constitute a bitter defeat for global Islamic fundamentalism itself.

The American persistence in Iraq under difficult circumstances might also explain why potential enemies farther afield, from Teheran to Pyongyang, have so far decided not to seize the moment to press their luck with the United States. Meanwhile, the world at large appears more, rather than less, disposed to stand up to Islamic fascism and the terror it wages. Even less ambiguously, Pakistan, though often playing a duplicitous role in the past, has remained a neutral in the war on terror if not at times an ally, while its nuclear guru, A.Q. Khan, is for the moment in retirement. On the issue of the dangers posed by Islamic extremism, nearly 3 billion people in India, China, Japan, and the former Soviet Union are more likely to favor than to oppose American counterterrorism efforts. Libya is suddenly coming clean about its own nefarious schemes and even opening its borders to African aid workers. Murmurs of democratic change are rumbling throughout the autocratic Gulf. Terrorists are not so welcome as they once were in Jordan, Yemen, or much of North Africa. Even Europe, stung by charges of profit-driven appeasement, and even the UN, reeling under financial and humanitarian scandals, are reconsidering their habitual modes of reflexive accommodation.

Do these developments guarantee a more secure world in the offing? Hardly. But they are positive indications of momentum – signs that themselves reflect the unexpected forcefulness of the American response to Islamic terrorism and its dictatorial supporters. Stop, or pull out of Iraq before a free society is secure, and the entire sequence of reform could operate in reverse, leading four or five Middle Eastern states instead to become either nuclear-armed or open havens for anti-Western terrorists – or both. The task of stabilizing Iraq is thus of enormous significance in a region that, thanks only to the United States and its coalition allies, may yet be forced to confront its dictators' worst nightmare: not terrorist violence but televised coverage of citizens queuing up to vote in free elections and then arguing in an unfettered parliament.

* * *

There are lessons here for those who claim that American flexibility has become increasingly constricted and American choices all but foreclosed. In fact, as Iraq comes slowly under control, the opposite prognosis is at least as likely to be the case. Precisely *because* of proven American resolve in Iraq, the United States now commands both military and diplomatic options – well short of another Iraq-style invasion – that were not at its disposal previously.

The new stature enjoyed by America is especially germane in the Middle East itself. There, the first place where diplomatic and political initiatives could usefully be exercised is in the problematic triad of Syria, Lebanon, and Iran. The U.S. might, to begin with, pressure the UN Security Council to go beyond its recent call for Syria to end its occupation of Lebanon by demanding internationally supervised elections, to follow immediately upon the departure of the Baathists.

Both Iran and Syria, through their terrorist ganglia on the ground in the Bekka valley, can be counted on to try to strangle any such effort. But this is not 1983, when America retreated after Marines were murdered in Beirut and later bargained for hostages. Today the Lebanese, returning to their wonted entrepreneurialism, are tiring of the Baathist Syrians. Yasir Arafat is dead. And the Iranians are leery of American strikes against their nuclear facilities. It is thus a singularly opportune moment to stir worries about principled democratization; for nothing could be more dangerous to an untested dictatorship like Syria's than to ring it with an enlarging circle of autonomous countries with free elections, unbridled radio and television, and uncensored Internet service. To Arabs in Syria and elsewhere who are increasingly aware that they enjoy neither the freedoms nor the prosperity that billions elsewhere take for granted, the appeal of such reform is potentially explosive.

Other equally bold diplomatic initiatives could be undertaken, their credibility similarly enhanced by the operations in Afghanistan and Iraq. For example, the present Middle-East-aid policy of the United States is a relic both of the cold war (pump oil and keep out Communists) and the 1979 Camp David agreements (subsidize Egypt). Such short-term measures, carrying the odor of entreaty if not of bribery, hardly reflect our current aim of promoting consensual government. With both Saddam and the Soviets gone, granting weapons and money to the regime in Cairo – nearly $50 billion since 1979 – is becoming counterproductive. What advantages the United States receives in "moderation" is overshadowed by the venomous anti-Americanism that is the daily fare of millions of Egyptians, whipped up and manipulated by state-sponsored clerics and media.

As several congressional critics, most prominently Tom Lantos, have pointed out, America loses both ways: the money and the business-as-usual attitude send a message to others in the region that the United States will willingly subsidize anti-American hatred and promote an anti-democratic government in one place while trying to create the opposite elsewhere. True, a Hosni Mubarak is not an Assad or a Rafsanjani, and that must count for something in the volatile Middle East; but under the reign of Mubarak, Egypt has been turned into a kind of Afghanistan-of-the-mind, the intellectual and media mecca for anti-American and anti-Semitic hatred spread throughout the Arab world. We are in a war with both Islamic fascism and Arab autocracy for the hearts and minds of the Arab people, and sincere advocacy of the interests of the latter is the only way to head off a devil's partnership of the former.

As part of President Bush's democratic initiatives in the Middle East, financial or military support from the United States could, instead, be tied far more closely to constitutional reforms in places like Egypt, the Gulf States, North Africa, and Jordan. Such a policy, appealing directly to the citizenry of the Arab world, would also be invaluable when it comes to dealing with looming requests from the Palestinian Authority for still more cash aid. But the point is also general. Rather than cherry-picking the autocracies of the Middle East, with aid lavished on those who *sound* most moderate, it makes far more sense to calibrate help with evidence of concrete steps toward democratization.

Elections have their place in such a policy, but, alone, they are not the be-all and end-all. Ten years ago, "one man, one vote, one time" was a valid description of so-called democratic reform in the Arab world. The risk then was that, through our fixation with plebiscites, we would become complicit in bringing to power not a democracy but a "demonocracy" in the form of anti-democratic clerics or Arafat-like killers. In the case of Arafat himself, crowned president of the Palestinian Authority in a "democratic" election with Jimmy Carter's seal of approval, that deformity is precisely what happened.

Nor has the risk of democratic distortion abated. But we can hedge our coveted financial and diplomatic support with demands not merely for elections but for constitutional guarantees of human rights, market reforms, and free expression. In addition, though this is a trickier proposition, we can insist on evidence of liberalization as a precondition for continuing to pour billions of petrodollars into the region.

Pundits speak of poverty as the catalyst for terrorism in the Islamic world; in fact, far more often it is not the dearth but the spectacular abundance of wealth in Middle Eastern societies that has incited and then fueled the killers. In theocratic Iran, oil money is recycled both to Hizballah and the nuclear-weapons program. In Saudi Arabia, Western dollars translate into Wahhabi mosques and madrassas all over the world. Saddam Hussein not only corrupted much of the industrialized Western world via the UN's Oil-for-Food program but had earlier attacked four countries with his petrodollar-acquired arsenal. *Al-Jazeera*, the propaganda successor to

Pravda, and critical to the insurrectionists' efforts in the Sunni triangle, is an indirect dividend from Qatar's oil revenues.

If Americans have learned anything from the careers of Qaddafi, the Saudi royal family, Saddam Hussein, and the Iranian clergy, it is that huge petroleum profits accruing among illegitimate autocrats are a recipe for global terrorism and regional havoc. One way to end the present pathology is for the United States, accepting that concerns for our national survival can sometimes trump the logic of finding the cheapest energy source, to develop a policy that helps drive down world petroleum prices. Another option is far more aggressively to promote democratic reforms among the petrol sheikdoms themselves. A third is to do both. Given the entry of India and China into the world petroleum market, fostering tighter global demand while potentially circumscribing our own clout, the hour is more urgent than ever; but the Middle East is also, and once again thanks to the ongoing reform of Iraq and Afghanistan, more fluid and perhaps more promising than ever.

* * *

Political initiatives come in more than one form. A more muscular way of dealing with autocratic regimes involves direct support for dissidents and pro-democratic reformers, including elected ones. Fair elections that lead to constitutional government should be a non-negotiable proposition; if Sunni or other extremists object, as in Iraq, then it might be made clear that they will be left to carry on a struggle not only against the majority of the local population but also against an internationally recognized government backed in the last resort by the American military. We wish to avoid civil war; but, like it or not, in championing the formerly despised of Iraq, the United States is engaged in landmark social, political, and cultural upheavals, and it is naive to think that the Kurdish-Shiite coalition will be denied majority rule.

Iran is a *locus classicus* of what might be accomplished by encouraging indigenous grassroots reformers. The dilemma facing the United States is well known: stopping Iran's nuclear program is vital, yet both action and inaction have their unsavory costs. Unlike in Syria or in Saddam's Iraq, there is, by every credible report, broad and active internal opposition to the Iranian mullocracy. But not only would military action against Iran's dispersed nuclear installations be operationally difficult, but the ensuing worldwide hysteria would possibly embolden the regime to move against the dissidents (they were nearly wiped out during the 1980's under cover of Iran's war with Iraq).

Yet inaction, leading to an Iran armed with nuclear weapons, could yield the same deleterious effect: a triumphant regime now feeling secure enough to deal summarily with its internal opponents. In this wait-and-see moment, it is therefore all the more incumbent on the United States to step up its covert support for democratic dissidents. Even more importantly, today's underground reformers could be helped to evolve into openly organized groups, analogous to the refuseniks in the former Soviet Union, Solidarity in Poland, or the *contras* in Nicaragua – human-rights cadres capable of mounting a public campaign against the Iranian regime that might resonate in European capitals as well as among our own elites. Such advocacy does not mean we should be in the business of selecting the leaders of these groups, let alone dictating their agendas or masterminding their tactics; those who suffer first-hand repression know better than we what needs to be done and how to go about doing it. But if America is to win the current death struggle in the Middle East, we must aggressively promote democratization in Iran – and Syria – before both of them undermine it across the border in Iraq.

In line with this ambitious agenda, there are also military options available. Bill Clinton's cruise missiles and four-day bombing campaigns – complete with mandatory cessations before Ramadan or reprieves when Arab royalty was reportedly lunching with would-be targets – were poor substitutes for real action. But under the present, radically changed conditions, stand-off bombing remains a valuable consideration. Unlike in the 1990's, the United States has *already* shown that it can and will topple Islamic fascists on the ground – that no tactic is any longer taboo for Americans. The old, post-Mogadishu charge that the United States will not risk a fight on the ground has been disproved. Thus, bombing can be an end in itself or a precursor to something more, and we can leave it to others to do the guessing as to which course we will follow.

Targets of retaliation from the air include potential nuclear-weapons plants, identified nationals conducting terrorist bombing operations abroad, or visible signs of material aid flowing to jihadists across a border. Military action of this kind would serve not only to erode a country's military assets and damage its infrastructure but to bring humiliation upon its ruling power. In some cases, the threat of retaliation might itself suffice. If Syria, for example, continues to allow ex-Baathists to plot and fund insurrection in Iraq or to serve as a transit station for jihadists out to kill Americans, then Secretary of State Rice might present Bashar Assad with a list of military targets that could, without warning, be systematically destroyed from the air.

The problem with our 1990's air campaigns in Afghanistan, Iraq, and North Africa was transparent: our enemies knew that this was the last, not the first, stage of American retaliation and comprised the full extent of our military options. That perception is why we derived only a partial punitive benefit from Operation Desert Fox in Iraq or from striking back in Afghanistan and Sudan, and sparked little interest among the targeted in changing their ways. In the pre-9/11 world, such tactics were also largely predicated on the promise of few if any casualties, for us or even for our adversaries. Today's goal, by contrast, is to protect the democratic process in Afghanistan and Iraq against any in the region who threaten it, and to do so without necessarily investing American ground troops in additional theaters. For this, air power once again is a condign instrument.

* * *

Flexibility in response is essential in a war against diverse enemies. After the success of air campaigns in Kosovo and Serbia, some observers proclaimed a new age of Air-Force exclusivity. In Afghanistan, Americans riding on donkeys and calling in GPS coordinates from their laptops suggested still another radically new military paradigm. After the 2003 race to Baghdad and the retaking of Falluja in late 2004, we were happy we still had retrograde standbys like Abrams tanks and up-armored Humvees. The simple conclusion is that all assets and options are necessary, but not necessarily all the time.

America can always use more combat troops, planes, and ships, even if it is not advisable in every circumstance to pour assets into a theater in hopes that numbers can make up for what fighting alone can accomplish; the desirable size of the American military is not entirely the same issue as the proper number of soldiers to be deployed in any given situation. On the other hand, fighting need not take the identical form or incur the same costs everywhere. Another age-old lesson relearned from our experience in Iraq and Afghanistan is that victory in one battle increases the range of options in the next and lessens the military adventurism of our enemies – just as an American setback does the reverse.

The removal of the Taliban and the election of Hamid Karzai were of historic importance. So too was the end of the Saddam Hussein mafia, and so, following the present long ordeal, will be the Iraqi elections. Without a doubt, Saddam's Iraq was the most challenging of all the Middle East rogue regimes. The next step, reforming or changing the governments in Lebanon, Syria, and Iran demands its own flexible strategy and its own proper diplomatic and military calculus. But, contrary to the imagining of critics, the post-Iraq reformation of the Middle East will not necessarily have to be accomplished by the invasion of tens of thousands of American troops. Other remedies may well suit our national and humanitarian interests – strategies opened up, ironically, by our previous determination to *use* our ground forces in Afghanistan and Iraq, as well as by our will to see the process through to its end, without hesitation, apology, or compromise.

CHARLES R. KESLER

20 Democracy and the Bush Doctrine

GEORGE W. BUSH'S FIRST PRESIDENCY, DEVOTED TO COMPASSIONATE conservatism and to establishing his own bona fides, lasted less than eight months. On September 11, 2001, he was reborn as a War President. In the upheaval that followed, compassionate conservatism took a back seat to a new, more urgent formulation of the Bush Administration's purpose.

The Bush Doctrine called for offensive operations, including preemptive war, against terrorists and their abetters - more specifically, against the regimes that had sponsored, encouraged, or merely tolerated any "terrorist group of global reach." Afghanistan, the headquarters of al Qaeda and its patron the Taliban, was the new doctrine's first beneficiary, although the president soon declared Iraq, Iran, and North Korea (to be precise, "states like these, and their terrorist allies") an "axis of evil" meriting future attention. In his stirring words, the United States would "not permit the world's most dangerous regimes to threaten us with the world's most dangerous weapons."

The administration's preference for offensive operations reflected a long-standing conservative interest in taking the ideological and military fight to our foes. After all, the Reagan Doctrine had not only indicted Soviet Communism as an evil empire but had endeavored to subvert its hold on the satellite countries and, eventually, on its own people. The Bush Administration's focus on the states backing the terrorists implied that "regime change" would be necessary, once again, in order to secure America against its enemies. The policy did not contemplate merely the offending regimes' destruction, however. As in the 1980's, regime *change* implied their replacement by something better, and the Bush Doctrine soon expanded to accommodate the goal of planting freedom and democracy in their stead.

Reprinted from the *Claremont Review of Books*, Winter 2004/05, by permission.

Captive Nations

On this point, the Bush Doctrine parted company with the Reagan Doctrine. Although the Reagan Administration's CIA and other agencies had worked to build civil society and to support democratic opposition groups in Eastern Europe, Central America, and other strategic regions, these efforts were directed mostly to helping "captive nations" escape their captivity. That is, they presupposed a latent opposition against foreign, usually Soviet, oppression, or as in the satellite and would-be satellite countries, against domestic oppressors supported by the Soviets. The Russian people themselves counted as a kind of captive nation enslaved to Marxism's foreign ideology, and Reagan did not flinch from calling for their liberation, too. He always rejected a philosophical détente between democracy and totalitarianism in favor of conducting a vigorous moral and intellectual offensive against Communist principles.

But as a practical matter, the Reagan Doctrine aimed primarily at supporting labor unions, churches, and freedom fighters at the Soviet empire's periphery - e.g., Poland, Czechoslovakia, Afghanistan, Nicaragua, Grenada - rather than at its core. Even in these cases, the administration regarded its chief duty to be helping to liberate the captive nations, that is, expelling the Soviets and defeating their proxies, rather than presiding over a proper democratization of the liberated peoples. Not unreasonably, the Reaganites thought that to those freed from totalitarian oppression, America's example would be shining enough, especially when joined to their visceral, continuing hatred for the Soviet alternative.

In countries where bad or tyrannical regimes were homegrown or unconnected with America's great totalitarian enemy, the administration's efforts in support of democratization were quieter and more limited still. These involved diplomatic pressure, election-monitoring, and occasional gestures of overt support, such as the administration's endorsement of "people power" in the Philippines. Most importantly, Reagan wanted to avoid the Carter Administration's hubris in condemning the imperfect regimes of America's friends, while neglecting the incomparably worse sins of America's foes.

The distinction between authoritarian and totalitarian regimes, classically restated by Jeane Kirkpatrick in her article that caught Reagan's eye, "Dictatorships and Double Standards," provided intellectual support for his administration's policies. Authoritarian regimes, like Iran's Shah or Nicaragua's Somoza, though unsavory, were less oppressive than totalitarian ones, Kirkpatrick argued. What's more, countries with homegrown monarchs, dictators, or generalissimos were far more likely to moderate and perhaps even democratize themselves than were societies crushed by totalitarian governments. And it was this potential of non-democratic but also non-totalitarian states to change their regimes for the better, in their own good time, that helped to justify America's benign neglect of or, at most, episodic concern with their domestic politics. Once freed from the totalitarian threat, countries like Nicaragua or Afghanistan could more or less be trusted to their own devices.

The wave of democratization that occurred in the 1980's, especially in Asia and South America, seemed to confirm the wisdom of the administration's approach. Even when America was called to play a role, as it was in the Philippines, our intervention was short and sweet, confined mainly to persuading Ferdinand Marcos to leave office.

By comparison, the Bush Doctrine puts the democratization of once totalitarian, quondam authoritarian, and persistently tribal societies at the center of its objectives. The case of Afghanistan shows, to be sure, that the Reagan Doctrine had its drawbacks. Left to itself, Afghanistan after the Soviets' withdrawal did not resume its former ways, at least not for long, and certainly did not evolve into a democracy. Instead, it succumbed to the Taliban's peculiar Islamic totalitarianism. Nevertheless, the Bush Administration's policy is not merely to expunge the totalitarians there and in Iraq, but to ensure that they never return by reconstructing their societies along democratic lines. Authoritarianism (at least in the Middle East) is no longer acceptable. The U.S. now proposes to liberate these nations from the captivity of their own unhappy traditions.

So far as it goes, that policy, or some version of it, might be justified by the circumstances and stakes of U.S. involvement, even as the American refoundings of Germany and Japan after the Second World War were justified on prudential grounds. Occasionally, the Bush Administration makes this kind of argument. (The analogies are not exact, of course - about which more anon.) But usually this claim is mixed up with a very different one that is more characteristic of the Bush Doctrine as such: America's supposed duty, as the result of our respect for human rights, to help the Iraqis and others realize their democratic entitlement and destiny.

Rights and Republicanism

Political scientists James W. Ceaser and Daniel DiSalvol draw attention to this dimension of the Bush Doctrine when they observe, in a recent issue of the *Public Interest*, that "President Bush has identified the Republican party with a distinct foreign policy, which he has justified by recourse to certain fixed and universal principles – namely that, in his words, 'liberty is the design of nature' and that 'freedom is the right and the capacity of all mankind.' "

Bush's appeal, in their words, to "the universality of democracy and human rights" is a watershed moment in the history of American politics, with enormous significance for the Republican Party and the conservative movement. "Not since Lincoln has the putative head of the Republican party so actively sought to ground the party in a politics of natural right."

Bush's revival of natural or human rights as the foundation of political morality is welcome, and should be taken seriously. Like Lincoln, Bush is, in his own way, looking to the American Founding for guidance in charting his course through the dire circumstances that confront him. But there is, in his use of these noble ideas, a certain ambiguity or confusion between the natural *right* to be free and the *capacity* to be free. The two are not quite the same.

The founders affirmed that every human being has, by nature, a right to be free. Unless men were endowed by nature with a certain minimum of faculties, inclinations, and powers, that right would be nugatory. Taken together, those endowments – which include reason, an access to morality (variously traced to reason, conscience, or the moral sense), a spirited love of freedom for its own sake, passions (especially the powerful desire for self-preservation), and physical strength – constitute the capacity or natural *potential* for human freedom. But this potential needs to be made *actual*, needs to be awakened by practice and habit.

James Madison, for example, writes in *The Federalist* of "that honorable determination which animates every votary of freedom to rest all our political experiments on the capacity of mankind for self-government." In the largest sense, those experiments aim to prove whether the latent capacity of mankind for self-government can, at last, after centuries of slumber, be activated, realized, and confirmed by the conduct of the American people – in particular, by their ratification of the newly proposed Constitution. Alexander Hamilton underlines the point in that work's famous opening paragraph: "It has been frequently remarked that it seems to have been reserved to the people of this country, by their conduct and example, to decide the important question, whether societies of men are really capable or not of establishing good government from reflection and choice, or whether they are forever destined to depend for their political constitutions on accident and force."

The human right to be free, in other words, does not guarantee the human capacity to be free. That capacity must be elicited and demonstrated, and its noblest and most persuasive proof is by the establishment of "good government," along with the habits necessary to perpetuate it; the habits of heart and mind that, among other things, allow a people's "choice" to be guided by "reflection."

Notice, too, that the founders are not content with (merely) democratic regimes, i.e., with governments that hold elections and empower majorities to rule. The test of mankind's political capacity is that its self-government should culminate in good government, in regimes that not only have elections but actually achieve the common good and secure the rights of individuals, whether or not they belong to the ruling majority. This blend of constitutionalism and republicanism is extremely difficult to attain. Well acquainted with the history of failed republican regimes, the founders by and large thought it the *most difficult* of all forms of government to establish and preserve. Hence good, republican government is an achievement, not an entitlement.

The Limits of Regime Change

Thus even with the improvements in political science celebrated by Madison, Hamilton, and the other founders, most of them never expected republican government to spread easily and universally across the globe. Though fervent believers in universal moral principles, they knew that these had to be approximated differently in different political situations. In this sense, they were students of Montesquieu and Aristotle, who taught that governments have to be suited to a people's character and conditions.

None of this implies, of course, that dramatic political change is not possible. America's founders could not have been *founders* if they did not think regime change possible and, in their own case, desirable. Founding is possible because culture is not destiny; politics can reshape a nation's culture. But they knew also that no founding is completely *de novo*. Every attempt at regime change begins from the existing habits and beliefs of the people for whom you are trying to found a new way of life. Accordingly, the founders would have been cautious, to say the least, about America's ability to transform Iraqis into good democrats.

In the last century, we saw in the cases of Germany and Japan that it is possible to remake even Nazi and imperial Japanese institutions into democratic regimes. But these are really exceptions that prove the rule that it is very difficult to pull off this kind of transformation. Germany and Japan were exceptional, first, because the U.S. and its allies had beaten them into complete submission. Then we occupied them for decades – not merely for months or years, but for the better part of a half-century. And both were civilizations that had the advantage of having enjoyed beforehand a high standard of living, widespread literacy, and considerable political openness. Besides, America was reorganizing them at the beginning of the Cold War, when circumstances compelled them, as it were, to choose between the West, with its democratic institutions, and the East, with its bleak tyranny.

To his credit, President Bush recognizes the difficulty of the task in Iraq. He acknowledged to the National Endowment for Democracy that "the progress of liberty is a powerful trend," but that "liberty, if not defended, can be lost. The success of freedom," he said, "is not determined by some dialectic of history." In his elegant speech at Whitehall Palace, he affirmed that "freedom, by definition, must be chosen and defended by those who choose it." And he warned that "democratic development" will not come swiftly, or smoothly, to the Middle East, any more than it did to America and Europe.

Nonetheless, he finds strong support for the "global expansion of democracy" in human nature itself. "In our conflict with terror and tyranny," he said at Whitehall, "we have an unmatched advantage, a power that cannot be resisted, and that is the appeal of freedom to all mankind." In a speech in Cincinnati, he declared, "People everywhere prefer freedom to slavery; prosperity to squalor; self-government to the rule of terror and torture." Aboard the *U.S.S. Abraham Lincoln*, after announcing that "major combat operations in Iraq have ended," he said, "Men and women in every culture need liberty like they need food and water and air."

Democratic Feelings

Here he stumbles. It is one thing to affirm, as the American Founders did, that there is in the human soul a love of liberty. It is another thing entirely to assert that this love is the main or, more precisely, the naturally predominant inclination in human nature, that it is "a power that cannot be resisted." In fact, it is often resisted and quite frequently bested, commonly for the sake of the "food and water and air" that human nature craves, too. The president downplays the contests within human nature: conflicts between reason and passion, and within reason and passion, that the human soul's very freedom makes inescapable. True enough, "people everywhere prefer freedom to slavery," that is, to their *own* slavery, but many people everywhere and at all times have been quite happy to enjoy their freedom and all the benefits of someone else's slavery.

In his 2002 State of the Union Address, one of his best speeches, he amplified his point. "All fathers and mothers, in all societies, want their children to be educated and live free from poverty and violence. No people on earth yearn to be oppressed, or aspire to servitude, or eagerly await the midnight knock of the secret police." There is truth in the president's words, but not the whole truth. No one may want to be oppressed, but from this it does not follow that no one yearns to oppress. The love that parents feel for their children does not necessarily transfer to benevolence, much less equal solicitude, for the children of others. This is why "do unto others" is not a moral rule automatically or easily observed. This is why, when Abraham Lincoln distilled his moral teaching to its essence, he did not confine himself to the wrongness of slavery simply. "As I would not be a slave," he wrote, "so I would not be a master. This expresses my idea of democracy. Whatever differs from this, to the extent of the difference, is not democracy."

In other words, that "people everywhere" or "all fathers and mothers" have the same *feelings* for themselves and their own kind does not (at least not yet) make them believers in human equality, human rights, or democracy. President Bush, in effect, plants his account of democracy in common or shared human passions, particularly the tender passions of family love, not in reason's recognition of a rule for the passions. He does not insist, as Lincoln and the founders did, that democracy depends on the mutual recognition of rights and duties, grounded in an objective, natural order that is independent of human will. Bush makes it easy to be a democrat, and thus makes it easier for the whole world to become democratic.

History and Culture

Yet democracy based on feelings or compassion has obvious limits. What takes the place of the rigorous moral teaching that once lifted compassion to the level of justice? What summons forth the embattled statesmanship and republican striving that sustain democracy, especially in crises? Despite his comments that democratic progress is not inevitable and that "the success of freedom is not determined by some dialectic of history," Bush finds himself appealing again and again to a kind of providential or historical support for democracy. In the same speech in which he uttered the words just quoted, he concluded by saying: "We believe that liberty is the design of nature; we believe that liberty is the direction of history."

At Goree Island, Senegal, the slave ships' point of departure from Africa, Bush declared:

> We know that these challenges can be overcome, because history moves in the direction of justice. The evils of slavery were accepted and unchanged for centuries. Yet, eventually, the human heart would not abide them. There is a voice of conscience and hope in every man and woman that will not be silenced - what Martin Luther King called a certain kind of fire that no water could put out. . . . This untamed fire of justice continues to burn in the affairs of man, and it lights the way before us.

In this eloquent address, the president praises the role that John Quincy Adams and Lincoln, among others, played in the fight against slavery, but he salutes their "moral vision" as though that alone had been sufficient to doom the peculiar institution. In his words, "Their moral vision caused Americans to examine our hearts, to correct our Constitution, and to teach our children the dignity and equality of every person of every race." What happened to the Civil War, not to mention Jim Crow? Bush leaves the impression that "history moves in the direction of justice," and that once Americans were awakened to the Truth, they went with the flow. Yet the anti-slavery cause, at least in Lincoln's mind, did not depend in the slightest on history's support for the triumph of free labor and free men. Rather, it was a very close issue, requiring for its resolution all of Lincoln's genius and the Union's resources, not forgetting a considerable measure of good luck. And the triumph, so dearly won, soon gave way to tragedy and renewed tyranny in the South.

Bush's position recalls the important recent dispute between Francis Fukuyama and Samuel Huntington. Huntington insists that, after the Cold War, international politics will be marked by the inevitable clash of civilizations, e.g., between the Islamic and non-Islamic nations. Fukuyama argues that history is overcoming all such cultural clashes and culminating in liberal democracy, which is destined to spread all over the world. In this dispute, Bush seems to be firmly on Fukuyama's side. At West Point, the president explained, "The 20th century ended with a single surviving model of human progress, based on non-negotiable demands of human dignity, the rule of law, limits on the power of the state, respect for women and private property and free speech and equal justice and religious tolerance. . . . When it comes to the common rights and needs of men and women," he said, "there is no clash of civilizations."

If not dialectical, Bush's account of history certainly seems Darwinian; history has winnowed itself down to a "single surviving model of human progress." He dismisses doubts that the Middle East will grow increasingly democratic as narrow-minded, if not downright prejudiced. From his 2004 State of the Union Address: "[I]t is mistaken, and condescending, to assume that whole cultures and great religions are incompatible with liberty and self-government. I believe that God has planted in every human heart the desire to live in freedom." Yes, but the question is whether some cultures and religions are less compatible with freedom and democracy than others, and if so, how in his second term the president ought to adjust our foreign policy. Granted, too, that God has implanted in men a love of freedom, but cultures, rulers, and religions each diffract that love, accentuating, obscuring, or perverting it. Bush calls those who raise such contentions "skeptics of democracy," when in fact they are skeptical mostly of his easy-going account of democracy.

James Q. Wilson, with his usual insight and learning, takes an empirical look in the December *Commentary* at the relation between Islam and freedom. He declines to inspect Islam and democracy, on the grounds that there are too few examples from which to generalize and that, in the long run, personal liberty is more important. From liberty, liberal democracy may spring; democracy without liberty is despotic (Fareed Zakaria's recent book, *The Future of Freedom*, reinforces this point). Wilson proffers Turkey, Indonesia, and Morocco as reasonably liberal Muslim states; of these only one, Morocco, is both Muslim and Arab. What these cases have in common, he suggests, is a "powerful and decisive leader" who can "detach religion from politics"; an army that "has stood decisively for secular rule and opposed efforts to create an Islamist state" (a condition that Morocco does not quite meet); the absence of "a significant ethnic minority" demanding independence; and the lack of major conflicts between Sunni and Shiite Muslims.

Iraq shares *none* of these advantages. Straining to find some cause for optimism, Wilson notes that in one opinion poll more than 75% of Iraqis express support for liberties like free speech and freedom of religion. In the same poll, about 40% endorse a European-style parliamentary democracy.

Rethinking the Doctrine

In this vein, it is heartening to see elections in Afghanistan, with thousands upon thousands lining up to vote. It is encouraging, too, that elections are about to be held for the new Iraqi national assembly. As the president says, "it is the practice of democracy that makes a nation ready for democracy, and every nation can start on this path." But not every nation will finish it, because democracy is not just a matter of elections. Democracy requires that majorities restrain themselves and practice sometimes disagreeable tasks out of respect for law and for their fellow citizens. These tasks, in turn, require a willingness to trust one's fellow citizens that comes hard to tribal societies, whose members are not used to trusting anyone who is not at least a cousin.

Of course, it is a wonderful thing to hear President Bush reassert the natural-rights basis of just government and, incidentally, of the Republican Party. As against today's shallow culture of liberal relativism, his willingness to point out the plain difference between good and evil is bracing, and recalls Ronald Reagan's denunciation of the Evil Empire. The worry is that in tracing the individual right to be free to ordinary human compassion or fellow-feeling, and then confounding that right with an entitlement to live in a fully democratic regime, Bush promises or demands too much and risks a terrible deflation of the democratic idealism he has encouraged.

As he begins his second term, the president and his advisors must take a hard, second look at the Bush Doctrine. In many respects, it is the export version of compassionate conservatism. Even as the latter presumes that behind the economic problem of poverty is a moral problem, which faith-based initiatives may help to cure one soul at a time, so the Bush Doctrine discovers behind the dysfunctional economies and societies of the Middle East a moral problem, which "the transformational power of liberty" may cure, one democrat and one democracy at a time. "The power of liberty to transform lives and nations," he admonishes, should not be underestimated. But it may be that the administration underestimates the difficulty of converting whole societies in the Middle East into functioning democracies. By raising expectations – by making democracy appear as an easier conversion and way of life than it really is – Bush risks not only the erosion of liberal and pro-democratic support within Iraq, but also at home a loss of public confidence in the whole war effort.

One wonders, for example, whether his version of compassionate democracy is sufficiently alert to the problem of security. In most American wars, the reconstruction did not begin until the fighting had ended, until the enemy was subjugated and peaceful order imposed on the country. Vietnam was an exception, but not a very helpful one. Bush criticizes previous administrations for making short-sighted bargains with Mideast kings and dictators, trading security for liberty in the region. Without liberty, he argues, there is no long-term security. Although he has a point, liberty itself presupposes a certain minimum security for life, liberty, and property that is woefully absent in much of Iraq. Earlier American statesmen, including the founders, would have been keenly aware of this requirement because their argument for republican government put great weight on the passion, and the right, of self-preservation. A government that could not protect the life and liberty of its citizens (better than they could left to themselves) was no government at all.

But in its first term the Bush Administration underestimated the problem of security because it overestimated the sentimental or compassionate grounds of democracy. Expecting the Iraqis quickly and happily to get in touch with their inner democrat, the administration was surprised that so many of them took a cautious, more self-interested view, preferring to reserve their allegiance for whichever side would more reliably protect them from getting killed. In general, the Bush team needs to recall that weak, contemptible, authoritarian regimes are not the only breeding grounds of trouble in the Middle East or elsewhere. Weak, contemptible democracies can be the source of great evil, too, as Weimar Germany attests.

Finally, the Bush Doctrine's all-absorbing focus on bringing democracy to Iraq tends to crowd out concern for the kind of constructive, wide-ranging statesmanship that is needed there and in other Islamic nations. Unfortunately, the administration has never thought very seriously about constitutionalism, either at home or abroad, except for the narrow, though important, issue of elections. As the example of Turkey suggests, it may take many years, if ever, before Iraq is capable of a fully-functioning liberal democracy. In the meantime, the Iraqis need to adopt what arrangements they can to create strong executive powers; security forces able to protect their countrymen's life, liberty, and property; a free, prosperous economy; local experience in managing local affairs; and impartial courts. Better regimes than the Taliban or Saddam Hussein are surely attainable, and are being attained. But these new governments are haunted by dire threats, including the danger of civil war and national disintegration.

Aboard the *U.S.S. Abraham Lincoln*, President Bush promised, "we will stand with the new leaders of Iraq as they establish a government of, by, and for the Iraqi people." But let us not expect that they will reform themselves – much less that we shall transform them – all at once up to the standards of the Gettysburg Address.

ELIOT A. COHEN

21 A Time for Humility

A MILESTONE DOES NOT INFORM US WHETHER THE TRAIL AHEAD IS smooth or rocky, well marked or obscure, but it provides a place to pause and reflect. So too with the Iraqi election. It may weaken the insurgency by endowing the Iraqi government with a legitimacy and authority it now lacks, or by reinforcing Sunni resentment, strengthen it. But the election indubitably demonstrates the power of freedom, and the courage that love of it can elicit even in a terrorized population. Surely, even those so-called realists who disparage the project of building civil society in Iraq share Lincoln's wish, expressed about another group, also believed incapable of self-rule, "that all men every where could be free."

This is a victory, no doubt about it. Iraq's journey may take many turnings, but it will not return to a past in which a totalitarian regime brutalized 85% of the population. It may, in the future, have its Salazar or Pinochet, it may writhe in anarchy or civil war, but Saddam Hussein and the Baath Party are gone. That is an achievement which, however perilous their condition now, most Iraqis do not wish to reverse. The menace of an Iraqi regime that intended to rebuild and extend its most dangerous capabilities has been removed, and possibly forever. Most of the Arab world may hate America, but a disjointed yet palpable movement for reform has gathered strength. This movement has broken through in a few countries; it has sympathizers in the rest, who note the irony of free elections as a byproduct of American occupation.

The war has achieved important results, wrongly minimized or dismissed by the administration's critics. But this is not, alas, the whole story.

Reprinted from the *Wall Street Journal*, January 31, 2005.

For us too the Iraq elections provide an opportunity, more proper than arbitrary anniversaries, to reckon with our failures as well as our achievements. If the war has had its great successes, it has also had more than its share of bungles, evident in the chaos and suffering in Iraq, heavy loss of American life, and a battered reputation for the United States abroad. Bloody mistakes occur in all wars, as some point out – an easy wisdom that flows most easily from those who have no loved ones in harm's way. Even such philosophers, however, should honor the 8,000 families of dead and wounded American soldiers by facing the unpleasant truths, because even if blunders characterize all wars, blunders they remain.

* * *

The argument about the merits of going to war will continue for many years. The overthrow of Saddam's regime represented the least unpalatable choice in the face of a regime that was about to slip as completely out of a leaky and corrupt U.N. sanctions regime as it had a U.N. inspections regime. It embodied a decision based on bad intelligence, but the best available. It reflected suppositions about linkages to the 9/11 plotters that were, at least, plausible. But war emerged, most of all, from the view that by removing Saddam's regime and replacing it with something reasonable – not Sweden, but, say, Romania circa 1993 – the broader political dynamics of the Arab world could be altered, profoundly and perhaps decisively. We do not know, and will not know for years whether that strategy will work, but it had much to be said for it.

Before the war reasonable people disagreed about these arguments for war; they still do. But good idea or bad, the handling of the war has made an admittedly risky strategy far more precarious and costly than it need have been. Some of those failures persist, and others could recur all too easily. They fall into two classes:

The first consists of waging war with the mentality and practices of peace. Because we choose to cut taxes in wartime, we have a ballooning deficit; because we have a ballooning deficit we cannot expand the active-duty military on a permanent basis; because we cannot expand the active-duty military we call up hundreds of thousands of reservists to fight an optional war half a world away, sending part-time soldiers – some ready for this mission, others not – off for a year of combating guerrillas in a limited war, a concept at odds with all previous notions of what citizen-soldiers do. Because we cannot substantially increase the defense budget we may fail to replace equipment worn down by months of active service in a harsh climate, and we have even begun to drain our military-school system of leaders. Signs of strain appear in retention rates; but it becomes most clear, if you talk to soldiers, in the disgust and anger of the Army's best mid-level leaders, and in the institutional leukemia that has begun to sap the vitality of a military educational system that was once, deservedly, the pride of our armed forces.

In past conflicts, civilian and military leaders ruthlessly pruned the ranks of generals who, though competent in peace, could not adapt to the novel conditions of war. They promoted rapidly the lieutenant colonels and colonels who could. George Marshall did this in World War II, and pillars of the old Army like 62-year-old Hugh Drum gave way to hard 36-year-olds like James Gavin. A few happy but nonetheless regular promotions aside, this has not happened here. Nor is the issue military leadership alone: Ambassador Paul Bremer, an intelligent and self-sacrificing man, accepted the call to go to Iraq, with neither the time nor the authority to build a staff and a plan. Still, the Coalition Provisional Authority he ran was a disaster, a micromanaged American enterprise too often out of touch with Iraqi realities. The U.S. government that had not provided the structure needed to administer postwar Iraq would not admit his deficiencies and replace him. Instead, he, like George Tenet and Gen. Tommy Franks - equally able and patriotic men, who also failed in key aspects of the Iraq war - received the Presidential Medal of Freedom.

Carl von Clausewitz, the Prussian military philosopher, declared that statesmen and commanders must establish "the kind of war on which they are embarking; neither mistaking it for, nor turning it into, something that is alien to its nature." Here came the second class of failures. For a very long time, the U.S. government would not even use the word insurgency. Until recently it insisted that we faced only 5,000 "former regime loyalists, jihadis, and released criminals." We have killed or captured more than three times as many, and yet the insurgency rages. In a war where, as one successful commander has put it, "dollars are bullets," bureaucrats spent months ponderously awarding giant contracts to multinational corporations that would hire expatriates from around the world, rather than Iraqis who could get angry young men off the street. In guerrilla war nothing matters more than raising and training indigenous forces; we passed that job off to Vinnell Corporation, and only belatedly realized that we needed our best general, supported by American soldiers and Marines, to do the job.

* * *

The failure to accept this war's nature as an insurgency rests with civilians and soldiers, individuals and institutions. It has many causes, to include memories of Vietnam that have prevented Americans from thinking straight in peacetime about the challenges of guerrilla warfare. Nor is it certain that the lessons will stay with us: Having built and celebrated a military designed to win battles, but less adroit at winning wars, it is entirely possible that the Pentagon will revert to a military obsessed with stupendous deeds of fire and movement, rather than winning the wars we face.

In part because it corrected belatedly many, though not all of these mistakes, the United States may still achieve a tolerable outcome in Iraq, albeit at the cost of far too much American and Iraqi blood, far too much treasure, far too much political capital. We remain big, rich, and determined; above all, we have tapped a yearning for freedom in Iraq. But as we celebrate this historic poll, honoring the courage of the millions of Iraqis who risked their lives to vote, and the bravery and skill of our soldiers and public servants who helped them do so, we should, in all humility, look at our failures as well as our successes, call them by that name, and learn from them.

REUEL MARC GERECHT

22 Birth of a Democracy

ALL RIGHT. LET US MAKE AN ANALYTICAL BET OF HIGH PROBABILITY and enormous returns: The January 30 elections in Iraq will easily be the most consequential event in modern Arab history since Israel's six-day defeat of Gamal Abdel Nasser's alliance in 1967. Israel's pulverizing defeat of the Arab armies dethroned Nasserism, the romantic pan-Arab dictatorial nationalism that had infected much of the Arab world, particularly its intelligentsia, during the 1950's and 60's. With the collapse of Nasserism, the overtly secular socialist-cum-fascist age in the Middle East closed – except in Iraq under Saddam Hussein. Its spirit would soon die there, too, a victim of Saddam's long and disastrous war against Iran (1980–88), which encouraged the Butcher of Baghdad to emblazon "God is Great" upon the Iraqi flag. Responding to the spiritual agony and internal rot of the pan-Arab dream, Islamic activism gained speed throughout the Middle East and has remained – outside of Iraq and now possibly Palestine – the only serious opposition to the vagaries, incompetence, and corruption of princely and dictatorial rule.

The January 30 elections will do for the people of Iraq, and after them, in all likelihood, the rest of the Arab world, what the end of the European imperial period did not: show the way to sovereignty without tyranny. For the first time really in Arab history, people power has expressed itself democratically. Say whatever you want about the coverage of the Arabic-language satellite channels, *Al Jazeera* and *Al Arabia*, they relayed quite well stunning democratic imagery – the repeated shots of entire families voting together, from pregnant mothers with babies to grandparents in wheelchairs. The rulers of the Middle East will no doubt try to depict

Iraq's democratic experiment as a vehicle of anti-Sunni Shiite extremism, but the U.S. government - parts of which (the State Department and the CIA) have a tendency to project the rulers' views onto their people - would be well advised to turn a deaf ear. Anyone who watched the satellite coverage knew those families were putting themselves into harm's way, as were even more the Sunni Arabs, who voted in greater numbers than many expected. Arab satellite television, which is Sunni-dominated except for the Lebanese Hezbollah's *Al Manar* service, has been playing a game - and *Al Jazeera* is more dedicated to this game than *Al Arabia* - of pretending that the insurgents in Iraq were the real Iraqis and that all Iraqis really in their hearts supported the insurgents. The savagery of the suicide bombers has undoubtedly complicated this good guy-bad guy scenario, but the easiest way out of this ethical pit has been to suggest that only the over-the-top holy warriors, like Abu Musab al Zarqawi, kill barbarically. Most insurgents, the good patriotic ones defending the fatherland and the fatherland's true faith, just kill American occupiers and their Iraqi lackeys - this has been, at least up to January 30, the reflexive *Al Jazeera* spin.

Arab satellite television has accordingly not liked to have long, thoughtful discussions about Iraq's Shia Arabs and their near universal approval of the Anglo-American invasion of Iraq. Not much really about Grand Ayatollah Ali Sistani, the preeminent Shiite divine, who has usually encouraged cooperation with the Americans and always encouraged the advance of democracy. Not much either on the failure of Moktada al-Sadr, the rabble-rousing young cleric, to oppose violently the American presence in Iraq. (As long as Sadr could be depicted as an insurgent in the Sunni Arab media, he was a hero.)

January 30 and the coming of Iraq's newly elected national assembly will make the past prejudice extremely difficult to maintain. A decent bet today would be that most of the Sunni Arabs who watched the Iraqi elections on satellite television probably both admire and feel ashamed of what happened. However much they may admire the Iraqis for defying the violence to vote in massive numbers, they are also probably ashamed that the Shia displayed such courage, while they in their own countries do not. (It's not at all contradictory for an Egyptian to hope that January 30 will help end President Hosni Mubarak's despised dictatorship and yet feel a bit sickened that it is Shiite Arabs - the black sheep of the Arab Muslim family - who are leading the faithful to a democratic rebirth.) And it is certainly true that the enabling hand of the United States provokes great waves of contradictory passion. It is worthwhile to note that these same emotions are common among the Iraqi Shia: The more religious and nationalistic they are (and the two impulses are quite harmonious among the Shia), the more difficult they find it psychologically to accept their freedom from the Americans. But the Shia have – with the possible exception of the followers of Moktada al-Sadr – gotten over it. So likely will the average non-Iraqi Sunni Arab who wants to see elected leadership in his native land.

But our Muslim "allies" in the Middle East are much less likely to get over it. They saw on television what their subjects saw: The American toppling of Saddam Hussein has allowed the common man to become the agent of change. This is particularly gripping in a region historically addicted – at least the leaders would like to so believe – to a top-down political identity. Go to Jordan, one of the more "progressive," "pro-American" states in the region, and the omnipresence of pictures of King Abdullah, often next to pictures of his late father, King Hussein, does the opposite of what the picture-hangers intend: It suggests a fundamental uneasiness about the monarchy's legitimacy. (As the Hashemite state continues to spend much more than the state can earn, this sense of unease will undoubtedly rise even further. Fiscal profligacy, both in Egypt and Jordan, will continue to be a driving force behind the popular desire to see the political systems open up.)

* * *

Just imagine the possibilities of pan-Arab dialogue when Iraq begins to broadcast the debates within the new national assembly. And remember, the Iraqi national assembly, not the new president, prime minister, and other cabinet officials, is likely to remain the real power center in Iraq, at least until a new constitution is written. Iraqis are a diverse people – though not as diverse as many civil-war-is-here! Western commentators would like us to believe – and they will have vivid arguments about what belongs in their basic law. It will not be hard for Arabs elsewhere, even for the most Shiite-cursing, American-hating Arab Sunnis who loathe the American-supported dictators above them, to find common ground and aspirations in these debates, which will likely be the most momentous since Egypt's literary and political elite started taking aim at (and advantage of) British dominion over the Nile Valley in the early twentieth century. If the Bush White House were wise, it would ensure that all parliamentary debates are accessible free via satellite throughout the entire Middle East. Such Iraqi C-SPAN coverage could possibly have enormous repercussions. For just a bit of extra money, Washington should dub all of the proceedings into Persian, remembering that Baghdad's echo is easily as loud in Tehran as it is in Amman and Cairo. The president has stated that he wants to stand by those who want to stand by democratic values. This is easily the cheapest and one of the most effective ways of building pressure for democratic reform.

Recalling 1967, or for that matter virtually any memorable date in contemporary Arab history before the Anglo-American invasion of Iraq in 2003, reminds one acutely how painful the process of Westernization has been in the Near East since Napoleon landed at Alexandria in 1798. The Muslims of the Middle East have tried variations of every intoxicating bad Western idea that promised quick power to peoples, especially to their leaders, whose historical memories were built by a militarily victorious faith. By and large, certainly among the elites, they drank voluntarily and rapaciously. And the results have been awful.

There are many reasons why the World War II generation of Western diplomatic and journalistic Arabists hated Zionism and the creation of Israel with a passion that occasionally rivaled the Austrian anti-Semitism of the 1920's and 1930's. But among the most important reasons is that they could see the old Middle East, with all its complexities and warmth, coming apart. Zionism and Israel became the cutting edge of the Western whirlwind that was robbing them of their beloved world. By the late 1960's, ugliness was on the march, in architecture, language, culture, politics, and manners, and the old-school Arabists locked onto Israel, and later the United States, as the culprit. This was an odd inversion of history - making Arab Muslim pride and curiosity about the secrets of the West derivative of Zionism - but the sadness that often drove this anger is understandable. The January 30 elections in Iraq are probably the first truly happy, powerful echo of Napoleon's invasion of Egypt. In this at least, the French today can take pride.

The democratic ethic is trying now to put down deep roots in Iraq; the democratic spirit, however, has been present in the Middle East for a lot longer. The understanding of it has grown as tyrannies have failed (but continue to rule on), elite corruption has skyrocketed, and the number of those who have known the penalties for political deviation has risen to produce a counterculture of resistance, pride, and small-scale heroism. Not that long ago, Muslim Arabs could look at Asia and feel no shame. Not now. The civilizational gap has become too wide. And unlike 50 years ago, when Arab dictators and their peoples could believe that state power could raise nations up, now they know - and they really do know it - that their societies cannot produce capitalist dictatorships that work. Hosni Mubarak probably doesn't really care about this. That he rules is enough. But the apparatus below him does. What the Bush administration wants to do is target its message at that apparatus, particularly at the security service that must evolve or crack for there to be political change in Cairo. Rapid change in Egypt is certainly possible. Go into the streets of Cairo and ask the poor urbanized *fellah* whether he understands one man, one vote, and you will discover that he has an understanding that vastly exceeds his experience of democratic politics (zero). He has learned by seeing the opposite. So let us bring on C-SPAN Iraq, and let his education grow the only way it now can.

In Iraq, where Middle Eastern tyranny reached its zenith, the appreciation of democracy's possibilities is surely the most acute. America's presence in the country – its political guidance, however errant – has been essential in setting the stage for the great debates that will shortly be upon the Iraqis, the Arab world, and us. As those debates unfold, we would be wise to remember a few simple truths about Iraq, and particularly about the Iraqi Shia.

*First, contrary to the rising chorus of Democratic commentary on the Iraqi elections, Iran was the biggest loser last Sunday. The United Iraqi Alliance, which seems certain to capture the lion's share of the vote, is not at all "pro-Iranian." Neither is it any less "pro-American" than Prime Minister Iyad Allawi's al-Iraqiyya list, unless you mean that the various members of the Alliance have been and will continue to be less inclined to chat amicably with the Central Intelligence Agency, which has been a longtime backer of Allawi and his Iraqi National Accord. (This is not to suggest at all that Allawi is a CIA poodle.) A better way to describe the United Iraqi Alliance, if it lasts, is as Iran's worst nightmare. It surely will cause the clerical regime enormous pain as the Iraqis within it, especially those who were once dependent on Iranian aid, continue to distance themselves ever further from Tehran. Primary point to remember: Grand Ayatollah Ali Sistani, who is now certainly the most senior Shiite cleric in both Iraq and Iran, who is of Iranian birth and early education, has embraced a democratic political creed that is anathema to the ruling mullahs of Tehran. Ali Khamenei, Iran's senior political cleric, is in a real pickle since he cannot openly challenge Sistani and his embrace of democracy. Iran's relations with the new Iraq would cease to exist. Also, the repercussions inside the Iranian clerical system would not be healthy. Sistani is the last of the truly great transnational Shiite clerics, and his following inside Iran, particularly since he has so publicly backed a democratic franchise, which if it were applied in Iran would shatter clerical power, should not be underestimated. Sistani and his men know very well that the political game they play in Iraq will have repercussions throughout the Arab world and Iran. He and his men are not rash, but there will be no tears shed on their side if Iraq's political advancement convulses those clerics in Iran who believe in theocracy.

*Second, we are lucky that Iyad Allawi's moment has passed. Spiritually and physically, Allawi would have kept the new government in the Green Zone, the surreal, guarded compound in central Baghdad where the American embassy is located. The United Iraqi Alliance will ensure that it is in all aspects pulled out. No real political progress among Iraqis can be made unless the Green Zone becomes a memory of occupation.

*Third, the United Iraqi Alliance and the Kurdish slate will probably start to review closely America's and Allawi's army, police, and intelligence training programs. This is all to the good. We have had enormous problems with these programs, in part because we have tried to incorporate Sunni Arabs who were not loyal to the new Iraq. The Alliance and the Kurds will be much more demanding than was Allawi, who built his outreach program to Sunnis in large part on bribery. By offering them jobs in the new army, police force, and intelligence service, Allawi led Sunnis to believe their positions in these organizations would not be subject to democratic politics. Allawi actually created the opposite dynamic among the Sunnis from what he intended. The Sunni insurgency was emboldened. Those elite Sunnis who should have felt the need to compromise and come on board did not do so. With the January 30 elections, the Sunni Arabs now know the old order is dead. The Shia and the Kurds will certainly reach out to them - Sistani has been doing so since Saddam fell - but they are unlikely to continue any form of bribery that touches upon Iraq's military services. Washington should welcome any change of tactics in this direction. Allawi's way was not working.

*Fourth, if Ahmed Chalabi gains a position of influence inside the new national assembly, it would be wise for State and the CIA to ensure that any and all officials who were involved in his regular trashings - particularly the trashing of his home - do not serve in Iraq. The Bush administration is going to have a hard time working with and figuring out the Iraqi Shia (it is striking how thin U.S. embassy coverage of the Shia still seems), and it does not need to further antagonize one of the few Iraqis capable of appreciating both the religious and secular sides of the Iraqi Shiite family and who can present his understanding to the Americans in a way they can understand. Ahmed Chalabi may be wrong in his assessments - he has certainly made mistakes in the past - but the Bush administration is doing itself an enormous disservice if it allows the old State-CIA animus against Chalabi to continue any further. Irony is always both bitter and sweet. Tell Langley to live with it before Chalabi has the will and allies to get even.

*And fifth, continue to pray every night for the health, well-being, and influence of Grand Ayatollah Sistani. Not surprisingly, there seems to be an increasing body of American liberals out there who foretell the end of a "liberal Iraq" because religious Shia now have a political voice. It is a blessed thing that Sistani and his followers have a far better understanding of modern Middle Eastern history than the American and European liberals who travel to Iraq and find only fear. There are vastly worse things in this world than seeing grown Iraqi men and women arguing about the propriety and place of Islamic family law and traditional female attire in Iraqi society. Understood correctly, it will be an ennobling sight - and a cornerstone of a more liberal Iraq and the Muslim world beyond.

Index